Equilibrium Exchange Rate Models,
the Euro and the 2004 Expansion of the EU

STUDIEN ZU INTERNATIONALEN WIRTSCHAFTSBEZIEHUNGEN

Herausgegeben von Prof. Dr. Michael Frenkel

Band 10

PETER LANG
Frankfurt am Main · Berlin · Bern · Bruxelles · New York · Oxford · Wien

Isabell Koske

Equilibrium Exchange Rate Models, the Euro and the 2004 Expansion of the EU

PETER LANG
Internationaler Verlag der Wissenschaften

Bibliographic Information published by the Deutsche Nationalbibliothek
The Deutsche Nationalbibliothek lists this publication in the Deutsche Nationalbibliografie; detailed bibliographic data is available in the internet at <http://www.d-nb.de>.

Zugl.: Vallendar, Wiss. Hochsch. für Unternehmensführung, Diss., 2006

ISSN 1618-503X
ISBN 978-3-631-56703-6

www.peterlang.de

Contents

List of Tables

List of Figures

List of Abbreviations

ADF	augmented Dickey-Fuller
ARCH	autoregressive conditional heteroskedasticity
ARDL	autoregressive distributed lag
ARIMA	autoregressive integrated moving average
AU	Australia
AUD	Australian dollar
AWM	Area-Wide Model
BEER	behavioral equilibrium exchange rate
BG	Bulgaria
BOFIT	Bank of Finland Institute for Economies in Transition
BPEER	balance of payments equilibrium exchange rate
BS	Balassa-Samuelson
CA	Canada
CAD	Canadian dollar
CEE	central and eastern Europe
CEEC	central and eastern European countries
CEPR	Center for Economic Policy Research
CH	Switzerland
CHEER	capital enhanced equilibrium exchange rate
CHF	Swiss franc
CIDEI	Centro Interdipartimentale Di Economia Internazionale
CLS	Continuous Linked Settlement
cont	continued
CPI	consumer price index
CY	Cyprus
CZ	Czech Republic
DE	Germany
DEER	desired equilibrium exchange rate
DEM	deutschmark

DIFF	differential
DKK	Danish krona
DM	Diebold-Mariano test statistic
DM*	modified Diebold-Mariano test statistic
DOLS	dynamic ordinary least squares
e.g.	for example
ECB	European Central Bank
ed.	editor
eds.	editors
EE	Estonia
EMU	European Economic and Monetary Union
EPRU	Efficiency and Productivity Research Unit
ERM	European exchange rate mechanism
EU	European Union
EUR	euro
FDI	foreign direct investment
FEER	fundamental equilibrium exchange rate
FIM	Finnish marka
FIML	full information maximum likelihood
GBP	British pound
GDP	gross domestic product
HIPC	Harmonized Index of Consumer Prices
HR	Croatia
HU	Hungary
I(0)	integrated of order 0
I(1)	integrated of order 1
i.i.d.	independently and identically distributed
IFS	International Financial Statistics
IMF	International Monetary Fund
IND	industry
JP	Japan
JPY	Japanese yen
KPSS	Kwiatkowski, Phillips, Schmidt, Shin
LHS	left-hand-side
LM	Lagrange multiplier
LOOP	law of one price
LT	Lithuania
LV	Latvia
$\max(r\|r+1)$	maximum eigenvalue statistic
MM	monetary model

NA	not available
NACE	nomenclature générale des activités économiques dans les Communautés européennes
NATREX	natural real exchange rate
VAR	vector autoregression
NBER	National Bureau of Economic Research
NCGDP	nominal consumption to GDP ratio
NEER	nominal effective exchange rate
NER	nominal exchange rate
NFA	net foreign assets
NIESR	National Institute for Economic and Social Research
NIGEM	National Institute's Global Economic Model
NO	Norway
NOK	Norwegian krone
OECD	Organization for Economic Cooperation and Development
OeNB	Österreichische Nationalbank
PEER	permanent equilibrium exchange rate
PL	Poland
PMGE	pooled mean group estimator
PPI	producer price index
PPP	purchasing power parity
PROD	productivity
R&D	research and development
REER	real effective exchange rate
RER	real exchange rate
RGDPEMP	real GDP per employment
RINT	real interest rate
RMSE	root mean squared error
RO	Romania
S	sign test statistic
SEK	Swedish krona
SER	services
SI	Slovenia
SIC	Swiss Interbank Clearing
SK	Slovak Republic
SUR	seemingly unrelated regressions
SVAR	structural vector autoregression
TFP	total factor productivity
TOT	terms of trade
TP	trading partner countries

trace(r|k)	trace statistic
UIP	uncovered interest rate parity
UK	United Kingdom
ULC	unit labor costs
US	United States
USD	United States dollar
VECM	vector error correction model

List of Symbols

A	productivity parameter
B	trade balance
$\mathcal{B}$	cointegrating vector
C	consumption
CA	current account
D	matrix
d	loss differential
E	expectation operator
$\mathcal{E}$	nominal exchange rate
e	nominal exchange rate (logarithm)
e_1	first unit vector
F	net foreign debt
g	growth rate of real output
h	forecast horizon
I	identity matrix (chapter 3)
I	investment
$I_+(d_t)$	binary scalar
i	nominal interest rate
j	parameter
K	capital stock
k	parameter
L	labor
m	money demand (logarithm)
$N(0,1)$	standard normal distribution
n	number of endogenous variables
P	price index
P^Q	output deflator
P^I	investment deflator

p	price index (logarithm)
Q	output
q	Tobin's q
q	real exchange rate (logarithm; chapter 2)
R	real exchange rate
r	real interest rate
r	number of cointegrating vectors
R_N	relative price of non-tradable to tradable goods
S	savings
S_{00}	residual moment matrix
S_{0k}	residual moment matrix
S_{kk}	residual moment matrix
T	sample size
T_h	number of forecasts with forecast horizon h
TOT	terms of trade
u	productivity
UCA	underlying current account
W	Wilcoxon's signed-rank test statistic
X	matrix of variables
x	cointegrating vector
Y	output
y	output (logarithm)
Z	vector of variables
z	variable

α	matrix of adjustment parameters
α_1	income elasticity of money demand
α_2	interest rate semi-elasticity of money demand
β	matrix of cointegrating vectors
Γ	coefficient matrix
γ	autocovariance
Δ	first difference operator
δ	rate of depreciation
ε	error term
ζ	coefficient vector
θ	share of capital's income in total income
ι	maximum lag
κ	maximum lag
λ	eigenvalue
μ	constant

ν	adjustment parameter
Π	coefficient matrix
π	expected inflation rate
ϖ	growth rate of output
ρ	time preference
σ	scalar of short-term dynamics
τ	parameter
ϕ	error correction parameter
φ	weight of the non-tradable good in the GDP deflator
ψ	coefficient vector
ω	time varying risk premium
$\hat{\bullet}$	estimated value
$\tilde{\bullet}$	medium-run value
$\bar{\bullet}$	long-run value
$\bullet'$	transpose
$\bullet^*$	foreign value
$\bullet^r$	real value
$\bullet^P$	permanent component
$\bullet^T$	transitory component
$\bullet_\perp$	orthogonal complement
$\bullet_1$	domestically produced tradable good (chapter 4)
$\bullet_2$	importable good (chapter 4)
$\bullet_N$	non-tradable good
$\bullet_T$	tradable good
$\bullet_t$	time index

Chapter 1

Introduction

On January 1, 1999 the euro was launched as the official currency in eleven countries of the European Economic and Monetary Union (EMU).[1] The euro is the second most important international currency after the U.S. dollar. By mid 2005, 31.5 percent of international debt securities and 24.9 percent of global foreign exchange reserves were denominated in euro (ECB, 2005, p. 10). The share of the euro in daily foreign exchange trades settled via Continuous Linked Settlement (CLS) amounted to 21.5 percent in mid 2005, compared to 45 percent for the U.S. dollar and 10 percent for the Japanese yen (ECB, 2005, p. 9).

The growing importance of the euro in international capital markets was accompanied by a growing interest of researchers, policy makers, and business analysts in the evolution of the external value of the euro. Since the beginning of the European Economic and Monetary Union, the external value of the euro has fluctuated considerably. During the first two years of its existence, the euro lost about 17 percent of its initial value in effective terms. This period of depreciation was followed by an equally remarkable period of appreciation. In mid 2003, the euro exceeded its initial value of 1999 for the first time. The effective exchange rate of the synthetic euro, which can be calculated as a trade-weighted average of the exchange rates of the euro area member countries, shows that significant changes in this exchange rate also occurred during the 1980s and 1990s

The significant changes in the value of the euro since its launch and of the synthetic euro before then raise the question of how much of these changes can

[1]These countries are Austria, Belgium, Finland, France, Germany, Ireland, Italy, Luxembourg, the Netherlands, Portugal, and Spain. Greece followed suit on January 1, 2001.

be explained by the underlying economic fundamentals. Knowing whether an observed change in the value of the euro is justified by a shock to the underlying fundamentals is essential in order to deduce the most appropriate policy response. Typically, the macroeconomic impact of an exchange rate change depends on the source of the shock that drives this change. Moreover, knowing where the current exchange rate stands relative to its equilibrium value can provide insights into the likely future movements in the exchange rate.

On May 1, 2004 the European Economic and Monetary Union expanded its membership with the accession of ten countries from central and eastern Europe and the Mediterranean - Cyprus, the Czech Republic, Estonia, Hungary, Latvia, Lithuania, Malta, Poland, Slovakia, and Slovenia. The new member states participate in the Economic and Monetary Union with derogation as they have not yet adopted the euro, but are committed to do so as soon as they fulfill the Maastricht convergence criteria.[2]

According to the Maastricht exchange rate criterion, each country must participate in the European exchange rate mechanism (ERM) II for at least two years before joining the common currency. The Estonian kroon, the Lithuanian litas, and the Slovenia tolar already entered the ERM II on June 28, 2004, followed by the Cyprus pound, the Latvian lats and the Maltese lira which entered on May 2, 2005. Participation in the ERM II necessitates a mutual agreement on a sustainable central parity, at which the currencies of the new member countries enter the ERM II. Deciding on the central parity requires information on the equilibrium values of these currencies with respect to the euro in order to set the central rate such that it is the least costly to sustain in terms of inflation differentials.

Knowledge of the equilibrium real exchange rate paths is also desirable in order to evaluate in how far the new member countries may encounter difficulties in complying with the convergence criteria laid down in the Maastricht Treaty. Over the past ten years, the currencies of the majority of these countries have heavily appreciated in real terms. If this appreciation represents an equilibrium phenomenon that is likely to continue over the near future, tying

[2] According to the Maastricht Treaty, any country that wants to adopt the euro has to meet the following five conditions: (i) the budget deficit must not exceed three percent of GDP; (ii) the national debt must not exceed 60 percent of GDP; (iii) the inflation rate must not exceed the average inflation rate of the lowest three inflation countries in the euro area by more than 1.5 percentage points; (iv) the long-term interest rate must be no more than two percent above the average of the three countries with the lowest inflation rates; (v) the fluctuation margins provided for by the exchange-rate mechanism must be respected without severe tensions for at least two years.

the nominal exchange rates to the euro within the ERM II means that the adjustment has to come through inflation rates that exceed the inflation rate in the euro area. Hence, the new member countries that participate in the ERM II may face difficulties in fulfilling the Maastricht inflation criterion.

This study addresses the questions raised above by estimating equilibrium exchange rate paths for the euro and for the currencies of the new EU member countries. Chapter 2 of this study starts with an overview on the various theoretical concepts of equilibrium exchange rates that have been put forward in the literature and their applications to the euro and to the currencies of the new EU member countries. Chapters 3 and 4 then take a closer look at recent movements in the external value of the euro. Chapter 3 investigates in how far variations in the nominal exchange rate of the euro vis-à-vis the U.S. dollar, the Canadian dollar, the British pound, the Norwegian krone, the Japanese yen, the Swiss franc, and the Australian dollar can be explained by monetary factors. The chapter examines the validity of several alternative versions of the monetary approach for the seven exchange rates. In those cases, in which the data lend support to the monetary approach, the estimation results are used to assess a possible under- and overvaluation of the euro and to investigate the out-of-sample forecasting performance of the monetary approach.

As the monetary approach assumes the real exchange rate to fluctuate around some constant value it cannot explain the large variations in the real exchange rate of the euro that could be observed over the past decades. Chapter 4 therefore takes a closer look at the real exchange rate of the euro and investigates in how far variations in this exchange rate represent movements in underlying fundamentals. Among the various concepts that have been proposed in the literature to estimate real equilibrium exchange rates, the chapter focuses on the natural real exchange rate (NATREX) approach advocated by Stein (1994) and Stein and Allen (1997). Compared to alternative concepts, the natural real exchange rate approach has the advantage that it explicitly distinguishes, within a structural model, between the medium-term and the long-term equilibrium exchange rate. The estimates are used to evaluate in how far recent movements in the real effective exchange rate of the euro represent movements in the underlying equilibrium rate or in how far they represent real exchange rate misalignments.

Chapters 5 and 6 of this study take a closer look at the currencies of the ten countries that joined the European Union in 2004. Both chapters make use of a small country version of the NATREX approach in deriving equilibrium real exchange rate paths for these currencies. In chapter 5, the model is estimated in reduced form for a set of 21 OECD countries and the obtained coefficients are then applied to data from the new member countries. This two-step estimation strategy has the advantage that time series starting in 1980 can be used for the regression analysis, which makes it more likely that it captures the long-term relationship between the real exchange rate and economic fundamentals, and that the influence of the transition effect present in the data of most of the new member countries is avoided. While the simplifications that reduced-from estimations impose on the theoretical complexity of models allow an intuitive interpretation of the results, they make it impossible to verify whether the analytical conditions for equilibrium are met. Chapter 6 therefore estimates the small country version of the NATREX model in structural form. This guarantees that the analytical conditions for equilibrium are satisfied and, additionally, makes it possible to verify, whether the underlying behavioral relationships are in line with the predictions of the structural model. Due to data availability problems, the structural estimation is only carried out for the Lithuanian economy.

Chapter 2

Equilibrium Exchange Rate Concepts

The literature on exchange rate economics has put forward a number of theoretical models that are commonly referred to as equilibrium exchange rate models (see, for example, the surveys by MacDonald, 2000; and Driver and Westaway, 2004). All of these models have in common that they aim at deriving an equilibrium level of the exchange rate which is related to some set of economic fundamentals. Exchange rate movements are then explained either by moving fundamentals or by the correction of an existing disequilibrium. The models do not attempt to explain exchange rate movements that result from transitory factors such as asset market bubbles (Driver and Westaway, 2004, p. 12). Rather, the focus is on the underlying trend movement.

If the actual exchange rate deviates from the equilibrium path implied by fundamentals it is said to be misaligned. Such a misalignment may occur because the fundamental factors that determine the exchange rate deviate from equilibrium themselves. In this case, adjustment does not fall on the exchange rate but on the fundamentals. The exchange rate may also deviate from its equilibrium level despite the fact that the fundamentals are in equilibrium. In this case, the warranted policy reaction depends on the magnitude of the misalignment as well as on the source and nature of the shock that caused the exchange rate misalignment in the first place.

This chapter does not explore the policy implications that might be associated with an observed exchange rate misalignment. Rather, it provides an introduction to equilibrium exchange rate concepts and their applications to the euro and to the currencies of the new EU member countries. Sections 2.1

and 2.2 first present some of the more popular methods of estimating equilibrium exchange rates. The presentation in these two sections is not meant to be conclusive or exhaustive, but rather to provide a brief overview on those equilibrium exchange rate models that have been the most widely employed in empirical work.

Section 2.1 starts with the purchasing power parity (PPP) hypothesis, the oldest concept for calculating equilibrium exchange rates. An important implication of purchasing power parity is that the real exchange rate is constant. The focus of the concept therefore lies in explaining nominal exchange rate movements by changes in relative prices. The section then continues by presenting two extensions of the purchasing power parity concept, the monetary exchange rate approach and the capital enhanced equilibrium exchange rate (CHEER) approach. The desire of the two models is to improve the ability of PPP to explain the behavior of nominal exchange rates (Driver and Westaway, 2004, pp. 35, 37).

The proposition of a constant real exchange rate made by PPP and its extensions is hardly reconcilable with the empirical evidence. Several authors have therefore developed exchange rate models that explicitly explain movements in the real exchange rate. These models do not say anything about the equilibrium level of the nominal exchange rate, since every given real exchange rate equilibrium is associated with an infinite number of combinations of the nominal exchange rate and relative prices. They are thus in sharp contrast to the earlier exchange rate concepts that all focused on the nominal exchange rate.

The most widely applied concepts to calculate *real* equilibrium exchange rates are presented in chapter 2.2. These are the behavioral equilibrium exchange rate (BEER) approach, the permanent equilibrium exchange rate (PEER) approach, the macroeconomic balance approach, and the natural real exchange rate (NATREX) approach. The BEER approach relies on a statistical notion of equilibrium. It tries to explain exchange rate movements based on a set of relevant explanatory variables that are selected according to what economic theory stipulates as variables that play a role in determining the real exchange rate in the short to medium term. The PEER approach aims at decomposing the exchange rate into its permanent and transitory components. The permanent component is then taken to be a measure of equilibrium. The equilibrium is a purely statistical concept and in this sense the PEER is similar to the BEER approach. The macroeconomic balance approach puts more structure on the computations of the equilibrium real exchange rate in that it assumes the economy to be in internal and external equilibrium. The NATREX approach is similar to the macroeconomic balance in that it starts from a medium-term equilibrium where internal and external balance prevail, but extends the macroeconomic balance approach to the long term when net foreign debt and the capital stock have reached their steady state values.

The last section of this chapter finally presents empirical applications of equilibrium exchange models to the euro and to the currencies of the new EU member countries. The focus is on the methodology applied to estimate the equilibrium exchange rate path as well as on the findings regarding any possible under- or overvaluation of the currencies.

2.1 Concepts explaining Movements in the Nominal Exchange Rate

2.1.1 Purchasing Power Parity

The measure economists usually first turn to when asked to think about the equilibrium value of the exchange rate is purchasing power parity. The central idea of purchasing power parity dates back to the 18th century (Officer, 1976, p. 5; Brisman, 1933, p. 72), though the term 'purchasing power parity' was originated by Cassel (1918, p. 413). He was also the first to place PPP within a coherent framework and to make it an operational concept (Officer, 1976, p. 5).

In its absolute version, PPP states that the price levels in different countries should be the same when expressed in a common currency:

$$e_t = p_t - p_t^*. \tag{2.1}$$

Here, e is the logarithm of the domestic currency price of a unit of foreign currency, p is the domestic price index, p^* is the foreign price index, and t is the time index.

The PPP hypothesis is build upon the law of one price (LOOP), which claims that identical goods sold at different geographical locations should sell for the same price if prices are expressed in the same currency and if no transaction costs are present. The theoretic rational behind the law of one price are arbitrage activities that eliminate any price differences for individual goods. In reality, transportation costs, tariffs and non-tariff barriers, and pricing-to-market may drive a wedge between prices at different locations, thereby causing violations of the LOOP. Moreover, even if the law of one price holds for individual goods, purchasing power parity may not hold due to differences in the composition of consumption baskets across countries. These limitations are acknowledged in the relative version of the PPP hypothesis, stating that the change in the exchange rate should equal the inflation differential:

$$\Delta e_t = \Delta p_t - \Delta p_t^*, \tag{2.2}$$

where Δ is the first difference operator.

A large body of literature deals with empirically testing the purchasing power parity hypothesis (see the surveys by Sarno and Taylor, 2002; Taylor and Taylor, 2004; and Taylor, 2006). The studies date back until the late 1970s when researchers began to exploit the data on floating exchange rates that became available after the collapse of the Bretton Woods system. While early results were encouraging (Frenkel and Johnson, 1978), studies from the early 1980s that drew on data from the late 1970s when the dollar became more volatile showed that PPP was easily rejected by the data (Frenkel, 1981), a phenomenon that became known as the PPP puzzle.

Acknowledging that PPP does not hold in the short run, the literature shifted towards PPP as a long-run phenomenon with the aim of solving the PPP puzzle. Two types of formal tests of long-run PPP have dominated the literature. The first type of test examines the unit root properties of the real exchange rate, defined as $q_t = e_t - p_t + p_t^*$. PPP implies that the real exchange rate is a constant, so that movements in the real exchange rate represent deviations from PPP. Therefore, if the real exchange rate is found to be stationary (i.e., to fluctuate around some constant value) this can be interpreted as evidence in favor of long-run PPP. The second type of test relies on cointegration analysis (Engle and Granger, 1987) and tests for the existence of an equilibrium relationship between the nominal exchange rate and domestic and foreign prices. The main difference between the two approaches in testing for PPP is that unit root tests of the real exchange rate restrict the nominal exchange rate and the price differential to move proportionally and are thus a test of PPP in its absolute version, while cointegration tests do not impose this restriction and thus test PPP in its relative version. Early studies yielded conflicting results regarding the validity of the purchasing power parity hypothesis (e.g., PPP is rejected by Darby, 1980; Adler and Lehmann, 1983; MacDonald, 1985; Enders, 1988; Taylor, 1988; Mark, 1990; Edison and Pauls, 1993, but supported by Huizinga, 1987; Corbae and Ouliaris, 1988; Kim, 1990; Chowdhury and Sdogati, 1993; Cheung and Lai,

1993a). By contrast, later studies that increased the power of the tests by using long-time spans of data or by examining several currencies simultaneously within a panel framework usually found evidence in favor of the PPP hypothesis (e.g., Abuaf and Jorion, 1990; Diebold, Husted, and Rush, 1991; Glen, 1992; Levin and Lin, 1992, 1993; Lothian and Taylor, 1996; Jorion and Sweeney, 1996; Flood and Taylor, 1996; Wu, 1996; Frankel and Rose, 1996; Lothian, 1997; Coakley and Fuertes, 1997; O'Connell, 1998; Papell, 1998; Taylor and Sarno, 1998).

Even if the long-time-span and panel-data studies of the 1990s were considered as having solved the original PPP puzzle, a second puzzle was brought up which relates to the high persistence of deviations from PPP. Among the studies that find evidence in favor of PPP, there appears to be a consensus that deviations from PPP are highly persistent with half life times of three to five years (Rogoff, 1996). Recent studies on PPP therefore focus on the high persistence of deviations from PPP. A promising attempt is to allow for nonlinear dynamics in the adjustment process. From a theoretical point of view, nonlinearities can be rationalized by transactions costs (e.g., Williams and Wright, 1991; Dumas, 1992), technical traders (Kilian and Taylor, 2003), and central bank interventions (Taylor, 2004); and from an empirical point of view, nonlinearities seem to produce half-life estimates well below the Rogoff consensus (e.g., Obstfeld and Taylor, 1997; Michael, Nobay, and Peel, 1997; Taylor, Peel, and Sarno, 2001).

2.1.2 The Monetary Approach

The monetary approach essentially augments the purchasing power parity relationship with a theory that specifies how prices are determined in the countries. Specifically, demand for money relationships for the home and foreign country are added to the model. Assuming that money markets clear continuously so that the demand for money always equals supply, prices are determined by the money stock and by a set of economic fundamentals that affect money demand.

The monetary approach is not a single model but in fact covers a number of differing approaches. Depending on the degree of price flexibility, two main versions of the monetary approach can be distinguished. The models by Frenkel (1976) and Bilson (1978) presume that prices are perfectly flexible, so that purchasing power parity holds continuously. By contrast, the models by Dornbusch (1976) and Frankel (1979) assume sticky prices, so that purchasing power parity only holds in the long run.

Applications of the approach center on estimating a reduced-form equation that relates the nominal exchange rate to a set of economic fundamentals. The composition of this set of fundamentals depends on whether price adjustment is assumed to take place slowly or instantaneously and on how the demand for money relationships are specified. The set of fundamentals always includes relative money stocks and relative output, though it may also include the nominal interest differential (Bilson, 1978; Dornbusch, 1976), the expected inflation differential (Frenkel, 1976), or both (Frankel, 1979).

A large number of researchers have tested the propositions of the monetary model empirically (see, for example, the survey by MacDonald and Taylor, 1992). While early studies that look at data from the interwar period or from the early years of the floating period are largely supportive of the monetary model (e.g., Bilson, 1978; Hodrick, 1978; Putnam and Woodbury, 1979; Dornbusch, 1979; and Frankel, 1979), studies that extend the data set beyond the late 1970s often report wrongly signed or insignificant coefficients (e.g., Haynes and Stone, 1981; Frankel, 1984; Backus, 1984; and, more recently, Chinn, 2000; Chinn and Alquist, 2000). Three exceptions are Husted and MacDonald (2000), van Aarle, Boss, Hlouskova (2000), and Groen (2005) who, when applying the monetary model to east Asian currencies and to the euro, respectively, report coefficients that are in line with the predictions of the monetary approach.

2.1.3 The Capital Enhanced Equilibrium Exchange Rate

The capital enhanced equilibrium exchange rate concept has been popularized by Juselius (1991, 1995), Johansen and Juselius (1992), MacDonald and Marsh (1997, 1999), and Juselius and MacDonald (2000), though the term 'capital enhanced equilibrium exchange rate' was first introduced by MacDonald (2000). The starting point of the CHEER approach is the observation that purchasing power parity only holds in the long run. The persistent deviations of the actual nominal exchange rate from its PPP implied level are then attributed to non-zero interest differentials.

Specifically, the concept combines the purchasing power parity condition (2.1) with the uncovered interest rate parity (UIP) condition, which states that the expected change in the nominal exchange rate should equal the interest rate differential between domestic and foreign securities:

$$E_t(\Delta e_{t+k}) = i_t - i_t^*. \tag{2.3}$$

Here, Δe_{t+k} is the exchange rate change over the time interval k, i_t is the interest rate on a domestic bond of maturity $t+k$, i^* is the interest rate on a foreign bond of the same maturity, and E is the expectation operator. Assuming that the expected level of the exchange rate at any future point in time is given by PPP, equation (2.3) can be written as:

$$i_t - i_t^* = E_t(e_{t+k}) - e_t = p_{t+k} - p_{t+k}^* - e_t. \tag{2.4}$$

The CHEER approach therefore involves estimating the cointegrating vector

$$x' = [e, p, p^*, i, i^*] \tag{2.5}$$

and then solving for the nominal exchange rate, which is the CHEER.

Empirical applications of the CHEER approach have generally suggested higher speeds of convergence than the simple PPP approach (e.g., MacDonald and Marsh, 1997; Juselius and MacDonald, 2000). Moreover, out-of-sample forecasts of the nominal exchange rate tend to dominate the random walk at horizons as short as two months (e.g., MacDonald and Marsh, 1997).

2.2 Concepts explaining Movements in the Real Exchange Rate

2.2.1 The Behavioral Equilibrium Exchange Rate

The BEER approach was originally developed by Clark and MacDonald (1998, 2000). The starting point of the model is the risk-adjusted uncovered interest rate parity condition

$$E_t(\Delta e_{t+k}) = (i_t - i_t^*) + \omega_t, \tag{2.6}$$

where ω is a time-varying risk premium, commonly approximated by the ratio of the outstanding domestic government debt to foreign government debt, both as ratio to GDP. Equation (2.6) says that the expected change in the exchange rate should equal the interest differential plus a risk premium. Subtracting the expected inflation differential $E_t(\Delta p_{t+k} - \Delta p_{t+k}^*)$ from both sides of the equation and then setting $r_t = i_t - E_t(\Delta p_{t+k})$, $r_t^* = i_t^* - E_t(\Delta p_{t+k}^*)$, and $E_t(\Delta q_{t+k}) = E_t(q_{t+k}) - q_t = E_t(\Delta e_{t+k}) - E_t(\Delta p_{t+k}) + E_t(\Delta p_{t+k}^*)$ gives:

$$q_t = E_t(q_{t+k}) + (r_t - r_t^*) + \omega_t. \tag{2.7}$$

Assuming that the expected exchange rate at any future point in time is equal to the long-run equilibrium rate $\overline{q}$, equation (2.7) can be written as:

$$q_t = \overline{q} + (r_t - r_t^*) + \omega_t, \qquad \overline{q} = f(TOT, R_N, NFA). \tag{2.8}$$

The long-run equilibrium rate $\overline{q}$ is assumed to depend on a set of economic fundamentals, which in the original papers by Clark and MacDonald (1998, 2000) comprises the terms of trade TOT, the relative price of non-traded to traded goods R_N, and the net foreign asset position NFA, although the authors acknowledge that this choice is not exhaustive. In empirical applications of the BEER approach, the set of fundamentals is commonly extended to factors such as the productivity differential between the tradable and non-tradable sector (as an alternative to the relative price of non-tradable goods), government expenditure, openness, government debt (as a measure of fiscal sustainability), per capita GDP (as a measure of the stage of development), and the dependency ratio. Table 2.1 provides an overview on these factors and their expected impact on the real exchange rate.

Equation (2.8) suggests that the actual real exchange rate q_t should move in accordance with the real interest rate differential, the risk premium, and the economic fundamentals that explain the equilibrium real exchange rate:

$$q = f(TOT, R_N, NFA, r - r^*, \omega_t). \tag{2.9}$$

To put it differently, the framework implies the existence of a cointegrating relationship between the actual real exchange rate and the set of fundamentals. Although the theoretical background of the BEER approach stipulates that the set of fundamentals should at least comprise the real interest differential and a measure of the risk premium, the BEER terminology is often used in a more general sense, where all studies that relate the real exchange rate to some set of fundamentals without specifying an explicit underlying model are categorized as BEER studies.

A central question that arises is how to evaluate the estimated cointegrating relationship. A first possibility is to evaluate the cointegrating vector at actual values of the economic fundamentals in order to calculate a short-term equilibrium real exchange rate that would prevail under current economic settings after abstracting from the influence of unexpected shocks (Driver and Westaway, 2004, p. 12). Any deviation of the observed real exchange rate from this short-term equilibrium rate would, thus, be entirely due to unexpected shocks. However, the equilibrium level of the real exchange rate obtained by using actual values of the fundamentals is a disequilibrium in the sense that it is associated with a disequilibrium of the whole economy. A second possibility therefore is to derive a medium-term equilibrium real exchange rate

Table 2.1: Factors commonly included in Reduced-From Equilibrium Exchange Rate Estimations

Factor	Impact on the real exchange rate
Terms of trade	A rise in the terms of trade, measured as export prices over import prices, leads to an improvement in the current account and, hence, causes an appreciation of the real exchange rate in order to restore equilibrium.
Net foreign asset position	A country's net foreign asset position is supposed to be positively correlated with the real exchange rate. The idea is that a decline in net foreign assets - or, equivalently, a rise in net foreign liabilities - requires a depreciation of the real exchange rate in order to generate the trade surpluses needed to finance the higher interest payments and more generally to increase external sustainability.
Productivity differential	Balassa (1964) and Samuelson (1964) argue that a productivity increase in the tradable sector relative to the non-tradable sector induces a rise in wages in this sector. If labor moves freely between sectors, the higher wage level in the tradable sector spills over to the non-tradable sector. If productivity in the non-tradable sector remains constant, this rise in wages brings about higher prices of non-tradable goods. The overall price level in the economy rises and the real exchange rate appreciates. However, these propositions hinge on three key assumptions: (i) PPP holds for the tradable sector, (ii), both the tradable and the non-tradable sector are governed by market forces, and (iii) wages tend to equalize across sectors.
Real interest rate differential	According to the uncovered interest rate parity hypothesis, a rise in domestic real interest rates stimulates net capital inflows and, thereby, causes an appreciation of the real exchange rate. It should be noted that the impact of the real interest rate differential on the real exchange rate is predominantly a short-term phenomenon as arbitrage opportunities tend to be explored rather quickly.
Openness	A rise in openness is assumed to exert competitive pressure on an increasing range of tradable goods in the domestic economy, thereby leading to a decline in prices and wages and, hence, to a depreciation of the real exchange rate.

Table 2.1: Factors commonly included in Reduced-From Equilibrium Exchange Rate Estimations (cont.)

Factor	Impact on the real exchange rate
Fiscal sustainability	Fiscal sustainability might influence the real effective exchange rate through several channels. First, a deterioration in fiscal sustainability could entail a rise in the domestic risk premium, requiring a depreciation of the equilibrium real exchange rate to generate expectations of a future appreciation. For this first channel to work, a high degree of capital mobility and some degree of substitutability between different government papers are required. The second channel rests upon the idea that a deterioration in fiscal sustainability might give rise to expectations of fiscal adjustment. As public consumption falls to a large extent on non-tradable goods, these expectations of fiscal adjustment might be accompanied by expectations of declining relative prices for non-tradable goods and, hence, of a real exchange rate depreciation.
Government consumption	If government consumptions mainly falls on non-tradable goods, a rise in government consumption is associated with a rise in the demand for non-tradable goods and thus puts upward pressure on the price of non-tradable goods, resulting in a real exchange rate appreciation.
Stage of development	The hypothesis is that at an early stage of development, countries typically import capital and, hence, run current account deficits. At a later stage of development, countries run current account surpluses in order to pay off accumulated external liabilities and also to export capital to less advanced economies. To bring about this intertemporal adjustment, the real exchange rate has to depreciate over time as the economy moves from current account deficits to current account surpluses.
Demographic structure	Countries with higher relative dependency ratios are expected to exhibit lower levels of domestic savings and, thus, to run smaller current accounts surpluses (or larger deficits). Here, the intertemporal adjustment would imply that countries with an aging population experience an appreciation of the real exchange rate.

from the cointegrating vector which is compatible with the whole economy being in equilibrium. This can be done by replacing the actual values of the fundamentals with estimates of their trend levels.

An inherent drawback of the BEER approach is the lack of an explicit underlying economic model. As a result, the choice of fundamentals that are included in the regressions is, in most cases, rather ad-hoc. This is problematic as the signs of the estimated coefficients may be affected by this choice. Moreover, the concept relies on reduced-form estimates that only provide information about the general interrelationship between the real exchange rate and economic fundamentals. They cannot give any insight into the various forward and backward channels through which the real exchange rate and the fundamentals are connected, which makes interpretation rather difficult, especially because both are endogenous in most cases.

2.2.2 The Permanent Equilibrium Exchange Rate

The permanent equilibrium exchange rate approach aims at decomposing the real exchange rate into its permanent and transitory components. The permanent component is then taken as a measure of equilibrium and is called the PEER (MacDonald, 2000, p. 26).

Two distinct approaches for calculating the PEER have been put forward in the literature. The first one involves a direct decomposition of the real exchange rate q_t into its permanent components q_t^P and its transitory components q_t^T:

$$q_t = q_t^P + q_t^T. \tag{2.10}$$

A number of different econometric techniques have been proposed in the literature for extracting the permanent component q_t^P. Several researchers have applied the Beveridge-Nelson decomposition (e.g., Huizinga, 1987; Cumby and Huizinga, 1990; Clarida and Gali, 1994). The approach rests on the idea that any autoregressive integrated moving average (ARIMA) process can be represented as the sum of a stationary component and a random walk component (Beveridge and Nelson, 1981). The random walk component is then interpreted as the permanent component of the process. Clarida and Gali (1994) propose an alternative technique which involves estimating a structural vector autoregression (SVAR) model and then extracting demand and supply shocks, where the latter are taken to be the permanent components of the real exchange rate (e.g., MacDonald and Swagel, 2000; Detken et al., 2002).

The second approach for calculating the PEER is due to Clark and MacDonald (2000) who suggest decomposing the cointegrating vector obtained from a BEER-type estimation into its permanent and transitory components. The decomposition is implemented using the methodology proposed by Granger and Gonzalo (1995) who have demonstrated that the elements of the cointegrating vector can be explained in terms of some common factors which are I(1) and, hence, have a permanent impact on the real exchange rate, and some transitory factors which are I(0). The approach does not attempt to measure the equilibrium levels of the fundamentals and as such is a statistical rather than an economic concept of equilibrium (Driver and Westaway, 2004, p. 47).

2.2.3 The Macroeconomic Balance Approach

The macroeconomic balance approach overcomes the deficiencies of the BEER and the PEER approaches in that it derives the equilibrium level of the real exchange rate from an explicit economic model. The approach dates back to the early writings of Nurkse (1945) and Metzler (1951) and was later refined by various authors including Swan (1963), Artus (1978), Artus and Knight (1984), and Williamson (1985, 1994). The central idea is that a country's current account balance is equal the excess of domestic savings over domestic investment. The real equilibrium exchange rate is defined as the exchange rate that equates the current account to its target, given by the structural saving-investment balance in the medium run, when the economy is producing at potential output. Hence, the equilibrium real exchange rate is the level of the exchange rate that ensures both external and internal balance.

The workings of the model can be illustrated with the help of Figure 2.1. The equilibrium saving-investment balance is assumed to be independent of the real exchange rate R (here defined in quantity quotation), as depicted by the vertical SI line, while the underlying current account is assumed to deteriorate with an appreciation of the real exchange rate, as depicted by the negatively sloped line labelled UCA. The equilibrium real exchange rate $\tilde{R}$ corresponds to the exchange rate at which the UCA and SI lines intersect. Changes in economic fundamentals that shift either the position of the SI line or the UCA line will alter the equilibrium real exchange rate. For example, demographic changes that lead to a higher dependency ratio will be associated with a decrease in savings and, hence, with a shift of the SI line to the left. The result is an appreciation of the equilibrium real exchange rate which stimulates imports and dampens exports. The current

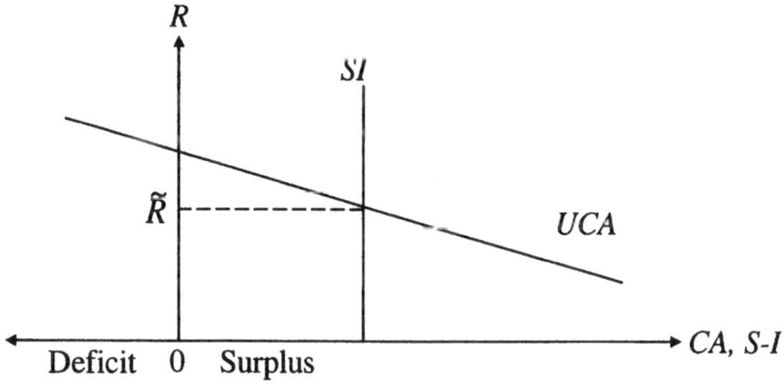

Figure 2.1: Stylized model of the macroeconomic balance approach

account deteriorates and external equilibrium is restored. Other factors that are commonly considered as important determinants of the real exchange rate within the macroeconomic balance approach are per capital GDP, the output gap, and the fiscal position (Isard and Faruqee, 1998, p. 12). Although this collection of variables is similar to the one commonly employed in a BEER estimation, the reasons for their inclusion and the way in which they feature are less ad hoc than would be true for a BEER analysis (Driver and Westaway, 2004, p. 39).

The macroeconomic balance approach can be implemented either within a fully specified macroeconomic model (e.g., Coudert and Couharde, 2003; Šmídková, Barrell and Holland, 2002) or within a partial equilibrium framework (e.g., Wren-Lewis and Driver, 1998; Isard and Faruqee, 1998). The former involves imposing internal and external balance on the macroeconomic model and solving for the real exchange rate which is the equilibrium rate. The latter involves a three step procedure. In the first step, a trade equation model is applied to calculate the underlying current account position that would emerge at prevailing exchange rates if the country were producing at potential output. In the second step, the target current account position is specified, also assuming that the country is operating at potential output. Finally, in the third step, the trade elasticities that were estimated in the first step are used to calculate the change in the exchange rate that is required to adjust the underlying current account position to its target level.

Applications of the approach can be distinguished based on the way the target current account is identified. One possibility is to set the target current account equal to sustainable capital flows, in which case the derived equilibrium exchange rate is usually referred to as the fundamental equilibrium exchange rate, or simply the FEER (Williamson, 1985, 1994). In early applications of the approach, the level of sustainable capital flows was simply assumed to be a constant proportion of GDP (e.g., Barrel and Wren-Lewis, 1989; Currie and Wren-Lewis, 1989; Williamson and Miller, 1987; Williamson, 1994). A less ad hoc alternative is to set the target current account equal to the equilibrium savings-investment balance, where the equilibrium values of savings and investment are determined in terms of demographic factors, the fiscal stance, and income per capita (e.g., Faruqee and Debelle, 1998; Masson, 1998, Wren-Lewis and Driver, 1998).

An alternative way is to set the target current account equal to some optimal or desired level of capital flows, in which case the resulting equilibrium real exchange rate is called the DEER, or the desired equilibrium exchange rate (Bayoumi et al., 1994). The idea is to condition the real exchange rate on some measure of optimal policy, which inherently makes the equilibrium exchange rate a normative concept. In empirical applications of the approach, the DEER is usually conditioned on some measure of optimal fiscal policy (e.g., Bayoumi et al., 1994; Artis and Taylor, 1995). It should be noted that the terminology does not imply that the calculated exchange rate should be seen as a target in itself, but rather as facilitating the achievement of certain macroeconomic objectives (Bayoumi et al., 1994, p. 20).

2.2.4 The Natural Real Exchange Rate Approach

The NATREX approach was originally developed by Stein (1994) and later extended by Stein and Allen (1997). It is similar to the macroeconomic balance approach in that it starts from the concept of a medium-term equilibrium in which internal and external balance prevail. It extends the macroeconomic balance approach to the long term in which net foreign debt and the real capital stock have reached their steady state values. Like in the macroeconomic balance framework, internal balance refers to the concept of a non-accelerating inflation rate of unemployment, while external balance refers to a situation in which the current account balance is equal to the ex ante difference of saving and investment, where these are evaluated at the level implied by fundamentals. In the NATREX approach, these fundamentals relate to productivity, the time preference rate, the world real interest rate, and the terms of trade.

The NATREX approach is not represented by a single model, but rather by a group of models, each of which is tailored to the specific features of the country under consideration. The different versions of the NATREX approach can be categorized based on how goods markets and asset markets are modelled (Allen, 1997, p. 19). With respect to goods markets, two main types of countries can be distinguished: (i) large and/or specialized countries that are able to influence the world market price of their products (e.g., Stein, 1994, United States; Fischer and Sauernheimer, 2002, Germany), and (ii) small countries that face perfectly elastic world demand for and supply of tradable goods (e.g., Lim and Stein, 1997, Australia).

With respect to asset markets, three main types of countries can be distinguished: (i) countries that have high capital mobility and are small in world asset markets (e.g., Fischer and Sauernheimer, 2002, Germany), (ii) countries that have high capital mobility and are large in world asset markets (e.g., Stein, 1994, United States), and (iii) countries with less than perfect capital mobility (e.g., Lim and Stein, 1997, Australia). Countries from the first group can borrow as much as they wish at the given world real interest rate. Since the domestic real interest rate is tied to the world rate, a lasting change in the domestic real interest rate cannot occur and market adjustments entirely fall on the real exchange rate. Countries from the second group, by contrast, are large enough to influence the world real interest rate. The real interest rate and the real exchange rate are thus determined simultaneously and adjustment falls on both of them. The third group of countries faces a limited foreign supply of capital. World asset markets impose a risk premium on the domestic real interest rate. A rise in desired borrowing will induce a rise in the domestic real interest rate over the world real interest rate thereby reducing the necessary adjustment of the real exchange rate.

This study makes use of two different versions of the NATREX approach that relate to different combinations of the goods and asset market specifications. First, in chapter 4, the euro area is modelled as small in the sense that foreign output and the world interest rate are exogenous (asset market specification (ii)), but large in the sense that it has the ability to influence the world market price of its products so that the terms of trade are endogenous (goods market specification (i)). Second, in chapters 5 and 6, the new EU member countries are modelled as small in the sense that they cannot influence the world market prices of their products so that the terms of trade are exogenous (goods market specification (ii)). In addition, it is assumed that these countries face a limited foreign supply of capital implying that world asset markets impose a risk premium on the domestic real interest rate (asset market specification (iii)).

2.3 Empirical Applications of Equilibrium Exchange Rate Models to the Euro and to the Currencies of the New EU Member Countries of 2004

The theoretical concepts discussed in the previous section have been extensively used in the literature to evaluate in how far observed exchange rate movements are in line with underlying economic fundamentals. This section provides an overview on this literature focusing on those currencies that are in the center of this study, i.e., the euro (section 2.3.1) and the currencies of the new EU member countries (section 2.3.2).

2.3.1 Empirical Studies of the Euro

The rapid depreciation of the euro after its launch in 1999 motivated many economists to estimate models of the euro exchange rate to ascertain whether the decline in its value could be explained by movements in the underlying economic fundamentals. Studies that examine the nominal exchange rate of the euro mostly rely on some version of the monetary approach (e.g., van Aarle, Boss, Hlouskova, 2000; Chinn, 2000; Chinn and Alquist, 2000; Groen, 2005). By contrast, assessments of movements in the real exchange rate are based on a wide variety of different models, including the BEER approach (e.g., Alberola et al., 1999; Clostermann and Schnatz, 2000; Lorenzen and Thygesen, 2000; Detken et al., 2002; Alquist and Chinn, 2002; Maseo-Fernandez, Osbat, and Schnatz, 2003; Osbat, Rüffer, and Schnatz, 2003; Schnatz, Vijselaar, and Osbat, 2004), the PEER approach (e.g., Alberola et al., 1999; Maseo-Fernandez, Osbat, and Schnatz, 2001), the macroeconomic balance approach (e.g., Detken et al., 2002; Borowski and Couharde, 2003), and the NATREX approach (e.g., Duval, 2002; Detken and Marín Martínez, 2001; Detken et al., 2002).

Among the studies that apply the monetary approach to assess movements in the nominal exchange rate of the euro, the most convincing results are obtained by van Aarle, Boss, Hlouskova (2000), Frenkel and Koske (2004), and Groen (2005). Van Aarle, Boss, Hlouskova (2000) estimate a general specification of the monetary exchange rate model, including money stocks, output, interest and expected inflation rates for the bilateral exchange rates of the euro against the British pound, the US dollar, the Swiss franc and the

Japanese yen for the period January 1980 - February 1999. The results are broadly in line with the monetary model and even out of sample forecasts of the exchange rates are able to beat a naïve random walk in a number of cases. Frenkel and Koske (2004) examine the validity of the monetary model for the bilateral exchange rates of the euro vis-à-vis the US dollar, the Canadian dollar, the British pound, the Norwegian krone, the Japanese yen, and the Swiss franc during the period 1980-2003. The authors find that a long-run equilibrium relationship does indeed exist between the variables of the monetary model, however, different versions of the model seem to be supported by the data in different countries. Groen (2005) applies a rational expectations-based monetary model to the bilateral exchanges rates of the euro vis-à-vis the Canadian dollar, the Japanese yen, and the US dollar. The obtained parameter estimates comply with the underlying model and out-of-sample forecasts show that the monetary model is superior to both the random walk model and a standard VAR model. Chinn (2000) and Chinn and Alquist (2000) who use a variation of the traditional monetary variables and apply their version to the bilateral exchange rate between the euro and the US dollar present less positive results. Using data for the 1990s, most of the estimated coefficients are not significant at conventional significance levels.

The majority of the studies that assess the development of the real exchange rate of the euro employ the BEER approach. Alberola et al. (1999) study bilateral euro exchange rates as well as the effective euro exchange rate over the period 1980Q1 to 1998Q4. The authors show that a significant cointegrating relationship exists between the real euro exchange rate, the net foreign asset position, and relative prices of tradable to non-tradable goods. By decomposing the observed real exchange rate into its transitory and permanent components, the authors derive the permanent equilibrium exchange rate and show that, just before the beginning of the European Economic and Monetary Union, the euro was overvalued against the Japanese yen and the Swedish krona, but undervalued against the US dollar, the Canadian dollar, the UK pound, and the Danish krona.

Lorenzen and Thygesen (2000) also estimate a BEER model but restrict their study to the real exchange rate between the euro and the US dollar. The authors find a significant correlation between the exchange rate and a set of fundamentals that consists of net foreign assets, the dependency ratio,[3] R&D expenditures, the internal relative price ratio, and the medium-term

[3]The dependency ratio is defined as the population under age 15 and above age 65 divided by the population aged 15 to 64.

real interest differential. The authors find that, at the beginning of 1999, the euro was undervalued against the US dollar. Clostermann and Schnatz (2000) apply a similar approach using the real interest differential, the relative price of traded to non-traded goods, the real oil price, and the relative fiscal position as fundamentals. For the third quarter of 1999, the authors estimate the equilibrium exchange rate of the euro against the US dollar to be around USD/EUR 1.20.

The analysis by Alquist and Chinn (2002) is also in the spirit of the BEER approach. The real exchange rate between the euro and the US dollar is related to the productivity differential, the real price of oil, and relative government spending. The authors find that each percentage point in the productivity differential between the US and the euro area results in a five percentage point real appreciation of the US dollar. The estimated model suggests that the exchange between the euro and the US dollar was close to equilibrium by the end of 2001.

Similar to Alberola et al. (1999), Maseo-Fernandez, Osbat, and Schnatz (2001) assess recent developments in the euro exchange rate within a BEER/PEER framework. The authors relate the real effective euro exchange rate to a number of fundamental variables. Overall, the exchange rate turns out to be mainly affected by productivity developments, the real interest differential, and oil prices. Decomposing the estimated exchange rate into its permanent and transitory part indicates an undervaluation of the euro by mid 1999 which even widened in the course of 2000. The extent of undervaluation depends heavily on the model specification.

Osbat, Rüffer, and Schnatz (2003) examine the long-run determinants of the bilateral exchange rate of the euro against the Japanese yen within a BEER framework. The authors identify a consistent and significant relationship between the real exchange rate and relative productivity, the net foreign asset position, relative government spending, and the terms of trade. The estimation suggests that the euro appreciation vis-à-vis the yen in 2001 represented an equilibrium correction from its previously undervalued position. Schnatz, Vijselaar, and Osbat (2004) make use of the BEER methodology to analyze the impact of productivity developments on the euro-dollar exchange rate. They find that productivity developments can explain only a fraction of the actual euro depreciation observed in 1999 and 2000, though the extent of the impact varies heavily with the productivity proxy.

Borowski and Couharde (2003) employ the macroeconomic balance approach to derive the fundamental equilibrium real exchange rate between the euro and the US dollar for the year 2001. The calculation of the FEER is implemented within a partial equilibrium framework, where the trade elasticities are obtained from the NIGEM model and the current account targets are taken from Williamson and Mahar (1998).[4] The calculations point to an undervaluation of the euro vis-à-vis the US dollar in 2001. Yet, this result heavily depends on the way the target current account is identified.

Detken and Marín Martínez (2001) present an empirical study that is based on the NATREX approach. The authors apply the NATREX model to the real effective euro exchange rate between 1970Q1 and 1999Q4. The authors estimate the model in structural form and conclude that the euro was increasingly undervalued during the period 1997-1999. Duval (2002) combines the BEER and the NATREX concepts and applies his model to the bilateral real exchange rate between the euro and the US dollar for the period 1970Q1 to 1999Q4. He estimates the equilibrium value of the euro based on a time preference variable, total factor productivity, the real interest differential, and the relative price of traded to non-traded goods. He finds that the euro became undervalued against the US dollar in the course of 1999. In 2000, the undervaluation widened and reached 25 percent in the third quarter of 2000.

Detken et al. (2002) employ four different models to examine the euro exchange rate against a basket of currencies consisting of the UK pound, the US dollar, the Japanese yen, and the Swiss franc over the period 1970Q1 to 2000Q4. The authors start their analysis by relating the real exchange rate to a number of candidate variables such as productivity, the relative price of tradable to non-tradable goods, interest rates, and consumption to GDP ratio. The authors generally have difficulties finding a significant cointegrating relationship between the real exchange rate and the candidate variables. The best specification relates the real exchange rate to interest differentials and the relative price of non-tradable to tradable goods. Next, the authors estimate a structural VAR model to extract the permanent equilibrium exchange rate and a structural NATREX model along the lines of Detken and Marín Martínez (2001). Finally, the authors simulate a macroeconomic model with stochastic and deterministic shocks to derive the desired equilibrium exchange rate. With all four models the authors find that the euro was undervalued at the end of 2000 against the basket of reference currencies, but the degree of undervaluation varies widely across the models, ranging from 5 to 28 percent.

Table 2.2 summarizes the key features of the various studies on the euro exchange rate. Comparing the findings of the studies shows that almost all of

[4]Williamson and Mahar (1998) calculate current account targets for all countries/regions in the world based on the condition of stabilizing debt-to-GDP ratios.

Table 2.2: Empirical Studies on the Equilibrium Exchange Rate of the Euro

Authors	Model	Exchange rate	Time period	Estimation technique	Explanatory variables	Main results
Chinn (2000)	Monetary model	Nominal vis-à-vis USD	1991-2000	Johansen	Money stock, output, nominal interest rate, expected inflation rate, relative price of non-tradable to tradable goods	Estimated coefficients hardly significant; undervaluation at the beginning of 2000
Chinn, Alquist (2000)	Monetary model	Nominal vis-à-vis USD	1991-2000	Johansen	Money stock, output, nominal interest rate, expected inflation rate, relative price of non-tradable to tradable goods	Estimated coefficients hardly significant
van Aarle, Boss, Hlouskova (2000)	Monetary model	Nominal vis-à-vis GBP, USD, CHF, JPY	1980-1999	Johansen	Money stock, output, nominal interest rate, expected inflation rate	Estimated coefficients broadly in line with monetary model; out-of-sample forecasts beat random walk in several cases
Frenkel, Koske (2004)	Monetary model	Nominal vis-à-vis CAD, CHF, JPY, NOK, GBP, USD	1980-2003	Johansen	Money stock, output, nominal interest rate, expected inflation rate	Different versions of the model are supported by the data in different countries

Notes: USD = US dollar, JPY = Japanese yen; GBP = British pound; CHF = Swiss franc; CAD = Canadian dollar

Table 2.2: Empirical Studies on the Equilibrium Exchange Rate of the Euro (cont.)

Authors	Model	Exchange rate	Time period	Estimation technique	Explanatory variables	Main results
Groen (2005)	Monetary model	Nominal vis-à-vis USD, CAD, JPY	1975-2000	Johansen	Money stock, output	Coefficients in line with monetary model; cut-of-sample forecasts beat random walk and standard VAR model
Alberola et al. (1999)	BEER, PEER	Real vis-à-vis JPY, SEK, USD, CAD, GBP, DKK, real effective	1980-1998	BEER: Johansen; PEER: Gonzalo-Granger	NFA, relative price of tradable to non-tradable goods	In 1998, the euro was overvalued vis-à-vis JPY and SEK, but undervalued vis-à-vis USD, CAD, GBP, DKK
Clostermann, Schnatz (2000)	BEER	Real vis-à-vis USD	1975-1998	Johansen	Real interest differential, relative price of tradable to non-tradable goods, oil price, fiscal position	Equilibrium exchange rate estimated at USD/EUR 1.20 in the third quarter of 1999
Lorenzen, Thygesen (2000)	BEER	Real vis-à-vis USD	1960-1999	Johansen	NFA, dependency ratio, R&D expenditures, relative price of tradable to non-tradable goods, real interest differential	Undervaluation vis-à-vis USD at the beginning of 1999

Notes: SEK = Swedish krona; DKK = Danish krona

Table 2.2: Empirical Studies on the Equilibrium Exchange Rate of the Euro (cont.)

Authors	Model	Exchange rate	Time period	Estimation technique	Explanatory variables	Main results
Maseo-Fernandez, Osbat, Schnatz (2001)	BEER, PEER	Real effective	1975-2000	BEER: Johansen; PEER: Gonzalo-Granger	Productivity, real interest differential, oil price, relative price of tradable to non-tradable goods, public consumption	Undervaluation of the euro by mid 1999 which widened in the course of 2000
Detken, Marín Martinez (2001)	NATREX	Real effective	1970-1999	Structural estimation	Nominal and real interest rates, productivity, TOT	Undervaluation in 1999
Duval (2002)	BEER/ NATREX	Real vis-à-vis USD	1970-1999	Johansen	Time preference, total factor productivity, real interest rate differential, relative price of tradable to non-tradable goods	Undervaluation vis-à-vis the USD in 1999, which widened in 2000 and reached 25% in 2000Q3
Alquist, Chinn (2002)	BEER	Real vis-à-vis USD	1985-2001	Johansen, DOLS	Productivity, oil price, government spending	By the end of 2001, the euro was in equilibrium with respect to the USD
Borowski, Couharde (2003)	FEER	Real vis-à-vis USD	2001	Partial equilibrium approach	–	Undervaluation of the euro in 2001

Note: DOLS = dynamic ordinary least squares

Table 2.2: Empirical Studies on the Equilibrium Exchange Rate of the Euro (cont.)

Authors	Model	Exchange rate	Time period	Estimation technique	Explanatory variables	Main results
Detken et al. (2002)	BEER, PEER, NATREX, DEER	Real effective	1973 - 2000	BEER: Johansen; PEER: SVAR; NATREX: structural estimation; DEER: AWM macromodel	BEER: interest rate differential, relative price of tradable to non-tradable goods; PEER: output, inflation; NATREX: nominal and real interest rates, productivity, TOT	Estimates are model dependent and surrounded with high degree of uncertainty; undervaluation at the end of 2000
Osbat, Rüffer, Schnatz (2003)	BEER	Real vis-à-vis JPY	1975 - 2001	Johansen	Productivity, NFA, real interest rate differential, oil price, public spending	Apart from the interest differential all variables are very important; undervaluation of the euro in 2000
Schnatz, Vijselaar, Osbat (2004)	BEER	Real vis-à-vis USD	1981 - 2001	Johansen	Productivity, real interest rate differential, oil price, public spending	Productivity changes can only explain fraction of euro depreciation in 1999/2000

them point to an undervaluation of the euro in 1999 which further widened in the course of 2000. Hence, as regards the direction of the misalignment, the studies yield a rather uniform picture. Yet, the extent of the estimated misalignment varies widely across the studies. The source of this variations seems to be rooted in differing underlying models and in differing sets of economic fundamentals that are employed to explain exchange rate movements.

2.3.2 Empirical Studies of the Currencies of the New EU Member Countries of 2004

After the breakdown of communism in 1990, the exchange rates of central and eastern European economies underwent a sharp real depreciation, followed by a continuing real appreciation. This phenomenon encouraged a large number of researchers to examine in how far these developments were supported by underlying fundamentals (see the surveys by Égert, 2004; and Égert, Halpern, and MacDonald, 2006).

The first study to estimate equilibrium exchange rates for a broad group of central and eastern European countries is the one by Halpern and Wyplosz (1997). Instead of directly focusing on real exchange rates, the authors look at dollar wages in the manufacturing sector as an alternative measure of a country's competitiveness. They estimate equilibrium dollar wages for eighty countries and then apply the obtained coefficients to data from ten transition countries between 1991 and 1996. They find that in all countries the equilibrium dollar wage increased during the observation period due to gains in economic efficiency and that it nearly reached its equilibrium level by 1996 in the Czech Republic, Hungary, Poland, and Slovenia. The analysis of Halpern and Wyplosz (1997) was later extended by Begg, Halpern and Wyplosz (1999) who find similar results. Krajnyák and Zettelmeyer (1998) use a similar methodology to Halpern and Wyplosz (1997) to estimate equilibrium dollar wages for 15 transition countries as a function of productivity measures. They find that dollar wages were initially undervalued with the degree of undervaluation decreasing over time.

A major conclusion that could be drawn from these early studies was that the real exchange rate appreciations observed in central and eastern European countries were largely driven by productivity gains in line with the Balassa-Samuelson hypothesis. This finding motivated a large number of additional studies that tried to estimate the size of the Balassa-Samuelson effect directly by employing data from the central and eastern European economies themselves. The simplest approach adopted in the literature to assess the Balassa-Samuelson effect relies on a descriptive comparison of average productivity growth rates in the open and in the sheltered sectors with average inflation rates in the two sectors (e.g., Kovács, 2002; Backé et al., 2003; Burgess, Fabrizio, and Xiao, 2003). A more sophisticated way to analyze the size of the Balassa-Samuelson effect is the application of time-series, cross-section, or panel data techniques (e.g., Halpern and Wyplosz, 2001; De Broeck and Sløk, 2001; Mihaljek and Klau, 2004; Égert, 2002a,b; Égert et al. 2003; and Égert 2005). Overall, these studies suggest that the Balassa-Samuelson effect can a at least partially explain the real exchange appreciations observed in central and eastern European economies. De Broeck and Sløk (2001) use their estimates to also assess a possible undervaluation and overvaluation of the currencies in central and eastern European countries. They conclude that the real effective exchange rates in most countries have moved towards equilibrium from an initially undervalued position, but that there is scope for further appreciation.

With the Balassa-Samuelson effect not fully accounting for the real exchange rate appreciations in central and eastern European countries, several authors carry out a more broadly-based analysis in a behavioral equilibrium exchange rate framework (e.g., Lamdany et al., 1998; Filipozzi, 2000; Kemme and Teng, 2000; Coricelli and Jazbec, 2001; De Broeck and Sløk, 2001; Alonso-Gamo et al., 2002; Jazbec, 2002; Égert and Lahrèche-Révil, 2003; Égert, Lommatzsch, 2003; MacDoland and Wójcik, 2004; Rahn, 2003; Dobrinsky, 2003; Égert, Lahrèche-Révil, Lommatzsch, 2004; Fischer, 2004; Lommatzsch and Tober, 2004; Kim and Korhonen, 2005; and Oomes, 2005). The economic fundamentals included in the regressions vary widely across the studies and comprise the relative price of non-tradable goods, the terms of trade, private consumption relative to GDP, government debt relative to GDP, the current account position, net foreign assets relative to GDP, the real interest rate differential, per capita GDP, and openness. The estimated relationships between these fundamentals and the real exchange rate are used to determine whether there were any major real exchange rate misalignments in central and eastern European countries. The analysis by Égert and Lahrèche-Révil (2003) suggests that in mid 2001, the currencies of the Czech Republic, Poland, and Slovakia were overvalued in effective terms, while the currencies of Hungary and Slovenia were close to their equilibrium level. Kemme and Teng (2000) who focus on the bilateral exchange rate between the Polish zloty and the US dollar find that the zloty was slightly undervalued in real terms until the mid-1990s and then, with the adoption of the gliding band, started to become overvalued. In mid 1999, the overvaluation was in the order of 1.5 to 12 percent, depending on which price deflator is used in the calculation of the real exchange rate. Alonso-Gamo et al. (2002) examine the real effective exchange rate of the Lithuanian litas and find that the currency was overvalued by about 10 percent in 1994 and between 1999 and 2000. For the period 1995 to 1998 and for 2001, the authors find an undervaluation of the litas which amounted to roughly 5 percent in the third quarter of 2001.

A number of authors make the attempt to put more structure on the assessment of the real exchange rate appreciations observed in the central and eastern European economies. Coudert and Couharde (2003) and Šmídková, Barrell and Holland (2002) apply the fundamental equilibrium exchange rate approach to assess a possible undervaluation and overvaluation of the currencies in central and eastern European countries. Both studies make use of the NIGEM model of the National Institute for Economic and Social Research (NIESR) to derive their FEER estimates. Coudert and Couharde (2003) examine the currencies of the Czech Republic, Hungary, Poland, Slovenia, and Slovakia in 2001 and 2002 and cannot find any major misalignments. Šmídková, Barrell and Holland (2002) look at the Czech Republic, Estonia, Hungary, Poland, and Slovenia. For each country, the authors derive two equilibrium real exchange rate corridors up to 2005. For the period 2003 to 2005, the forecasts reveal that economic fundamentals are in line with a further appreciation of the Slovenian exchange rate, while for Hungary and Poland real exchange rate depreciation might be necessary.

Bulíř and Šmídková (2005) assess recent exchange rate developments in the Czech Republic, Hungary, Poland, and Slovenia based on a model that focuses on the role of foreign direct investment and external debt in explaining real exchange rate movements. The authors find that the Czech, Hungarian, and Polish currencies were overvalued in 2003, whereas the Slovenian tolar was close to equilibrium. Rubaszek (2004) develops the so-called balance of payments equilibrium exchange rate (BPEER) model that is similar to the BEER model in that the equilibrium exchange rate is derived from a reduced-form cointegrating relationship. The difference between the two concepts lies in the theoretical foundation: The starting point for the BEER is the risk-adjusted uncovered interest rate parity condition, whereas the BPEER roots in the balance of payments identity. Rubaszek (2004) applies his model to the Polish zloty and finds that the currency was close to equilibrium until 1999. Then, with the introduction of the crawling band in 1999, the currency became overvalued but, after a period of considerable depreciation, returned to equilibrium in 2002.

Recently, Crespo-Cuaresma, Fidrmuc, and MacDonald (2005) have investigated the ability of the monetary model to explain exchange rate developments in six central and eastern European countries: the Czech Republic, Hungary, Poland, Romania, Slovenia, and Slovakia. The analysis reveals that the monetary model can convincingly explain long-run exchange rate developments in these countries, particularly if the model is augmented by a Balassa-Samuelson effect. Comparing actual nominal exchange rates with the estimated equilibrium rates indicates that all exchange rate were overvalued against the euro in 2003, with the extent of overvaluation being particularly pronounced for the Czech Republic and Slovenia.

Table 2.3 provides an overview of the empirical studies discussed above, focusing on the countries and periods examined, the theoretical background, the fundamentals included in the analysis, and the main findings. As can be seen from the table and also from the discussion above, a huge number of empirical studies on equilibrium exchange rates in central and eastern European economies exists. The studies differ widely in the theoretical concepts that underly the analysis as well as in the econometric techniques employed to derive the equilibrium path of the exchange rate. Égert and Halpern (2006) make the attempt to empirically analyze a subset of these studies within a meta regression analysis. The authors find that the reported misalignment figures are systematically influenced by the theoretical background, the econometric estimation technique, and the choice of time series, cross-sectional, or panel data. The conclusion that can be drawn from their analysis is that any thorough assessment of equilibrium exchange rates in central and eastern European economies should make use of several alternative economic and econometric specifications.

Table 2.3: Empirical Studies on the Equilibrium Exchange Rate of the New EU Member Countries

Authors	Country	Period	Model	Exchange Rate	Variables	Main Findings
Alonso-Gamo et al. (2002)	LT	1994-2001	BEER	REER (CPI)	CPI/PPI, NFA/GDP	Overvaluation of roughly 10% in 1994 as well as from 1999 to 2000 and undervaluation in the order of 10% from 1995 to 1998 and of 5% in 2001
Backé et al. (2003)	CZ, HU, PL, SI	1990-2001	BS	Internal price ratio	Productivity tradables/non-tradables	BS effect can explain considerable portion of rise in internal price ratio
Begg, Halpern, Wyplosz (1999)	Panel of 85 countries, incl. CEEC8	1975,1980, 1985,1990, 1995	BS	Dollar wage	Per capita GDP, school enrolment, share of agriculture in GDP, government consumption/GDP, inflation, dependency ratio, openness, NFA of banking sector, credit to private sector, regional dummies	For EE, LV, LT overvaluation in early 1990s, but rapid convergence to equilibrium; slight overvaluation for HU, PL, SI from 1996 onwards

Notes: CZ = Czech Republic; HU = Hungary; EE = Estonia; LV = Latvia; LT = Lithuania; PL = Poland; SI = Slovenia; SK = Slovakia; CEEC8 = CZ, EE, HU, LV, LT, PL, SI, SK; REER = real effective exchange rate; BS = Balassa-Samuelson

Table 2.3: Empirical Studies on the Equilibrium Exchange Rate of the New EU Member Countries (cont.)

Authors	Country	Period	Model	Exchange Rate	Variables	Main Findings
Bulíř, Šmídková (2005)	CZ, HU, PL, SI	1992-2003	FEER	RER vis-à-vis EUR	NIGEM model	In 2003: overvaluation for CZ, HU, PL, no misalignment for SI
Burgess, Fabrizio, Xiao (2003)	EE, LV, LT	1997-2002	PPP, BS, BEER	REER (CPI)	BS: GDP per worker, TFP, sectoral productivity; BEER: productivity tradables/non-tradables, NFA	Productivity growth and rise in capital inflows have contributed to appreciation of equilibrium REERs
Coricelli and Jazbec (2001)	19 transition economies, incl. CEEC8	1990, 1995-1998	BEER	Internal price ratio	Sectoral labor productivity, non-tradable private consumption, government consumption, number of workers in industry vs. services, structural reform index	BS effect acconts for 1% of annual real appreciation
Coudert, Couharde (2003)	CEEC5	2000, 2001	FEER	REER (CPI)	Net external debt, net FDI, demand variables, NIGEM model	No major misalignments

Notes: CEEC5 = CZ, HU, PL, SI, SK; RO = Romania; MM = monetary model; NER = nominal exchange rate; TFP = total factor productivity; FDI = foreign direct investment; RER = real exchange rate

Table 2.3: Empirical Studies on the Equilibrium Exchange Rate of the New EU Member Countries (cont.)

Authors	Country	Period	Model	Exchange Rate	Variables	Main Findings
Crespo-Cuaresma, Fidrmuc, MacDonald (2005)	CEEC5, RO	1994-2002	MM, BS	NER vis-à-vis EUR	M2, real industrial production, deposit interest rates, CPI/PPI	NERs mainly driven by money supply and real industrial production; 2-3% of annual appreciation attributable to BS-effect
De Broeck, Sløk (2001)	17 OECD countries + 25 transition economies incl. CEEC8	1991-1998	BS, BEER	REER (CPI)	Sectoral productivity, oil price, openness, general government deficit, TOT, monetary aggregates/GDP	Movement towards equilibrium from initially undervalued position; scope for further appreciation
Dobrinsky (2003)	CEEC8, BG, HR, RO	1993-1999	BEER	RER vis-à-vis EUR (CPI)	TFP, per capita GDP, government expenditure/GDP, M1/GDP, exchange rate regime dummies	Proportionate relationship between productivity growth differential and real exchange rate
Égert (2002a)	CEEC5	1991-2001	BS	REER with basket of DEM and USD (CPI)	Labor productivity in industry, relative price of tradable to non-tradable goods	Observed real appreciation of the exchange rate can just partly be explained by BS-effect

Notes: BG = Bulgaria; HR = Croatia; USD = US dollar; DEM = deutschmark

Table 2.3: Empirical Studies on the Equilibrium Exchange Rate of the New EU Member Countries (cont.)

Authors	Country	Period	Model	Exchange Rate	Variables	Main Findings
Égert (2002b)	CEEC5	1991-2000	BS	REER with basket of DEM and USD (CPI), RER vis-à-vis DEM, USD (CPI)	Labor productivity in industry, relative price of tradables to non-tradables	Strong link between productivity and relative price of tradables, but weak link between relative price and RER
Égert (2005)	EE	1993-2002	BS	REER with basket of FIM, SEK, DEM, GBP (CPI)	Relative price of non-tradables (various measures), productivity tradables/non-tradables (various measures),	BS-effect can explain real exchange rate movements in the second half of the sample period, but not in the first half
Égert et al. (2003)	CEEC8	1995-2000	BS	RER vis-à-vis DEM (CPI), internal price ratio	Productivity tradables/non-tradables	BS-effect only plays minor role in explaining real appreciation in CEEC8
Égert, Lahrèche-Révil (2003)	CEEC5	1992-2001	FEER/BEER	REER (CPI)	TOT, relative price of tradables to non-tradables, per capita GDP, labor productivity, private consumption, current account, openness	Overvaluation for CZ, PL, SK, no major misalignment for HU, SI

Notes: FIM = Finnish marka; SEK = Swedish krona; GBP = British pound

Table 2.3: Empirical Studies on the Equilibrium Exchange Rate of the New EU Member Countries (cont.)

Authors	Country	Period	Model	Exchange Rate	Variables	Main Findings
Égert, Lahrèche-Révil, Lommatzsch (2004)	Panels of up to 35 countries, incl. CEEC8, CY	1992/1993-2002; CY: 1970-2002	BEER	REER (CPI, PPI)	Productivity tradables/non-tradables, non-price competitiveness, NFA	Real exchange rate is negatively related to NFA, but positively to non-price competitiveness and BS effect
Égert, Lommatzsch (2003)	CEEC8, HR	1993-2002	BEER	RER vis-à-vis EUR (CPI, PPI)	Industrial sector productivity, regulated prices, real interest rate differential, gross foreign debt/GDP, government debt/GDP, openness, TOT	Real exchange rate appreciation can be attributed to higher prices of tradable and non-tradable goods; estimated misalignments sensitive to model specification and estimation method
Filipozzi (2000)	EE	1993-1999	BEER	REER against 9 trading partners (CPI)	Nominal effective exchange rate, investment/GDP, current account balance/GDP, productivity tradables/non-tradables	25-30% overvaluation in 1993, 5-8% overvaluation in 1999

Note: CY = Cyprus; DE = Germany

Table 2.3: Empirical Studies on the Equilibrium Exchange Rate of the New EU Member Countries (cont.)

Authors	Country	Period	Model	Exchange Rate	Variables	Main Findings
Fischer (2004)	CEEC8, BG, RO	1993-2000	BEER	REER (CPI)	Sectoral labor productivity, total labor productivity, total consumption/GDP, government consumption/GDP, real interest rate (US, DE), TOT, raw material price index, private sector share in GDP, share of administered prices in GDP, tariff revenues as percentage of imports	Real exchange rate appreciation can be attributed to changes in productivity (50%), consumption demand (25%) and world real interest rate (25%); productivity effect works through BS-channel and through investment demand channel
Halpern, Wyplosz (1997)	Panel of 80 countries, incl. CEEC5	1975,1980, 1985,1990	BS	Dollar wage	Per capita GDP, school enrolment rate, share of agriculture in GDP, government consumption/GDP, inflation, regional dummies	Undervaluation at the beginning of the transition period, quasi-equilibrium in 1996
Halpern, Wyplosz (2001)	16 transition economies, incl. CEEC8	1991-1998	BS	CPI/PPI	Industrial sector productivity, services sector productivity, per capita GDP, inflation acceleration, exchange rate regime	Real equilibrium exchange rate appreciation of 3% p.a. due to BS-effect

Table 2.3: Empirical Studies on the Equilibrium Exchange Rate of the New EU Member Countries (cont.)

Authors	Country	Period	Model	Exchange Rate	Variables	Main Findings
Jazbec (2002)	19 transition countries, incl. CEEC8	1990/ 1995-1998, 1993-2001 (only SI)	BEER	RER vis-à-vis DEM (CPI, only SI), internal price ratio	Productivity tradables/non-tradables, labor market rigidity, non-tradable consumption/total consumption, government consumption/ GDP	1% increase in productivity differential contributes to 0.9% appreciation of internal price ratio; SI: 1% increase in productivity differential contributes to 1.5% appreciation of real exchange rate
Kemme, Teng (2000)	PL	1990-1999	PPP, BEER	RER vis-à-vis USD (wage rate, CPI, PPI, ULC)	Capital inflows, current account balance, wages/PPI, total trade/industrial production, government expenditure/industrial production, exchange rate regime dummies, devaluation dummies	Overvaluation at the beginning of the 1990s, then undervaluation in the mid 1990s; again overvaluation with the introduction of the crawling band
Kim, Korhonen (2005)	29 middle and high-income countries + CY, HU, PL, SI, SK	1975-1999	BEER	REER (CPI), RER vis-à-vis USD (CPI)	Per capita GDP, gross fixed capital formation/GDP, government consumption/GDP, openness	In 1999: no major misalignment vis-à-vis USD, substantial overvaluation of REER

Table 2.3: Empirical Studies on the Equilibrium Exchange Rate of the New EU Member Countries (cont.)

Authors	Country	Period	Model	Exchange Rate	Variables	Main Findings
Kovács (2002)	CEEC5	1994-2001	BS	RER vis-à-vis DEM (CPI, CPI tradables, CPI non-tradables)	Descriptive statistics	BS effect on CPI inflation vis-à-vis Germany smaller than 2%
Krajnyák, Zettelmeyer (1998)	15 transition economies, incl. CZ, EE, HU, LV, LT, PL, SK	1990-1995	BS	Dollar wage	GDP per capita, GDP per employment, GDP per total labor force, school enrolment, share of agriculture in GDP, regional dummies	1996 actual dollar wages were below equilibrium level in most countries
Lamdany, Mates, Wagner, Braumann (1998)	SK	1990-1997	BEER	REER (CPI, PPI, ULC), internal price ratio	Public consumption/GDP, investment/GDP, openness, real wage, M2/GDP	No major exchange rate misalignments
Lommatzsch, Tober (2004)	CZ, HU, PL	1994-2001	BEER, import/ export equations	REER (PPI)	Labor productivity in industry, foreign output, real interest rate differential, NFA	Movement of real exchange rate can at least partly be explained by productivity developments

Table 2.3: Empirical Studies on the Equilibrium Exchange Rate of the New EU Member Countries (cont.)

Authors	Country	Period	Model	Exchange Rate	Variables	Main Findings
MacDoland, Wójcik (2004)	Panel of EE, HU, SI, SK	1995-2001	BEER	REER (CPI), internal price ratio	Productivity tradables/non-tradables, productivity in the distribution sector, consumption/GDP, NFA/GDP, real interest rate differential, real wage, regulated prices	Both supply and demand side effects play an important role in explaining RER movements
Mihaljek, Klau (2004)	CEEC5	1992-2001	BS	Internal price ratio	Productivity tradables/non-tradables	Productivity differentials explain only about 0.2 to 2.0 percentage points of annual inflation differentials vis-à-vis euro area
Oomes (2005)	SK	1995-2004	BEER	REER vis-à-vis basket of EUR, USD (CPI, PPI, ULC)	Productivity tradables/non-tradables, government consumption	In 2004, the exchange rate was close to or slightly above equilibrium

Table 2.3: Empirical Studies on the Equilibrium Exchange Rate of the New EU Member Countries (cont.)

Authors	Country	Period	Model	Exchange Rate	Variables	Main Findings
Rahn (2003)	CZ, EE, HU, PL, SI	1990-2002	BEER, PEER	RER vis-à-vis EUR (CPI), REER (CPI)	CPI/PPI, NFA/GDP	In 2002: overvaluation in all 5 countries which is particularly pronounced for CZ, EE, and PL
Rubaszek (2004)	PL	1995-2002	BPEER		Domestic and foreign output, real interest differential, NFA	Zloty was close to equilibrium in 1995-1999, overvalued in 2000-2001, and back in equilibrium in 2002
Šmídková, Barrell, Holland (2002)	CZ, EE, HU, PL, SI	1994-1999, forecast until 2005	FEER	REER (import and domestic prices)	NIGEM model	Forecasts point to real appreciation for SI, real depreciation for HU and PL, and real exchange rate stability for CZ, EE

Chapter 3

The Application of the Monetary Exchange Rate Approach to the Euro

This chapter uses different versions of the monetary approach to the exchange rate in order to investigate how well this approach can explain the nominal exchange rate of the euro vis-à-vis the US dollar, the Canadian dollar, the British pound, the Norwegian krone, the Japanese yen, the Swiss franc, and the Australian dollar over the past 25 years. Testing the relevance of the monetary model in explaining the euro exchange rate is interesting because this model often represents an integral part of theoretical studies of open economies.

The analysis extends the existing literature in two directions. First, although it investigates a period of 25 years by including data on the synthetic value of the euro, a considerable period covering about one fourth of the data covers the time period since the beginning of the independent trading of the euro in foreign exchange markets. Second, it studies the nominal exchange rate of the euro not only vis-à-vis the US dollar but also vis-à-vis six other currencies. So far, other currencies than the US dollar have received fairly little attention in studies on the euro exchange rate. However, looking at other currencies too can lend insight into whether there are structural differences between the explanation of the euro exchange rate vis-à-vis the US dollar compared to the euro exchange rate vis-à-vis other currencies.

The chapter is structured as follows. Section 3.1 describes the different testable hypotheses all of which are consistent with a monetary view of the exchange rate. Section 3.2 then presents some empirical evidence on the validity of the assumptions that underly the monetary class of models. Section 3.3 briefly explains the econometric methodology as well as the data set employed in the empirical analysis. Section 3.4 presents the estimation results. Specifically, the validity of the monetary approach for the seven exchange rates is examined and in those cases, in which the data lend support to the monetary approach, the estimation results are used to assess a possible under- and overvaluation of the euro. Furthermore, the out-of-sample forecasting performance of the monetary approach is investigated and compared to the simple random walk model. Section 3.5 then presents several robustness tests and, finally, section 3.6 summarizes the main findings and concludes.

3.1 The Monetary Approach to the Exchange Rate

This section briefly derives different testable hypotheses of the monetary approach. Several versions of the monetary exchange rate model have been put forward, giving rise to two main types of models that can be distinguished. The first one is the flexible price monetary model of Frenkel (1976) and Bilson (1978), the second one is the sticky price model of Dornbusch (1976) with its modification as the real interest differential model of Frankel (1979).[5]

All of these models rest upon two major building blocks, the validity of purchasing power parity (PPP) and the existence of a stable money demand function. In Frenkel's and Bilson's model, prices are flexible and adjustment takes place instantaneously, implying that purchasing power parity holds at anytime:

$$e_t = p_t - p_t^*. \tag{3.1}$$

Here, e is the logarithm of the spot nominal exchange rate in price notation, p is the logarithm of the price level, t is the time index, and an asterisk denotes a foreign variable. The specification of the money demand function differs across the two models. The version presented by Frenkel (1976) assumes a Cagan-type money demand function which, including an income argument, leads to the money market equilibrium condition

$$m_t - p_t = \alpha_1 y_t - \alpha_2 \pi_t, \qquad \alpha_1, \alpha_2 > 0, \tag{3.2}$$

[5]Hooper and Morton (1982) develop another version of the sticky price monetary model that allows for shifts in the long-run equilibrium exchange rate in response to movements in the current account.

where m is the logarithm of money demand, y the is logarithm of output, and π is the expected inflation rate.[6] It is assumed that a similar equilibrium condition holds for the money market abroad:

$$m_t^* - p_t^* = \alpha_1^* y_t^* - \alpha_2^* \pi_t^*, \qquad \alpha_1^*, \alpha_2^* > 0. \tag{3.3}$$

The money market equilibrium conditions determine the price levels p and p^* which can be employed in the purchasing power parity expression (3.1) to yield:

$$e_t = m_t - m_t^* - \alpha_1 y_t + \alpha_1^* y_t^* + \alpha_2 \pi_t - \alpha_2^* \pi_t^*. \tag{3.4}$$

Equation (3.4) illustrates how the exchange rate is determined by the relative demand for and supply of the two monies. An increase in domestic money supply leads to a depreciation of the domestic currency as it induces a rise in the domestic price level. An increase in domestic output or a fall in the expected rate of inflation causes a rise in money demand and thus lowers the exchange rate. The Frenkel version of the monetary approach includes an unobservable variable, i.e., inflation expectations, so that estimating the exchange rate function requires the use of a proxy for this variable. Proxies for expected inflation rates could be past inflation rates or, assuming rational expectations, future inflation rates. Some authors also employ long-term interest rates as a proxy (e.g., van Aarle, Boss and Hlouskova, 2000).

Unlike Frenkel (1976), Bilson (1978) derives an exchange rate function that does not include any unobservable variables. He assumes that money demand depends on output and the nominal interest rate i, so that money market equilibrium can be written as

$$m_t - p_t = \alpha_1 y_t - \alpha_2 i_t, \qquad \alpha_1, \alpha_2 > 0. \tag{3.5}$$

Together with a corresponding money demand function for the foreign economy and purchasing power parity, this leads to the following exchange rate equation:

$$e_t = m_t - m_t^* - \alpha_1 y_t + \alpha_1^* y_t^* + \alpha_2 i_t - \alpha_2^* i_t^*. \tag{3.6}$$

An increase in the domestic (foreign) nominal interest rate lowers the demand for domestic (foreign) currency and causes a rise (fall) in the exchange rate. In estimating the Bilson model (3.6), short-term interest rates like, e.g., money market rates are employed as interest rate data.

[6]In the Cagan money demand function, the emphasis is on expected inflation as the decisive determinant of money demand.

The second class of monetary models differs from the first one in that it assumes a slow adjustment process of the exchange rate to its long-run equilibrium rate due to price stickiness. These models are associated with the contributions of Dornbusch (1976) and Frankel (1978). Both versions combine two building blocks to derive an expression for the exchange rate. The first building block includes the condition for uncovered interest parity and an expression for the exchange rate adjustment process. The former holds if

$$E(e_{t+1} - e_t) = i_t - i_t^*. \tag{3.7}$$

Here, $E(e_{t+1} - e_t)$ represents the expected exchange rate change. Concerning expectation formation, Frankel (1978) assumes that the expected exchange rate change is a function of the gap between the current spot rate and its long-run value and the expected long-run inflation differential:

$$E(e_{t+1} - e_t) = -\nu(e_t - \bar{e}) + \pi_t - \pi_t^*, \tag{3.8}$$

where $\bar{e}$ is the log of the long-run exchange rate. In equation (3.8), π and π^* represent expected long-run inflation rates. Combining equations (3.7) and (3.8) yields

$$\bar{e} = e_t + \frac{1}{\nu}[(i_t - \pi_t) - (i_t^* - \pi_t^*)]. \tag{3.9}$$

The term in brackets on the right-hand side of equation (3.9) presents the real interest rate differential.

The second building block of this second class of models is the determination of the long-run exchange rate along the lines of the monetary approach. As these models distinguish between short-run and long-run variables, long-run variables are indicated by a bar over the variables. It is assumed that purchasing power parity holds in the long run:

$$\bar{e} = \bar{p} - \bar{p}^*. \tag{3.10}$$

Long-run price levels are determined by money market conditions. Using the money demand functions given in equations (3.2) and (3.3), this yields

$$\bar{p} = \bar{m} - \alpha_1\bar{y} + \alpha_2\bar{i} \qquad \text{and} \tag{3.11}$$

$$\bar{p}^* = \bar{m}^* - \alpha_1^*\bar{y}^* + \alpha_2^*\bar{i}^*. \tag{3.12}$$

Assuming that the money market coefficients in both countries are the same, i.e. $\alpha_1 = \alpha_1^*$ and $\alpha_2 = \alpha_2^*$, purchasing power parity implies

$$\bar{e} = \bar{m} - \bar{m}^* - \alpha_1(\bar{y} - \bar{y}^*) - \alpha_2(\bar{i} - \bar{i}^*). \tag{3.13}$$

Frankel (1978) applies the Fisher relation (Fisher, 1930) to the long-run interest rates and, thus, uses $\bar{i} - \bar{i}^* = \pi - \pi^*$.[7] Together with the assumption that the long-run values of money and income are given by their current values, this implies for equation (3.13):

$$\bar{e} = m_t - m_t^* - \alpha_1(y_t - y_t^*) - \alpha_2(\pi_t - \pi_t^*). \tag{3.14}$$

This expression gives the long-run exchange rate level as a function of money, income and long-run inflation expectations. Substituting equation (3.14) for the long-run exchange rate in equation (3.9) yields

$$e_t = m_t - m_t^* - \alpha_1(y_t - y_t^*) - \frac{1}{\nu}(i_t - i_t^*) + (\frac{1}{\nu} + \alpha_2)(\pi_t - \pi_t^*). \tag{3.15}$$

Thus, the spot exchange rate is determined as a linear combination of the differences between domestic and foreign money supplies, output levels, interest rates and expected inflation rates. An increase in short-term interest rates leads to an appreciation of the domestic currency, while an increase in expected domestic long-run inflation leads to a depreciation. Unlike in Bilson's variant, the domestic interest rate here enters with a negative sign. This reflects the fact that price adjustment is slow. For example, if the domestic interest rate suddenly drops following an expansionary domestic monetary policy, uncovered interest parity continues to hold because a sharp rise in the exchange rate, i.e., the overshooting phenomenon, leads to appreciation expectations. As equation (3.15) includes expected domestic and foreign inflation which are unobservable, estimation requires proxies for these variables.

The framework of Dornbusch (1976) is very similar to Frankel's approach. Dornbusch assumes that the expected exchange rate change solely depends on the gap between the current spot rate and its long run value. Equation (3.15) then becomes

$$e_t = m_t - m_t^* - \alpha_1(y_t - y_t^*) - \frac{1}{\nu}(i_t - i_t^*). \tag{3.16}$$

On the basis of the four variants of the monetary model, four functional forms for the nominal exchange rate can be distinguished. These are equations (3.4), (3.6), (3.15), and (3.16). Together with proxies for the unobservable

[7] Fisher (1930) put forward that the nominal interest rate should equal the sum of the real interest rate and the expected inflation rate, i.e., $i = r + \pi$, where r is the real interest rate. Assuming that a similar equation holds for the foreign country and that capital movements lead to an equalization of real interest rates across countries, this leads to $i - i^* = \pi - \pi^*$.

Table 3.1: Effects of Different Variables on the Exchange Rate in the four Variants of the Monetary Model

	$m_t - m_t^*$	$y_t - y_t^*$	$i_t - i_t^*$	$\pi_t - \pi_t^*$
Frenkel	+	−	0	+
Bilson	+	−	+	0
Dornbusch	+	−	−	0
Frankel	+	−	−	+

variables in equations (3.4) and (3.15), this leads to four testable hypotheses for the monetary approach to the exchange rate. Table 3.1 summarizes the direction in which the different variables are expected to influence the exchange rate in these models.

3.2 The Validity of the Underlying Assumptions

As discussed in the previous section, all four variants of the monetary approach rest upon two major building blocks, the existence of a stable money demand function and the validity of purchasing power parity. Before estimating the monetary approach it is therefore essential to first investigate whether these two assumptions hold for the set of countries considered in the analysis.

3.2.1 The Stability of Money Demand

The existence of a stable long-run relationship between money, real income, interest rates, and prices has been extensively investigated in the literature. Empirical research on the euro area suggests that euro area money demand is a stable function of real income, interest rates, and prices (see Fagan and Henry, 1998; Coenen and Vega, 1999; Brand and Cassola, 2000; Calza, Gerdesmeier and Levy, 2001; and Bruggeman et al., 2003 for the monetary aggregate M3 and Stracca, 2001; and Golinelli and Pastorello, 2002 for M1). Several factors have contributed to the higher stability of money demand in the euro area than in other economies (see Calza and Sousa, 2003 for a detailed analysis). First, potential sources of instabilities such as financial innovation and banking sector reforms have been less prevalent in the euro area than in other economies. Second, Germany, the largest economy in the euro area, has historically had a remarkably stable money demand function (e.g., Scharnagl, 1998; Hubrich, 1999), thus contributing to the overall stability of euro area money demand. Third, by aggregating national money demand functions, de-synchronized shocks are averaged out leading to a more stable money demand function at the aggregate level than at the national level.

The stability of money demand has also been confirmed for the Norwegian economy with respect to the monetary aggregates M1 and M2. Bårdsen (1992) derives a money demand relationship for M1 that includes prices, real expenditure, and several interest rates. Although the author detects instabilities in the relationship in the first place, he is able to derive a conditional model with constant parameters in a second step. Eitrheim (1995, 1998) examines the monetary aggregate M2 and identifies a stable long-run demand for money relationship in which the real money is determined by real income, and nominal and real interest rates. The observation horizon of the studies by Bårdsen (1992) and Eitrheim (1995, 1998) end in 1989 and 1993, respectively. For the more recent period, no empirical evidence on the stability of Norwegian money demand is available.

Empirical research on the Canadian money demand suggests that the stability of money demand heavily depends on the choice of the monetary aggregate. Haug and Lucas (1996) and Crowder and Wohar (2004) identify a stable long-run relationship between the monetary aggregate M1, real income, and interest rates. However, there is hardly any evidence in favor of a cointegrating relationship when M2 is used instead (Haug and Lucas, 1996). In Switzerland, the stability of money demand also varies with the choice of the monetary aggregate. While M2 and M3 are found to be cointegrated with the price level, real income, and interest rates, with the estimated elasticities not exhibiting any structural breaks up to the mid-1990s (see, for example, Gerlach-Krisen, 2001 for the stability of M3, and Peytrignet and Stahel, 1998 for a comparison of the M2 and M3 cases), the demand for base money exhibited a major shift at the beginning of 1988, when the introduction of Swiss Interbank Clearing (SIC), a real-time gross settlement system for interbank payments, led to a massive reduction in the demand for base money (Rich, 2003).

For Australia and Japan empirical research has not yet provided a conclusive answer as to whether money demand can be assumed to represent a stable function of real income, prices, and interest rates or not. In the case of Australia, Asano (1999) identifies a stable long-run relationship between money, real income, and interest rates from the mid-1960s to the mid-1990s.

Orden and Fisher (1993), Karfakis and Parikh (1993), and Hoque and Al-Mutairi (1996), however, all find a structural break in the first half of the 1980s, when Australia deregulated its financial sector. Moreover, Felmingham and Zhang (2001) provide evidence of a second structural break in 1991, coinciding with a deep recession. Regarding the Japanese money demand, Miyao (1996) fails to detect a cointegrating relationship between the monetary aggregate M2, real income and interest rates over the period 1964 to 1993. Yamada (2000) attributes this result to the impact of the strong devaluation of yen-denominated foreign assets after the Plaza accord of 1985. In fact, when augmenting the model by the effective exchange rate, Bahmani-Oskooee and Shabisgh (1996) and Yamada (2000) are able to find a cointegrating relationship, comprising the stock of M2, real income, interest rates, and the effective exchange rate. Sekine (1998) provides an alternative explanation. He argues that the instability of money demand stems from the sharp rise in land and stock prices from the mid-1980s onwards and the subsequent decline. When including a wealth measure in the model, he finds a stable money demand function over the period 1975 to 1994. More recently, using more sophisticated estimation techniques than previous studies, Amano and Wirjanto (2000) and Bahmani-Oskooee (2001) are able to identify a stable cointegrating relationship between the stock of M2 and the traditional money demand determinants. However, the time horizon of both studies ends in 1993 and 1996, respectively, and, hence, does not include the severe recession of 1997-1998. Kimura (2001) studies the period 1977 to 1998 and identifies indeed a structural break in the broad money demand function in 1997.

For the two remaining countries in the sample, i.e., the United States and the United Kingdom, empirical results concerning the stability of money demand are even less encouraging. While the demand for M2 in the United States had been a stable function of real income and interest rates until the early 1990s (Carlson and Parrott, 1991; Duca, 1995; Whitesell, 1997; Dotsey, Lantz, and Santucci, 2000; Carlson et al., 2000), the deceleration in M2 growth observed in the late 1980s and early 1990s cannot be reconciled with historic money demand functions. The weakening in economic activity at that time was not sufficient to explain the slow-down in money demand, especially since interest rates plummeted. The instability in the early 1990s can be attributed to two factors: a restructuring of depository institutions resulting from financial difficulties (Mehra, 1997; Duca, 1995) and the emergence of bond and stock mutual funds that led to considerable shifts in the investment portfolios of households (Lown, Peristiani, and Robinson, 1999). More recent evidence indicates that the instability of money demand was only temporary and that money demand is behaving in line with historic trends again (Whitesell, 1997; Carlson and Schwarz, 1999; Orphanides and Porter, 2001).

In the United Kingdom, money demand has generally been found to be unstable at an aggregate level, while estimates of broad money demand at a sectoral level, i.e., when distinguishing between households and corporations, have yielded stable money demand functions. A potential explanation for this finding is provided by Fisher and Vega (1993) and Thomas (1997a,b) who argue that households, financial and non-financial corporations have different motivations for holding broad money. Some promising results regarding the stability of aggregate money demand are obtained by Hendry and Mizon (1998) who find evidence of a stable long-run relationship between interest rates and the velocity of money at an aggregate level.

Overall, the evidence on the stability of money demand in the set of countries examined in this study is mixed. For the euro area, there is widespread empirical support for a stable relationship between money, prices, real income, and interest rates. Hence, for the euro, which is in the center of this study, the assumption of a stable money demand function is met. The same holds true for Norway, for which empirical research has generally found a stable demand for money relationship. The money demand function in the United Kingdom, by contrast, is characterized by recurrent instabilities - at least at an aggregate level, which contradicts the assumption of the monetary approach. Hence, the empirical analysis carried out in section 3.4 might not be supportive of the monetary approach in the case of the bilateral exchange rate between the euro and the British pound. For the exchange rate of the euro vis-à-vis the US dollar, it might also be difficult to find evidence in favor of the monetary approach due to a temporary shift in the US demand for money relationship at the beginning of the 1990s. For Australia and Japan, the existing literature does not provide a conclusive answer as to whether money demand is stable or not. The results depend on the precise measurement of the different variables as well as on the econometric technique employed in the analysis. Thus, for these two countries, the monetary approach might well be supported by the data. In Canada and Switzerland, the stability of the money demand function depends on the choice of the monetary aggregate. As the empirical analysis carried out in section 3.4 draws on the monetary aggregate M2, this finding is unproblematic for the Swiss economy, where the demand for M2 has been shown to be stable, but problematic for the Canadian economy, where instabilities in the demand for M2 challenge the validity of the monetary approach.

3.2.2 Purchasing Power Parity

Although the number of empirical literature on the purchasing power parity hypothesis is tremendous (see the discussion in section 2.1.1) only two studies directly examine the validity of purchasing power parity for the euro versus other currencies. Lopez and Papell (2003) study the convergence to purchasing power parity for the euro area using quarterly data on exchange rates and CPI indices over the period 1973Q1 to 2001Q4. The authors first conduct unit root tests on real exchange rates for the period 1973Q1 to 1980Q1 and then add observations quarter by quarter. Examining the p-values of the unit root tests over time reveals that the bilateral exchange rates of the euro vis-à-vis the British pound and vis-à-vis the US dollar converge towards PPP from 1993 onwards. For the bilateral exchange rate between the euro and the Swiss franc, the authors find evidence of convergence towards PPP for the 1980s as well as for the more recent years. Regarding the exchange rate of the euro vis-à-vis the Japanese yen, there are signs of convergence from 1995 onwards, however, the unit root null is rejected only at the 20 percent significance level. The bilateral exchange rates of the euro vis-à-vis the Australian dollar, the Canadian dollar, and the Norwegian krone are not examined in the study.

Koedijk, Tims and van Dijk (2004) investigate the unit root properties of the real exchange rate of the euro relative to the British pound, the Canadian dollar, the Japanese yen, the Norwegian krone, the Swiss franc, the US dollar, the Danish krone, and the Swedish krona over the period 1979 - 2003. While the unit root hypothesis can be rejected for the euro area when the speed of mean reversion is assumed to be the same for all bilateral exchange rates, relaxing this restriction entails that PPP is supported only relative to Switzerland. The authors emphasize, however, that the power of the heterogenous SUR ADF test that is employed in the study is very limited.

Given the small number of studies that examine PPP for the euro area as a whole, it is useful to also take into account studies that look at individual EMU member countries. Jiménez Martín and Robles Fernández (2005) investigate the validity of purchasing power parity between 18 OECD countries (all euro area countries, Canada, Japan, Norway, Switzerland, and the United Kingdom, Sweden, and Mexico) and the United States. Using a first-order Fourier approximation, the authors find evidence of non-linear mean reversion in deviations from PPP in 12 of the 18 countries. Falk and Wang (2003) look at 12 OECD countries relative to the United States and implement residual-based and likelihood-ratio based cointegration tests of PPP that allow for infinite-variance innovations in the data. The estimation results are supportive of purchasing power parity in the cases of Belgium, Denmark, France, Italy, the Netherlands, Spain, the United Kingdom, and Japan, but not in the cases of Canada and Germany. Coakley and Snaith (2004) apply panel unit root tests that allow for cross section dependence to 16 OECD countries (the United States, Norway, Switzerland, and all members of the European Union except for Greece and the 10 new member countries). Using US dollar and deutschmark denominated exchange rates over the period 1977 to 2001, the authors conclude that long-run relative PPP holds in their sample.

Two studies that investigate the PPP hypothesis for the Australian dollar are Masih and Masih (2004) and Hasan (2006). Masih and Masih (2004) examine the validity of PPP for the exchange rates of the Canadian dollar and the Australian dollar vis-à-vis the British pound and find strong support for PPP across various specifications and testing procedures. Hasan (2006) examines the bilateral exchange rates of the Australian dollar and seven OECD trading partners (Japan, the United States, the United Kingdom, Germany, New Zealand, France, and Italy). The estimation results are mainly supportive of long-run PPP when deviations are allowed to follow a fractionally integrated process.

While the studies discussed so far are mostly supportive of long-run PPP, the analyses of Narayan (2005), Harris, Leybourne and McCabe (2005), and Franses and van Dijk (2006) yield less encouraging results. Narayan (2005) applies unit root tests that allow for a simultaneous structural break in the intercept and slope to 17 OECD countries (the United States, Canada, Japan, Norway, Switzerland, and all members of the European Union except for Greece, Luxembourg, Ireland, and the 10 new member countries). The authors reject the PPP hypothesis for 13 out of 16 countries when using the US dollar as numeraire currency and for 9 out of 16 countries when using the deutschmark as numeraire currency. Harris, Leybourne and McCabe (2005) investigate a panel of 18 OECD countries (the set of countries is identical to Narajan, 2005 plus Greece) and reject the PPP hypothesis, even when structural break models are incorporated to account for atypical episodes in the data. However, as the test employed by Harris, Leybourne and McCabe (2005) tests the null hypothesis that PPP holds for all exchange rate series in the panel, the rejection of the null does not imply that PPP may not hold at least for some of the exchange rates. Franses and van Dijk (2006) examine the validity of PPP among traded goods for 78 bilateral exchange rates between the currencies of 13 OECD countries and find evidence in favor of PPP only in about 20 percent of all cases.

Overall, it has to be concluded that, between the countries examined in this analysis, purchasing power parity holds reasonably well in the long-run, but not in the short run. This outcome suggests that the Dornbusch and Frankel versions of the monetary approach might be more suitable than the Frenkel and Bilson versions in modelling nominal exchange rate movements as they assume that prices are sticky and, hence, that PPP is a long-run phenomenon. This issue will be explored in detail in section 3.4.

3.3 Econometric Methodology and Data Set

Independent of the variant of the monetary model a test of the monetary approach to the exchange rate entails the testing for the existence of a long-run stable relationship between the exchange rate and monetary fundamentals. This is examined by applying the cointegration technique of Johansen (1988) which starts by specifying a k-th order vector autoregression (VAR) model for the vector of endogenous variables.[8] All four versions of the monetary model described in the previous section can be subsumed under the following general specification:[9]

$$e_t = \beta_1 + m_t - m_t^* + \beta_2(y_t - y_t^*) + \beta_3(i_t - i_t^*) + \beta_4(\pi_t - \pi_t^*). \tag{3.17}$$

Here, the signs of the coefficients β_j depend on the variant of the monetary model (see Table 3.1). Defining $X = [e - m + m^*, y - y^*, i - i^*, \pi - \pi^*]'$ as the vector of endogenous variables, the corresponding VAR model can be expressed as

$$X_t = \Pi_1 X_{t-1} + \Pi_2 X_{t-2} + \ldots + \Pi_k X_{t-k} + \varepsilon. \tag{3.18}$$

Each of the matrices Π_j is a $n \times n$ matrix of parameters, where n is the number of endogenous variables, and ε is a vector of residuals which are

[8]The methodology developed by Johansen (1988) is applied rather than the cointegration technique as pioneered by Engle and Granger (1987) and extended and refined by, among others, Stock and Watson (1988), because it has superior properties in testing for the presence of a cointegrating relationship and, in particular, allows testing restrictions on the cointegrating vector which is essential to discriminate between the different versions of the monetary approach to the exchange rate.

[9]Note that this specification implies the restriction that the coefficient on the domestic money supply variable is equal to one and the coefficient on the foreign money supply variable is equal to negative one.

assumed to be i.i.d. Gaussian. This system can be written in error correction form as

$$\Delta X_t = \Pi_1 X_{t-1} + \Gamma_1 \Delta X_{t-1} + \Gamma_2 \Delta X_{t-2} + \ldots + \Gamma_{k-1} \Delta X_{t-(k-1)} + \varepsilon. \tag{3.19}$$

In equation (3.19), Δ denotes first differences and $\Pi = \Pi_1 + \ldots + \Pi_k - I$ represents the coefficients of the long-run relationship between the variables contained in matrix X. In addition, $\Gamma_j = -(\Pi_{j+1} + \ldots + \Pi_k)$ captures the short-run dynamics. The rank of Π corresponds to the number of cointegrating vectors. If Π is of rank zero, no stationary linear combination of the variables can be found and, hence, no cointegrating relationship exists among them. If Π is of full rank, all series are stationary and, thus, no cointegration relationship exists either. If Π is of rank r (with $0 < r < n$) it can be decomposed as $\Pi = \alpha\beta$, where α and β are $n \times r$ matrices such that the columns of β are the cointegrating vectors and the elements of α are the adjustment parameters of the vector error correction model (VECM).

Johansen and Juselius (1990) demonstrate that the cointegrating vectors contained in the matrix β can be estimated as the eigenvectors associated with the r largest eigenvalues of $S'_{0k} S_{00}^{-1} S_{0k}$ with respect to S_{kk}, where S_{00}, S_{kk}, and S_{0k} are the residual moment matrices from a regression of ΔX_t and X_{t-k}, respectively, on $\Delta X_{t-1}, \ldots, \Delta X_{t-(k-1)}$. Equation (3.17) can also be extended to include constants or trend terms in the cointegration or error correction space.

To determine the number of cointegrating vectors, Johansen (1988) proposes two test statistics, the trace statistic and the maximum eigenvalue statistic:

$$\text{trace}(r|k) = T \sum_{j=r+1}^{n} \ln(1 - \hat{\lambda}_j), \tag{3.20}$$

$$\max(r, r+1) = -T \ln(1 - \hat{\lambda}_{r+1}), \tag{3.21}$$

where $\hat{\lambda}_{r+1}, \ldots, \hat{\lambda}_n$ are the smallest $n - r$ eigenvalues. The trace statistic tests the hypothesis that there are at most r cointegrating vectors while the maximum eigenvalue statistic tests the hypothesis of r cointegrating vectors against the alternative of $r + 1$ cointegrating vectors.[10] As the test statistics

[10] The critical values for both statistics are taken from MacKinnon, Haug, and Michelis (1999) and are adjusted for the sample size using the procedure suggested by Cheung and Lai (1993b). The asymptotic distribution of the critical values depends on $n - r$ as well as on the presence of deterministic regressors in the VECM.

are sensitive to the underlying assumption of i.i.d. Gaussian errors, the residuals are examined for autocorrelation, non-normality as well as heteroskedasticity. If a cointegrating vector is found this requires testing of whether this vector corresponds to one of the versions of the monetary model. This is done by examining the validity of exclusion restrictions on the coefficients using a likelihood ratio test.

In order to apply the methodology outlined in the previous paragraphs to the different variants of the monetary model, this chapter focuses on the exchange rate of the euro vis-à-vis seven currencies. Specifically, these currencies are the US dollar, the British pound, the Canadian dollar, the Japanese yen, the Norwegian krone, the Swiss franc, and the Australian dollar. Quarterly data for the period 1980Q1 to 2005Q1 is used in the analysis.[11] All data on exchange rates and monetary fundamentals are obtained from the International Financial Statistics (IFS) database. The euro exchange rate in price quotation is used and a synthetic euro exchange rate is calculated for the period prior to January 1999.[12] Money supply is measured as money plus quasi money for all countries except for the euro area. Here, no data on this measure are available and the monetary aggregate M2 is used instead. Output is measured as real GDP. For the euro area this variable is calculated as the sum of the GDPs of all euro area countries as no data on the GDP aggregate of the euro area are available prior to the first quarter of 1998. All money supply and real GDP series are seasonally adjusted. As short-term interest rates money market rates are employed. Prior to the first quarter of 1994, no data are available for the short term interest rate of the euro area; thus, the interest rate series is calculated as a trade-weighted average of the interest rates of the euro area countries. Regarding expected inflation rates, it is assumed that expectations are static and therefore expected inflation rates are proxied by past inflation rates.

3.4 Empirical Results

This section discusses the results of the empirical analysis. Section 3.4.1 first presents the VECM estimates and discusses whether the estimates are in line

[11]For Norway, the observation ends in 2004Q3, since data on money supply are not available for later periods.

[12]The calculations are based on the exchange rates of the previous national currencies weighted by the three-year average (1996-1998) of trade flows (exports + imports) of each euro area member country with the 13 most important trading partners outside the Euro area. Data on trade flows are obtained from the Direction of Trade Statistics.

Table 3.2: Augmented Dickey-Fuller Tests

	AU	CA	CH	JP	NO	UK	US
	with constant and time trend						
$e-m+m^*$	−3.13	−2.71	−1.94	−3.24	−1.60	−2.03	−2.09
$y-y^*$	−2.09	−1.99	−2.58	−1.65	−2.92	−2.57	−2.74
$i-i^*$	−2.30	−2.82	−3.90**	−2.94	−2.42	−2.45	−2.38
$\pi-\pi^*$	−2.08	−2.90	−2.57	−3.41	2.09	−4.29***	−4.72***
	with constant						
$e-m+m^*$	−2.13	−2.74	−2.95**	−3.01**	−3.42**	−0.95	−2.16
$y-y^*$	−0.71	−1.62	−1.69	−1.14	−0.46	−2.57	−0.95
$i-i^*$	−2.16	−2.55	−3.90***	−2.67	−3.42**	−2.99**	−2.77
$\pi-\pi^*$	−2.76	−2.51	−2.56	−3.00**	−3.02**	−3.46**	−2.69

Note: *** and ** denote rejection of the null hypothesis of a unit root at a one and five percent significance level, respectively.

with one of the versions of the monetary approach. Sections 3.4.2 and 3.4.3 take a closer look at those bilateral exchange rates, for which the estimates support one of the versions of the monetary model. Specifically, section 3.4.2 compares the actual bilateral exchange rates of the euro with the equilibrium values derived from the VECM estimates to assess the extent of any exchange rate misalignment. Section 3.4.3 then investigates the out-of-sample forecasting ability of the monetary approach in comparison to the random walk model.

3.4.1 VECM Estimates

As a preliminary step, augmented Dickey-Fuller (ADF) tests are conducted in order to investigate the presence of unit roots in each of the time series. The results are summarized in Table 3.2. For most of the series the tests indicate the presence of a unit root, supporting the application of cointegration techniques for analyzing the series. For several series, however, there is some evidence that the series are stationary. As the reliability of unit root tests is known to be rather poor, these series are, nevertheless, included in the cointegration analysis.

For the exchange rate of the euro vis-à-vis each of the seven currencies included in this study, a vector error correction model is estimated. All models contain a constant within the cointegration space and a separate constant

Table 3.3: Cointegration Test

H_0	AU	CA	CH	JP	NO	UK	US
			trace($r\|k$)				
$r=0$	47.111	52.999	60.646**	71.119***	52.877	34.649	51.612
$r\leq 1$	20.510	22.004	29.215	30.899	23.428	19.395	22.919
$r\leq 2$	6.246	6.643	8.711	12.942	7.831	7.452	6.933
$r\leq 3$	0.472	1.820	3.090	5.794	2.043	0.737	1.592
			max($r\|r+1$)				
$r=0$	26.601	30.994*	31.430*	40.220***	29.449	15.254	28.694
$r=1$	14.264	15.361	20.504	17.957	15.597	11.943	15.986
$r=2$	5.774	4.824	5.621	7.148	5.788	6.715	5.341
$r=3$	0.472	1.820	3.090	5.794	2.043	0.737	1.592

Note: ***, ** and * denote rejection of the null hypothesis of no unit root at a one, five and ten percent significance level, respectively.

within the error correction space. The residual tests suggest that a lag length of four quarters is appropriate for the estimations.

Table 3.3 shows the results of the trace and maximum eigenvalue tests. For the majority of the currencies, the tests are not able to reject the null hypothesis of no cointegration at conventional significance levels. The only exceptions are the Swiss franc and the Japanese yen, where the tests indicate the presence of a single cointegrating relationship at the 5 and 1 percent significance level, respectively. For Canada, the maximum eigenvalue tests points to a single cointegrating relationship at the 10 percent significance level, while the trace tests finds a cointegrating relationship only at the 12 percent significance level. For Norway, the United States, and Australia, a cointegrating relationship is found only at a significance level of around 13, 15, and 25 percent, respectively. Given the small sample size of just 92 observations, the failure to reject the null hypothesis at conventional significance levels might be due to a lack of power of the test statistics and should not be interpreted as evidence against the monetary approach. In the case of the United Kingdom, however, the tests clearly reject the existence of a long-run cointegrating relationship between the exchange rate and monetary fundamentals, implying that the cointegration tests do not support the monetary approach for the exchange rate between the euro and the British pound.

In order to investigate whether any of the variants of the monetary approach really applies to the individual countries, the normalized cointegrating vectors are examined. They are shown in Table 3.4 together with the p-values

Table 3.4: Normalized Cointegrating Vectors ($k = 4$, 1980Q1 - 2005Q1)

	$e - m + m^*$	$y - y^*$	$i - i^*$	$\pi - \pi^*$	α
AU	1.000	2.483	−0.030	0.005	−0.230
	[0.001]	[0.001]	[0.023]	[0.775]	[0.002]
CA	1.000	2.299	0.026	−0.103	0.008
	[0.000]	[0.010]	[0.101]	[0.002]	[0.883]
CH	1.000	8.333	0.758	−1.387	−0.009
	[0.663]	[0.010]	[0.005]	[0.001]	[0.059]
JP	1.000	−5.893	−0.205	0.231	−0.011
	[0.001]	[0.000]	[0.000]	[0.000]	[0.674]
NO	1.000	−0.106	0.033	0.462	−0.204
	[0.001]	[0.654]	[0.000]	[0.351]	[0.000]
UK	1.000	87.521	−1.552	0.753	0.000
	[0.406]	[0.083]	[0.080]	[0.372]	[0.953]
US	1.000	2.109	0.045	−0.210	−0.131
	[0.000]	[0.175]	[0.025]	[0.006]	[0.009]

Notes: The numbers in parentheses denote the p-values of likelihood-ratio tests of exclusion restrictions on the coefficients. All VECMs include a constant in the error correction space and a separate constant in the cointegrating space.

of likelihood ratio tests of exclusion restrictions on the coefficients.[13] For Australia, the data clearly support the Bilson version of the monetary approach. All variables except for the expected inflation differential are part of the cointegrating relationship. Furthermore, the short-term interest rate differential is positively related to the exchange rate term which is consistent with the propositions of Bilson's model. In the case of Canada, the data lend support to both the Frenkel and Frankel versions of the monetary model. An increase in the output-differential appreciates the exchange rate between the euro and the Canadian dollar, while an increase in the expected inflation differential depreciates it. The interest rate differential is negatively related to the exchange rate, but only at a 10 percent significance level. An insignificant coefficient could be interpreted as evidence in favor of the Frenkel version, while a significant coefficient would be in line with the Frankel version. In the following, I will assume the latter, i.e., that the Frankel version applies to the EUR-CAD exchange rate.

[13]Note that Table 3.4 shows the estimated cointegrating vectors. Thus, for the signs of the coefficients to be comparable to those in Table 3.1, they have to be multiplied by negative one.

In the case of Switzerland, the coefficients on the output differential, the short-term interest rate differential and the expected inflation differential are highly significant and consistent with the Frankel version. However, the term $e - m + m^*$ does not come out as significant which means that it is not part of the cointegration relationship. Thus, for the period examined in this study, the hypothesis that the monetary approach explains the bilateral exchange rate between the euro and the Swiss franc has to be rejected. For the Japanese yen, the results are not supportive of any of the tested models. The estimated coefficient on the interest rate differential is consistent with the Bilson version, but the signs of the estimated coefficients on both the output differential and the interest rate differential are not consistent with any of the four forms of the monetary model.

For the Norwegian krone, the estimation results lend some support to the Dornbusch version of the monetary model as the expected inflation differential does not come out as significant, while the interest rate differential enters the cointegrating vector with a negative sign and, hence, is positively related to the exchange rate between the euro and the Norwegian krone. However, the estimated coefficient on the output differential is insignificant. In the case of the United Kingdom, the expected inflation differential is insignificant, while the output differential and the interest rate differential enter the cointegrating vector with a positive and negative sign, respectively. Although these findings are consistent with the Bilson version of the monetary approach, the hypothesis that the term $e - m + m^*$ is not part of the cointegrating relationship cannot be rejected and, therefore, the data do not support the monetary approach. Finally, for the United States, the estimates support the Frankel version of the monetary model as the coefficients on the interest differential and the expected inflation differential are significant and of correct signs. The coefficient on the output differential is only marginally significant as indicated by the p-value of 0.17.

Table 3.4 also reports the error correction coefficients of the exchange rate equation (last column). Looking at the four currencies for which the estimated cointegrating vector is consistent with some variant of the monetary approach shows that the error correction parameter is significantly negative in the cases of Australia, Norway, and the United States. This means that any deviations of the actual bilateral exchange rate between the euro and these three currencies from its equilibrium value are corrected over time. The magnitudes of the error correction parameters suggest that mean reversion takes place rather quickly with half life times of 2.7, 3.0 and 4.9 quarters, respectively. For Canada, however, the error correction parameter is insignificant suggesting that the term $e - m + m^*$ is weakly exogenous to the system.

3.4.2 Exchange Rate Misalignment

Overall, the monetary approach is supported for four out of seven bilateral exchange rates examined in this study. These are the Australian dollar (Bilson version), the Canadian dollar (Frankel version), the Norwegian krone (Dornbusch version), and the US dollar (Frankel version).[14] The estimates for these four currencies are used to assess a possible undervaluation and overvaluation of the euro.[15] Figures 3.1 to 3.4 compare the actual nominal exchange rates of the euro with the equilibrium rates derived from the estimated cointegrating vectors. They also show two-standard error confidence bands that are derived based on the method suggested by Johansen (2001).[16]

The calculations suggest that during the past 25 years the actual exchange rate of the euro vis-à-vis the four currencies under examination deviated considerably from the value implied by monetary fundamentals at several points in time. However, in the cases of the EUR-AUD and the EUR-USD exchange rates, the estimates of the equilibrium paths are very imprecise as indicated by the wide confidence bands and, hence, the hypothesis that these exchange rates were fairly valued cannot be rejected. In the cases of the EUR-CAN

[14] Canada is included in this part of the analysis despite the weak exogeneity of the term $e-m+m^*$ as all roots of the characteristic polynomial lie outside the unit circle, implying that the system is stable. The intuition is that variables other than the term $e-m+m^*$ respond to deviations from the equilibrium and bring the system back to equilibrium.

[15] In the case of the Australian dollar and the Norwegian krone, the cointegrating relationship is first re-estimated without the expected inflation differential to obtain a specification that is consistent with the Bilson and Dornbusch versions, respectively. Dropping the expected inflation differential does not affect any of the remaining coefficients.

[16] Following Johansen (2001), the vector of endogenous variables X can be decomposed into a stationary and a nonstationary component. The decomposition is derived by first multiplying equation (3.19) by $\alpha'_\perp$, where $\alpha_\perp$ is the orthogonal complement of the matrix of adjustment parameters, i.e., $\alpha'\alpha_\perp = 0$, to obtain $\alpha'_\perp \Delta X_t = \sum_{j=1}^{k-1} \alpha'_\perp \Gamma_j \Delta X_{t-j} + \alpha'_\perp \sum_{j=1}^{t} \varepsilon_j$. Using the definition $\Gamma = I - \sum_{j=1}^{k-1} \Gamma_i$, this equation can be solved for the common trends as a function of levels, differences and initial values: $\alpha'_\perp \sum_{j=1}^{t} \varepsilon_j = \alpha'_\perp \Gamma X_t - \sum_{j=1}^{k-1} \alpha'_\perp \Gamma_j (X_{t-i} - X_t - X_{-j}) - \alpha'_\perp X_0$. Substituting $D \equiv \beta_\perp(\alpha'_\perp \Gamma \beta_\perp)^{-1} \alpha'_\perp$, where $\beta_\perp$ is the orthogonal complement of the matrix β of cointegrating vectors, into this equation yields $D \sum_{j=1}^{t} \varepsilon_j = D\Gamma X_t - \beta_\perp(\alpha'_\perp \Gamma \beta_\perp)^{-1} (\sum_{j=1}^{k-1} \alpha'_\perp \Gamma_j (X_{t-i} - X_t - X_{-j}) - \alpha'_\perp X_0)$. Taking a unit vector e_1 to select the first variable in the system, i.e., $X_{1t} = e'_1 X_t$, then the terms in this equation can be rearranged so that $X_{1t} - e'_1 D\Gamma X_t = e'_1 (I - D\Gamma)\beta' \bar{\beta} X_t$, where $\bar{\beta} = \beta(\beta'\beta)^{-1}$ such that $\beta'\bar{\beta} = I$ and $X_t = (I - D\Gamma)X_t + D\Gamma X_t$ is a stationary - nonstationary decomposition of X_t. The variance of the stationary part can be used to calculate confidence bands around the nonstationary part. The confidence bands are given by $\pm 2\sqrt{((I - D\Gamma)\bar{\beta}\mathrm{Var}(\beta' X_t)\bar{\beta}'(I - D\Gamma)')_{11}}$.

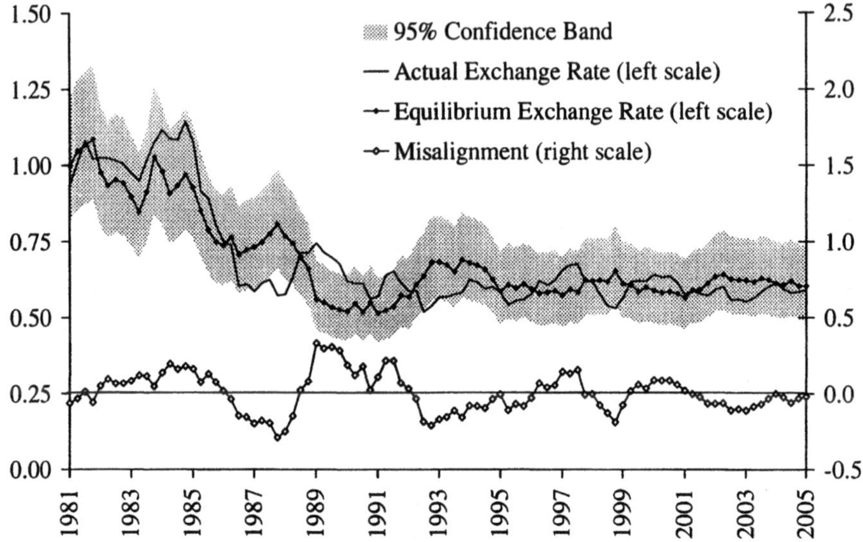

Figure 3.1: Actual and Equilibrium EUR-AUD Rate

and EUR-NOK exchange rates, however, significant exchange rate misalignments could be observed at several points in time. These misalignments were typically reversed within one to two years. For Norway this observation is consistent with the magnitudes of the estimated error correction parameter.

In order to evaluate whether the estimated equilibrium levels are reasonable, three different quarters of the sample that are of particular interest are examined in more detail. As the euro was launched at the beginning of 1999, the first quarter of 1999 is examined first. At least in hindsight, many observers felt that the euro started at a somewhat overvalued level. The calculations reveal that the euro was indeed overvalued against the Canadian dollar and the Norwegian krone. The overvaluation against the Canadian dollar is estimated at 7 to 20 percent with a point estimate of 13 percent and the overvaluation against the Norwegian krone is estimated at 14 to 24 percent with a point estimate of 19 percent. As the uncertainty surrounding the estimates for the Australian dollar and the US dollar is very high, the hypothesis that the actual exchange rate of the euro vis-à-vis these two currencies was in line with fundamentals at the beginning of 1999 cannot be rejected. Looking at the point estimates suggests that the euro was fairly valued against the US dollar and slightly overvalued against the Australian dollar.

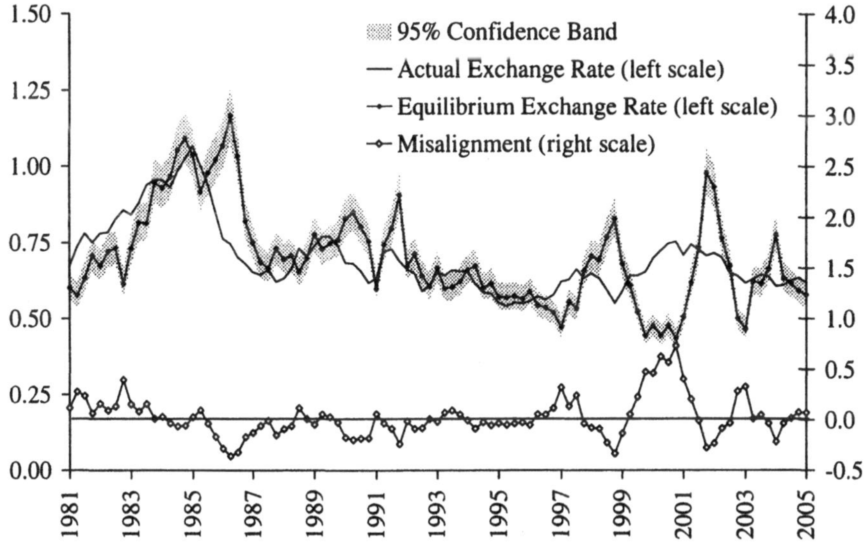

Figure 3.2: Actual and Equilibrium EUR-CAD Rate

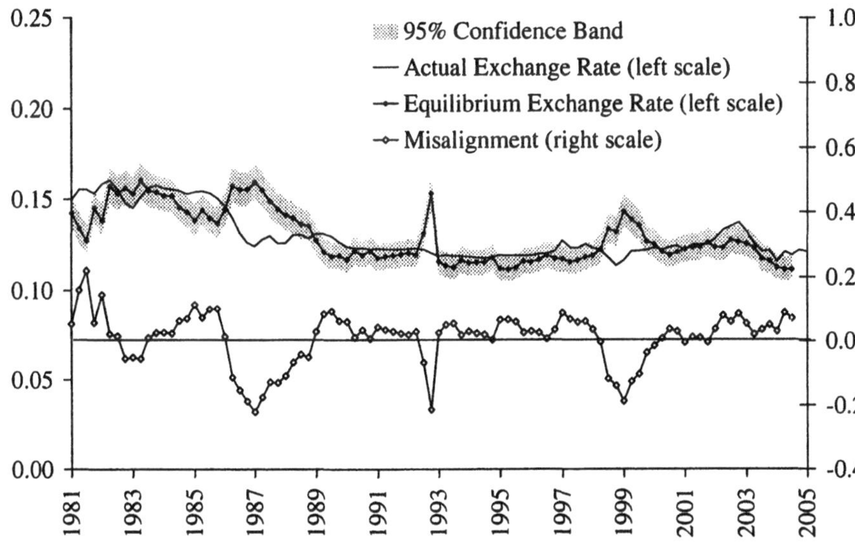

Figure 3.3: Actual and Equilibrium EUR-NOK Rate

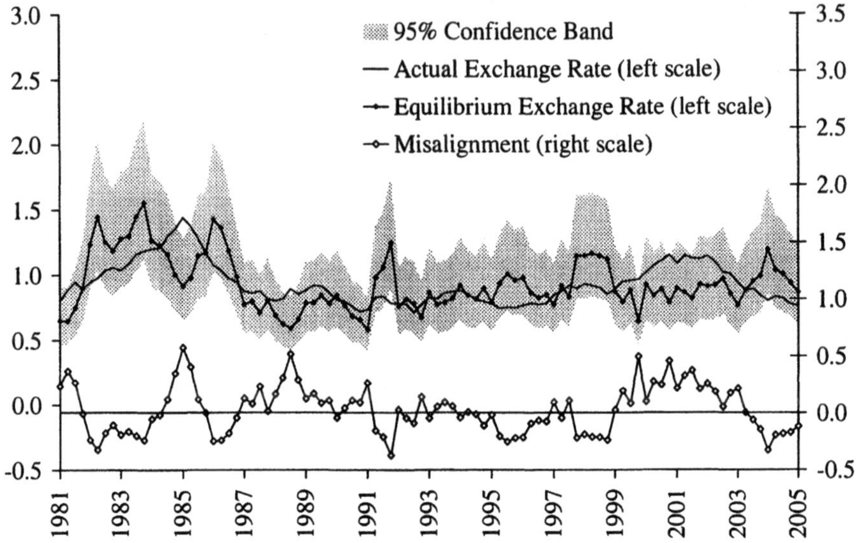

Figure 3.4: Actual and Equilibrium EUR-USD Rate

Another period that appears to be of particular interest in this context is the third and the fourth quarter of 2001, when the European Central Bank stated that the euro was heavily undervalued against all major currencies and intervened several times in the foreign exchange market to support the euro. This assessment was widely shared by economists and policymakers. The estimates of this study imply that the euro was fairly valued against the Australian dollar, the Canadian dollar, the Norwegian krone, and the US dollar when accounting for the uncertainty that surrounds the estimates. However, there are signs that the euro was heavily undervalued against the US dollar during the third and fourth quarter of 2001, as indicated by the point estimate of the undervaluation of 29 percent.

Finally, a third quarter examined here is the last quarter of the data set, i.e., the first quarter of 2005 for the Australian dollar, the Canadian dollar, and the US dollar and the third quarter of 2004 for the Norwegian krone. This seems to be interesting as the euro continuously strengthened during most of 2002 and 2003. The estimates suggest that the euro was back in equilibrium in the first quarter of 2005 with respect to the Australian dollar, the Canadian dollar, and the US dollar, but still slightly undervalued against the Norwegian krone in the third quarter of 2004.

3.4.3 Out-of-Sample Forecasting Performance

Since the finding of Meese and Rogoff (1983) that monetary models cannot outperform a simple random walk in predicting exchange rate movements, the literature has put a major interest in re-examining the forecasting performance of this class of models by varying the information set, the time horizon and the employed econometric techniques. Examples of recent papers that investigate the ability of the monetary approach to forecast bilateral exchange rates of the euro are Crespo-Cuaresma, Fortin, and Hlouskova (2004) and Groen (2005).

This section applies the VECM estimation results obtained for the bilateral exchange rates of the euro vis-à-vis the Australian dollar, the Canadian dollar, the Norwegian krone, and the US dollar to evaluate the out-of-sample forecasting performance of the monetary approach in comparison to the simple random walk. This exercise can give additional insight into the ability of the monetary approach to forecast bilateral exchange rates of the euro as the set of exchange rates differs from Crespo-Cuaresma, Fortin, and Hlouskova (2004) and Groen (2005) who focus on the exchange rate of the euro vis-à-vis the US dollar, the Japanese yen and, in the latter case, the Canadian dollar.

The analysis is based on a rolling estimation strategy in which the random walk model and the respective variant of the monetary model are estimated with data from the first quarter of 1980 up to the fourth quarter of 2000 in a first step. Based on these estimates an initial set of h-quarter ahead predictions is formed, $h = 1, 2, \ldots, 8$, where the actual values of the fundamentals are employed in the case of the monetary models. The sample is then updated with observations from the first quarter of 2001, and the forecast is repeated, continuing this way until the end of the data set.

The quality of the forecast values of the two alternative models are assessed using four different measures of forecasting accuracy. The first one is the frequently used root mean squared error (RMSE):

$$\text{RMSE}_h = \sqrt{\frac{1}{T_h}\sum_{t=1}^{T_h}(e_{t+h} - e_{t+h,t})^2}, \qquad (3.22)$$

where e_{t+h} is the actual value of the nominal exchange rate at time $t+h$, $e_{t+h,t}$ is its forecast value based on the estimation up to time t, and T_h is the number of forecasts. A smaller root mean squared error indicates that a given model has a better predictive capability. The upper part of Table 3.5 reports the RMSE of the monetary model relative to that of the random walk. A value

Table 3.5: Out-of-Sample Forecasting Performance

h	1	2	3	4	5	6	7	8
				RMSE ratio				
AU	0.88	0.88	0.91	0.96	1.06	1.20	1.06	0.96
CA	1.44	1.61	1.85	1.99	1.84	1.52	1.26	1.41
NO	1.10	1.01	0.96	0.96	0.94	0.89	0.85	0.84
US	1.02	1.10	0.95	0.89	0.86	0.75	0.65	0.52
				Sign statistic				
AU	−1.21	1.50	−0.26	1.07	0.83	−1.73*	−0.30	0.00
CA	−0.73	−1.00	−1.29	−1.60	−1.94*	−1.15	0.30	0.00
NO	−0.77	0.53	−0.28	0.00	0.30	0.00	0.33	0.71
US	−0.24	−1.00	0.77	1.60	0.83	1.15	2.11**	2.53**
				Signed rank statistic				
AU	−0.07	1.45	0.68	0.91	−0.24	−2.27**	−0.89	0.15
CA	−1.78*	−1.24	−1.87*	−2.10**	−1.43	−1.10	0.27	0.76
NO	−0.80	−0.16	0.17	0.16	0.36	0.46	0.77	0.84
US	−0.26	−0.72	0.40	1.22	0.80	1.41	1.78*	2.19**
				Modified Diebold-Mariano statistic				
AU	0.96	1.10	2.01	0.62	NA	−0.99	−0.41	0.18
CA	−1.89*	−1.77*	−1.38	−0.98	−0.46	−0.12	−0.03	−0.03
NO	−0.82	−0.04	0.15	0.11	0.15	0.20	0.18	0.00
US	−0.18	−0.34	0.08	0.16	0.16	0.21	0.22	0.17

Note: ** and * denote rejection of the null hypothesis of equal forecasting performance at the 5% and 10% significance level, respectively.

smaller than unity indicates that the predictions of the monetary model are more accurate than the predictions of the random walk model.

For the EUR-AUD exchange rate, the calculations reveal that the RMSE ratio is smaller than unity for forecasting horizons of 1 to 4 quarters as well as for a forecasting horizon of 8 quarters, meaning that at these forecasting horizons, the monetary model performs better than the random walk model. At forecasting horizons of 5 to 7 quarters, by contrast, the monetary model performs worse than the simple random walk. This result is rather surprising as fundamental-based models are generally found to outperform the random walk at longer time horizons - if at all. However, all values are rather close to unity indicating that the results might not be significant. In the case of Canada, the RMSE ratio is larger than unity for all forecasting horizons, implying that the monetary model is not able to beat the simple random walk. For Norway and the United States, by contrast, the calculations suggest that the forecasting ability of the monetary model improves relative to that of the random walk when the forecasting horizon is extended, and is better than that of the random walk at forecasting horizons of three quarters or more.

Since the root mean squared error criterion does not lend any insight into whether a model generates significantly better forecasts than another model at any point in time, three test statistics are calculated that formally test the hypothesis that two different models have equal forecasting performance. All three test statistics are based on the loss differential d_t which is the difference between the squared forecasting error of the random walk model and the corresponding value of the monetary model. A positive value of d_t means that the monetary model outperforms the random walk. The most simple test is the so-called sign-test. The test statistic is

$$\text{(3.23)} \qquad \mathrm{S} = \frac{\sum_{t=1}^{T_h} I_+(d_t) - 0.5T_h}{\sqrt{0.25T_h}} \sim N(0,1),$$

where $I_+(d_t) = 1$ if $d_t > 0$ and $I_+(d_t) = 0$ otherwise. In Table 3.5, the sign statistic indicates a significantly better forecasting performance of the monetary approach only for the 7- and 8-quarter forecasts of the EUR-USD exchange rate. In all other cases, the hypothesis of equal forecasting performance can either not be rejected or the monetary model performs significantly worse than the simple random walk (the latter is the case for the 6-quarter forecast of the EUR-AUD exchange rate and the 5-quarter forecast of the EUR-CAD exchange rate).

The power of the sign test is rather limited, since it does not take into account the magnitude of the forecasting errors. A test that overcomes this deficiency is Wilcoxon's signed-rank test. The test statistic equals the sum of the ranks of the positive loss differentials, where the ranks are calculated based on the absolute values of all loss differentials. Its studentized version is

$$\text{(3.24)} \qquad \mathrm{W} = \frac{\sum_{t=1}^{T_h} I_+(d_t)\mathrm{rank}(|d_t|) - \frac{T_h(T_h+1)}{4}}{\sqrt{\frac{T_h(T_h+1)(2T_h+1)}{24}}} \sim N(0,1).$$

The results of the Wilcoxon test are very similar to those of the sign test. The monetary approach is found to be superior to the random walk only for the 7- and 8-quarter forecasts of the EUR-USD exchange rate.

A last statistic that is calculated is the one suggested by Diebold and Mariano (1995):

$$\text{(3.25)} \qquad \mathrm{DM} = \frac{\frac{1}{T_h}\sum_{t=1}^{T_h} d_t}{\sqrt{\frac{1}{T_h}\left[\hat{\gamma}_0 + 2\sum_{\tau=1}^{h-1}\hat{\gamma}_\tau\right]}} \sim N(0,1),$$

where $\hat{\gamma}_0 = \frac{1}{T_h}\sum_{t=1}^{T_h}(d_t - \frac{1}{T_h}\sum_{t=1}^{T_h} d_t)^2$ and $\hat{\gamma}_\tau = \frac{1}{T_h}\sum_{t=\tau+1}^{T_h}(d_t - \frac{1}{T_h}\sum_{t=1}^{T_h} d_t)$ $(d_{t-\tau} - \frac{1}{T_h}\sum_{t=1}^{T_h} d_t)$. Harvey, Leybourne, and Newbold (1997) note that the Diebold-Mariono statistic could be seriously oversized in the case of two-step ahead predictions. The authors suggest the following modification of the original statistic:

$$\text{(3.26)} \qquad \mathrm{DM}^* = \left[\frac{T_h + 1 - 2h + T_h^{-1}h(h-1)}{T_h}\right]^{1/2} \mathrm{DM}.$$

The modified Diebold-Mariano statistic indicates that the monetary model is unable to beat the simple random walk at any forecasting horizon. This disappointing result is in line with previous research on the predictive ability of monetary models (see, for example, the overview by Neely and Sarno, 2002). One possible explanation for the poor forecasting performance of monetary models is provided by Kilian and Taylor (2001) who argue that exchange rates might revert nonlinearly to their equilibrium value. Nonlinear mean reversion would imply that monetary models provide better predictions when exchange rates deviate substantially from fundamentals. It also suggests that monetary models might be more informative at very long time horizons only.

3.5 Robustness Tests

As earlier studies have shown, the Johansen procedure may suffer from large variations in the estimates and a high probability of outliers (e.g., Maddala, 2001, p. 562). In order to assess the reliability of the estimation results, the lag structure of the VECM and the time horizon of the estimation are altered. Specifically, I change the lag length to 3 and 5, respectively, and drop the first and last three years of the sample, respectively.

The normalized cointegrating vectors and the error correction parameters of the exchange rate equations are displayed in Tables 3.6 to 3.9 for the four alternative specifications. Overall, the estimation results turn out to be

Table 3.6: Normalized Cointegrating Vectors ($k = 3$, 1980Q1 - 2005Q1)

	$e - m + m^*$	$y - y^*$	$i - i^*$	$\pi - \pi^*$	α
AU	1.000	2.306	−0.051	3.563	−0.214
	[0.086]	[0.098]	[0.051]	[0.333]	[0.038]
CA	1.000	6.817	0.010	−29.833	0.035
	[0.078]	[0.000]	[0.785]	[0.000]	[0.095]
CH	1.000	−6.843	−0.608	146.172	0.006
	[0.653]	[0.014]	[0.000]	[0.000]	[0.032]
JP	1.000	−4.681	−0.165	22.497	−0.049
	[0.001]	[0.000]	[0.000]	[0.000]	[0.066]
NO	1.000	1.870	0.002	−7.375	0.002
	[0.493]	[0.056]	[0.959]	[0.001]	[0.883]
UK	1.000	−145.635	2.114	208.496	−0.002
	[0.597]	[0.007]	[0.045]	[0.036]	[0.018]
US	1.000	11.014	−0.001	−57.524	0.014
	[0.034]	[0.000]	[0.981]	[0.000]	[0.394]

Notes: The numbers in parentheses denote the p-values of likelihood-ratio tests of exclusion restrictions on the coefficients. All VECMs include a constant in the error correction space and a separate constant in the cointegrating space.

somewhat sensitive to changes in the lag length of the VECM, though they are very robust to changes in the time horizon.

Looking at individual country results reveals that the estimates for Australia are very robust to variations in the model specification. All four alternative specifications confirm the finding of the baseline specification, i.e., that the EUR-AUD exchange rate is best modelled by the Bilson version of the monetary approach. In the case of Canada, the robustness analysis confirms the earlier impression that it is difficult to discriminate between the Frenkel and Frankel versions of the monetary approach. When changing the lag length to 3 or dropping the first three years of the sample, the coefficient on the interest rate differential becomes insignificant, thus supporting the Frenkel version. By contrast, with a lag length of 5 or an observation horizon that ends in 2002Q1, the coefficient comes out as significant which can be interpreted as evidence in favor of the Frankel version. Overall, it has to be noted that the results are inconclusive regarding the exact version of the monetary approach that applies to the EUR-CAD exchange rate.

As regards the euro exchange rates vis-à-vis the Japanese yen and the Swiss franc, changing the time horizon or the lag length does not alter the general impression given by the baseline specification, i.e., that the monetary

Table 3.7: Normalized Cointegrating Vectors ($k = 5$, 1980Q1 - 2005Q1)

	$e - m + m^*$	$y - y^*$	$i - i^*$	$\pi - \pi^*$	α
AU	1.000	2.566	−0.020	−1.161	−0.241
	[0.000]	[0.000]	[0.090]	[0.436]	[0.005]
CA	1.000	2.085	0.021	−8.871	0.011
	[0.000]	[0.016]	[0.094]	[0.006]	[0.880]
CH	1.000	−7.805	−0.910	62.560	−0.007
	[0.609]	[0.003]	[0.000]	[0.041]	[0.041]
JP	1.000	−4.799	−0.194	17.637	−0.025
	[0.017]	[0.033]	[0.012]	[0.061]	[0.579]
NO	1.000	−0.109	0.035	1.112	−0.164
	[0.269]	[0.827]	[0.251]	[0.509]	[0.197]
UK	1.000	95.245	−1.711	57.081	0.001
	[0.209]	[0.000]	[0.000]	[0.131]	[0.593]
US	1.000	10.277	−0.039	−56.136	0.010
	[0.533]	[0.150]	[0.709]	[0.188]	[0.846]

Notes: The numbers in parentheses denote the p-values of likelihood-ratio tests of exclusion restrictions on the coefficients. All VECMs include a constant in the error correction space and a separate constant in the cointegrating space.

model is not supported by the data. In the Japanese case, the direction of the impact of the fundamentals is not in line with the predictions of any of the versions of the monetary approach and in the Swiss case, the exchange rate term is not part of the cointegrating relationship throughout all specifications.

In the case of Norway, dropping the first or last three years of the sample does not affect the estimation results. The exchange rate term and the interest rate differential remain the only two variables to be significant, with the interest rate differential being negatively related to the exchange rate. However, when changing the lag length to 3 or 5, the exchange rate term becomes insignificant, implying that the monetary approach is no longer supported by the data.

For the bilateral exchange rate between the euro and the British pound, the robustness tests generally confirm the result of the baseline specification, i.e., that the monetary approach is not supported by the data due to the insignificance of the exchange rate term. The only exception is the regression that starts in 1983:1 as it lends some support to the Bilson version of the monetary model; the exchange rate term is marginally significant (p-value:

Table 3.8: Normalized Cointegrating Vectors ($k = 4$, 1980Q1 - 2002Q1)

	$e - m + m^*$	$y - y^*$	$i - i^*$	$\pi - \pi^*$	α
AU	1.000	2.530	−0.034	1.088	−0.234
	[0.002]	[0.003]	[0.022]	[0.574]	[0.003]
CA	1.000	0.143	0.049	−5.249	−0.038
	[0.000]	[0.902]	[0.011]	[0.052]	[0.578]
CH	1.000	2.738	0.285	−49.741	−0.027
	[0.440]	[0.109]	[0.038]	[0.016]	[0.121]
JP	1.000	−5.630	−0.204	21.747	−0.015
	[0.002]	[0.000]	[0.000]	[0.001]	[0.619]
NO	1.000	−0.294	0.032	0.437	−0.193
	[0.000]	[0.323]	[0.000]	[0.383]	[0.002]
UK	1.000	791.381	−12.828	705.030	0.000
	[0.939]	[0.048]	[0.053]	[0.264]	[0.722]
US	1.000	2.915	0.037	−23.316	−0.110
	[0.000]	[0.061]	[0.037]	[0.001]	[0.023]

Notes: The numbers in parentheses denote the p-values of likelihood-ratio tests of exclusion restrictions on the coefficients. All VECMs include a constant in the error correction space and a separate constant in the cointegrating space.

0.12) and an increase in the output differential or a decrease in the interest rate differential are associated with an exchange rate appreciation.

Finally, in the case of the United States, the analysis reveals that the results are highly sensitive to alterations in the lag length of the VECM, but not to alterations in the time horizon. The results strongly support the Frenkel version of the monetary model when setting the lag length to 3 quarters, while they clearly reject the monetary approach when setting the lag length to 5 quarters as none of the variables is significant in this case. By contrast, dropping the first or last three years of the sample confirms the finding of the baseline specification, i.e., that the Frankel version bests suits the data. The results even improve compared to the baseline specification in that the output differential becomes highly significant.

3.6 Concluding Remarks

This chapter examined how well monetary factors can explain the developments in the bilateral nominal exchange rate of the euro vis-à-vis the US

Table 3.9: Normalized Cointegrating Vectors ($k = 4$, 1983Q1 - 2005Q1)

	$e - m + m^*$	$y - y^*$	$i - i^*$	$\pi - \pi^*$	α
AU	1.000 [0.005]	2.527 [0.006]	−0.025 [0.142]	−0.220 [0.922]	−0.221 [0.018]
CA	1.000 [0.000]	2.371 [0.002]	0.017 [0.206]	−9.184 [0.001]	−0.020 [0.731]
CH	1.000 [0.303]	−6.973 [0.000]	−0.716 [0.000]	82.361 [0.000]	0.011 [0.057]
JP	1.000 [0.115]	−7.422 [0.001]	−0.230 [0.006]	30.389 [0.001]	−0.004 [0.885]
NO	1.000 [0.053]	−0.290 [0.436]	0.033 [0.035]	1.043 [0.228]	−0.181 [0.015]
UK	1.000 [0.121]	52.053 [0.012]	−0.928 [0.013]	47.537 [0.180]	0.000 [0.985]
US	1.000 [0.000]	2.899 [0.050]	0.035 [0.089]	−23.080 [0.001]	−0.112 [0.012]

Notes: The numbers in parentheses denote the p-values of likelihood-ratio tests of exclusion restrictions on the coefficients. All VECMs include a constant in the error correction space and a separate constant in the cointegrating space.

dollar, the Australian dollar, the Canadian dollar, the British pound, the Norwegian krone, the Japanese yen, and the Swiss franc over the past 25 years.

The results of the study are mixed. Overall, the monetary approach is supported for four out of seven bilateral exchange rates examined. These are the Australian dollar, the Canadian dollar, the Norwegian krone, and the US dollar. For the exchange rate vis-à-vis the Australian dollar, the Bilson version of the monetary model best suits the data, a result that is robust to changes in both the time horizon and the lag length of the VECM. For the exchange rate vis-à-vis the Canadian dollar, the results are ambiguous regarding the exact version of the monetary approach that applies to this exchange rate. Depending on the exact specification of the VECM, the data either support the Frankel or Frenkel version of the monetary model. For the exchange rate vis-à-vis the Norwegian krone, the results lend some support to the Dornbusch version of the monetary model, though this result is sensitive to the choice of the lag length in the VECM. Finally, in the case of the United States, the Frankel version best fits the data, which is, however, also sensitive to the lag length.

The estimated cointegrating vectors were used to calculate the equilibrium level of the exchange rate of the euro vis-à-vis the four currencies, for which the data lend support to the monetary approach. Although the estimates are surrounded by a high degree of uncertainty, they can give some insights into any exchange rate misalignments over the recent past. The calculations point to an overvaluation of the euro at the time of its launch, which was quickly reversed and turned into an undervaluation by 2001. By the end of the observation horizon, the euro was back in equilibrium.

Investigating the out-of-sample forecasting performance of the monetary model produced rather disappointing results. Comparing the quality of the out-of-sample forecasts of the monetary model to that of the random walk showed that the monetary approach is not able to outperform the random walk model at any forecasting horizon.

In sum, the results suggest that there is some scope for the monetary approach to explain the developments of the euro during the period examined in this study. However, for the purpose of exchange rate forecasting as well as the assessment of an undervaluation or overvaluation of the euro, the monetary approach should not be used as the exclusive tool. Two factors may explain this rather disappointing result. First, the two building blocks of the monetary model, i.e., a stable money demand function and purchasing power parity, do not work very well. Second, although the monetary model is intuitively appealing, it simplifies reality - like all models. Neely and Sarno (2002) argue that the amount of exchange rate variation that can be explained by monetary factors is at most small. In the short run, volatile expectations about future values of the exchange rate may detach the exchange rate from fundamentals (Frankel, 1996); and in the long-run, exchange rates may be affected by real factors that lead to movements in the real exchange rate. This latter issue is explored in more detail in the next chapter.

Chapter 4

The NATREX Approach and the Euro

In this chapter, I apply the natural real exchange rate approach advocated by Stein (1994) and Stein and Allen (1997) to evaluate recent movements in the real effective exchange rate of the euro. As shown in Figure 4.1, the real effective exchange rate of the euro has fluctuated considerably during the past 25 years, generally reflecting corresponding fluctuations in the nominal effective exchange rate.[17] The changes in the value of the euro have tended to be rather protracted, suggesting that the real exchange rate may not follow a stationary process. Augmented Dickey-Fuller unit root tests support this conjecture as they are unable to reject the null hypothesis of stationarity at conventional significance levels.[18] The nonstationarity of the real effective exchange rate calls into question the ability of traditional exchange rate models such as the monetary approach to explain movements in the euro exchange rate. These models claim that the real exchange rate converges to a constant mean, which cannot be reconciled with the empirical evidence on the behavior of the euro exchange rate. This view is supported by the analysis carried out in chapter 2 demonstrating that the ability of the monetary approach to explain movements in the euro exchange rate is rather limited.

[17]The nominal and real effective exchange rates are expressed in quantity quotation. The currency basket consists of the US dollar, the British pound, the Swiss franc, the Swedish krona, the Singapore dollar, the Norwegian krona, the Korean won, the Japanese yen, the Danish krona, the Canadian dollar, and the Australian dollar. Up to 1999, synthetic euro exchange rates are calculated based on the exchange rates of individual EMU member countries.

[18]The ADF is -0.058 with a 10% critical value of -1.615.

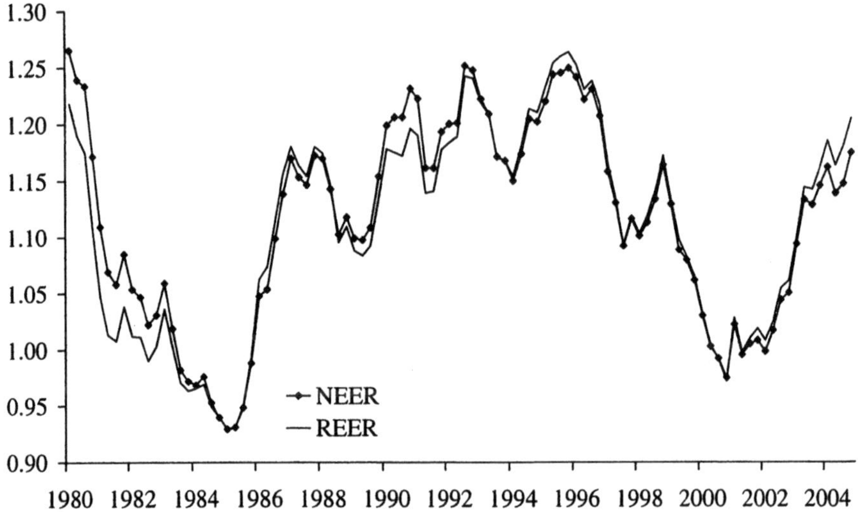

Figure 4.1: Actual Real and Nominal Effective Exchange Rates of the Euro

With the real exchange rate of the euro being non-stationary, an assessment of its equilibrium value should focus on models that do not assume the long-run real exchange rate to be constant, but allow it to change over time due to variations in underlying fundamentals. Among the three approaches that are commonly employed in the literature to explain movements in the real exchange rate, i.e., the BEER approach, the macroeconomic balance approach, and the NATREX approach, this study focuses on the NATREX approach. Compared to the other two approaches, the NATREX approach has the advantage that it explicitly distinguishes, within a structural model, between the medium-term and the long-term equilibrium exchange rate. While Stein (1994, 1997), who pioneered the work on the NATREX approach, presents reduced-form estimates for the effective exchange rate of the US dollar and the deutschmark, NATREX studies for the euro have, up to now, focused on estimating individual components of the model. By contrast, this study estimates the NATREX approach in reduced form for the effective exchange rate of the euro.

The outline of the rest of the chapter is as follows. Section 4.1 outlines the model which is employed in the empirical analysis and section 4.2 explains the estimation procedure and the data set. Section 4.3 then presents the estimation results. Section 4.4 compares the forecasting ability of the estimated model with that of the random walk. Finally, section 4.5 summarizes the main findings and concludes.

4.1 The NATREX Approach

The NATREX model was originally developed by Stein (1994) and later extended in Stein and Allen (1997). The approach aims at closing the gap in exchange rate economics between the medium and the long term and therefore explicitly distinguishes between a medium-term equilibrium, in which external and internal balance prevail and the domestic real interest rate is equal to the world real interest rate, and a long-term equilibrium, in which, in addition, net foreign debt and the capital stock are constant.

The empirical analysis in this study is based on a slightly modified version of Stein's (1994) model. It is assumed that the euro area is small in the sense that foreign output and the world interest rate are exogenous, but large in the sense that it has the ability to influence the world market price of its products so that the terms of trade are endogenous. I also abstract from population growth. The general structure of such a NATREX model is outlined in the section 4.1.1. Section 4.1.2 then discusses the adjustment of the endogenous variables to exogenous shocks, explicitly distinguishing between a medium and a long-term perspective.

4.1.1 The Model

The structure of the NATREX model employed in the empirical analysis can be expressed by the following four equations:

$$Y(\overset{+}{K},\overset{+}{u}) = C(\overset{+}{K},\overset{-}{F},\overset{\pm}{r},\overset{+}{\rho}) + I(\overset{-}{K},\overset{-}{r},\overset{+}{u}) + B(\overset{-}{R},\overset{+}{F},\overset{-}{K},\overset{-}{\rho},\overset{0}{r^*},\overset{+}{K^*},\overset{+}{\rho^*}), \tag{4.1}$$

$$S(\overset{+}{K},\overset{+}{F},\overset{\pm}{r},\overset{+}{u},\overset{-}{\rho}) - I(\overset{-}{K},\overset{-}{r},\overset{+}{u}) = B(\overset{-}{R},\overset{+}{F},\overset{-}{K},\overset{-}{\rho},\overset{0}{r^*},\overset{+}{K^*},\overset{+}{\rho^*}) - rF, \tag{4.1a}$$

$$\text{where } S(\overset{+}{K},\overset{+}{F},\overset{\pm}{r},\overset{+}{u},\overset{-}{\rho}) \equiv Y(\overset{+}{K},\overset{+}{u}) - C(\overset{+}{K},\overset{-}{F},\overset{\pm}{r},\overset{+}{\rho}) - rF;$$

$$(4.2)\quad \frac{dK}{dt} = I(\overset{-}{K}, \overset{-}{r}, \overset{+}{u});$$

$$(4.3)\quad \frac{dF}{dt} = I(\overset{-}{K}, \overset{-}{r}, \overset{+}{u}) - S(\overset{+}{K}, \overset{+}{F}, \overset{\pm}{r}, \overset{+}{u}, \overset{-}{\rho});$$

$$(4.4)\quad r = r^*.$$

Equation (4.1) reflects the condition for goods market equilibrium. The left-hand side represents aggregate supply Y which is a positive function of the capital stock K and a measure of productivity u. The right-hand side shows aggregate demand as the sum of consumption C, investment I, and the trade balance B. The signs over the different variables indicate the signs of the first derivative of the respective functions. Consumption depends positively on real[19] net wealth, which is the difference between capital K and real net foreign debt F, and positively on the time preference rate ρ.[20] The relation between consumption and the real interest rate r is ambiguous (indicated by a $\pm$ symbol) as the real interest rate positively affects consumption via an income and negatively via a substitution effect. Based on the idea of Tobin's q, investment is assumed to be a negative function of the capital stock K and the real interest rate r and a positive function of productivity u. Following the simplification of Stein (1994), it is assumed that the trade balance B is determined by the real exchange rate R (defined in quantity quotation) and domestic as well as foreign consumption (C and C^*). Hence, $B = B(R, C(F, K, \rho, r^*), C^*(F, K, r^*, K^*, \rho^*)) = B(R, F, K, \rho, r^*, K^*, \rho^*)$,where $\partial B/\partial F > 0$, $\partial B/\partial K < 0$, $\partial B/\partial K^* > 0$, $\partial B/\partial \rho < 0$, and $\partial B/\partial \rho^* > 0$. A normal reaction of the trade balance to exchange rate changes is assumed, i.e., $\partial B/\partial R < 0$. The impact of the interest rate on the trade balance is supposed to be rather small. For simplicity, it is assumed that $\partial B/\partial r^* = 0$.[21]

Goods market equilibrium is equivalent to balance of payment equilibrium, which is equation (4.1a). Equation (4.1a) implies that savings S de-

[19] 'Real' refers to a variable which is measured in units of the domestically produced good. This good is used for both consumption and investment.

[20] A consumption function of this type can be derived from intertemporal optimization considerations (Stein, 1997). Note that the NATREX approach does not distinguish between private and government consumption or investment, respectively. Hence, the variables C and I refer to the sum of private and government consumption or investment, respectively.

[21] This would for instance be the case if the ratio of consumption to wealth were the same in both countries and if the ratio of imports to consumption were reciprocally proportional to wealth.

pend on capital K, foreign debt F, the real interest rate r, and the exogenous factors ρ and u. A higher capital stock has a positive impact on S, i.e., $\partial S/\partial K > 0$, because it is assumed that a higher capital stock increases output by more than consumption. The impact of foreign debt on savings is theoretically ambiguous. However, to ensure that the debt level converges to a steady state level, a positive relationship between savings and foreign debt is necessary, $\partial S/\partial F = -r - \partial C/\partial F > 0$ (see, for example, Stein and Sauernheimer, 1996, p. 26). The reaction of S to a change in r depends on $\partial C/\partial r$ and on whether the country is a net debtor ($F > 0$) or a net creditor ($F < 0$).[22] The two remaining partial derivatives are unambiguous, i.e., $\partial S/\partial \rho < 0$ and $\partial S/\partial u = \partial Y/\partial u > 0$.

Equations (4.2) and (4.3) describe the evolution of the capital stock and the foreign debt level over time, respectively. The change in the capital stock equals investment, and the change in the net foreign debt level equals the excess of savings over investment. Equation (4.4) is the portfolio balance condition, stating that domestic and foreign real interest rates are equal.

The NATREX approach distinguishes between a medium-term and a long-term horizon. The crucial distinction is that the capital stock K and the stock of net foreign debt F are exogenous in what is referred to as the medium term. Although investment activities and current account balances can be different from zero in the medium term, their effects on the stocks of K and F are excluded from the analysis. The stock effects and their repercussions on other economic variables are included in the longer-run analysis. Finally, a long-run equilibrium is reached, when the stocks of K and F are at their steady state values.

More specifically, the medium-term equilibrium real exchange rate, i.e., the medium-term NATREX, denoted $\tilde{R}$, is defined as the exchange rate that equates the left-hand side and the right-hand side of equation (4.1) with portfolio balance (4.4) prevailing. The medium-term NATREX is not necessarily constant, but changes over time as the capital stock and net foreign debt

[22] For instance, if the country is a net debtor and consumption depends positively on the real interest rate, then savings depend negatively on the real interest rate.

evolve. The precise changes in the medium-term NATREX are given by

$$(4.5) \qquad \frac{\partial R}{\partial K} = \frac{\dfrac{\partial S}{\partial K} - \dfrac{\partial I}{\partial K} - \dfrac{\partial B}{\partial C}\dfrac{\partial C}{\partial K}}{\dfrac{\partial B}{\partial R}} < 0 \quad \text{and}$$

$$(4.6) \qquad \frac{\partial R}{\partial F} = -\frac{\left(1 + \dfrac{\partial B}{\partial C}\right)\dfrac{\partial C}{\partial F}}{\dfrac{\partial B}{\partial R}} < 0.$$

At the end of the adjustment process, the net foreign debt level as well as the capital stock reach their steady state levels so that their changes as expressed in equations (4.2) and (4.3) are equal to zero. As a consequence, the variables in equation (4.1) do not change anymore and, thus, the equilibrium real exchange rate is constant. This exchange rate is referred to as the long-term NATREX, $\bar{R}$. The reaction of the medium-term NATREX $\tilde{R}$ and the long-term NATREX $\bar{R}$ to exogenous shocks is discussed in the next section.

4.1.2 Adjustment to Exogenous Shocks

The main exogenous factors in the NATREX model are the time preference rate ρ, the productivity parameter u, and the world real interest rate r^* assuming the analyzed country is small in world capital markets and can, thus, not influence r^*. The effects of changes in these three factors on the other variables in the model are illustrated in Figures 4.2 and 4.3.

Figure 4.2 shows the medium-term equilibrium.[23] During the medium term, the real exchange rate adjusts to the level that equilibrates the ex ante savings-investment balance and the ex ante current account balance. The SI curve represents the difference between savings S and investment I, given $r = r^*$. As there is no relation between the real exchange rate and savings less investment, the curve is vertical. The CA curve shows the relation between the current account balance and the real exchange rate. An increase in R, i.e., an appreciation in real terms, leads to a decrease in the trade balance and, hence, to a deterioration in the current account. Both the SI curve and the CA curve are drawn for given values of the endogenous debt and

[23]Note that the NATREX approach only distinguishes between the medium and the long term.

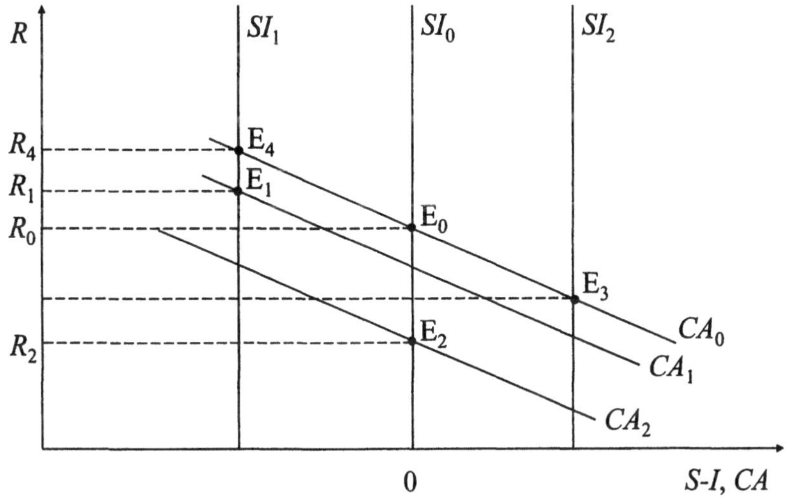

Figure 4.2: Portfolio and Current Account Balance

capital stock levels. It is assumed that debt and capital accumulation affect the decisions on investment, savings, and trade flows only with considerable delay. For a given world interest rate r^*, the intersection of the SI curve and the CA curve determines the equilibrium real exchange rate in the medium term.

The long-term adjustment of capital and debt is shown in Figure 4.3. Along the vertical curve $dK/dt = 0$, the q-ratio equals unity implying that the return on investment is equal to the cost of capital so that a change in the capital stock does not bring about any additional profit. Thus, in this situation, the capital stock does not change. To the left of the curve, i.e., at a lower capital stock, the q-ratio is above unity and additional investments are profitable. The capital stock therefore increases and moves towards its long-term equilibrium. To the right of the curve, the q-ratio is below unity and the capital stock decreases. The downward sloping curve $dF/dt = 0$ represents combinations of F and K for which the difference between savings and investment is equal to zero so that the foreign debt level does not change. A decline in F increases wealth and consumption so that savings decline. This would imply $S < I$ resulting in an increase in F. Then, the condition $S = I$ only remains satisfied if investment also declines. This requires a higher capital stock. Hence, in order for $S = I$ to hold, a lower level of F has to be

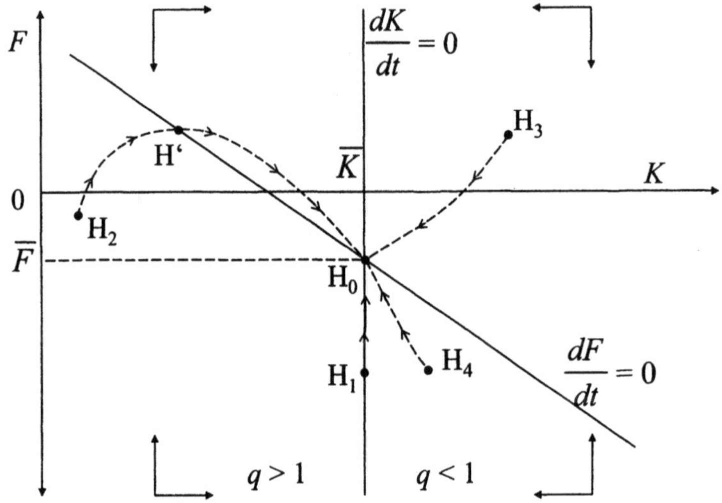

Figure 4.3: Net Foreign Assets and Capital Stock

associated with a higher level of K. This implies that the $dF/dt = 0$ curve is downward sloping.[24]

In the following, I briefly describe the effects of changes in the exogenous fundamentals time preference, productivity, and the world real interest rate. The effects are illustrated in Figures 4.2 and 4.3 and the analytical results are shown in Table 4.1.

First, an increase in the time preference rate is considered. Starting from an equilibrium in which $CA = S - I = 0$, the lower time preference rate decreases savings and leads to a negative savings less investment balance. This is depicted by a curve such as SI_1 to the left of the initial SI_0 curve. In addition, as part of the additional spending translates into imports, the CA curve shifts to the left from CA_0 to CA_1. At the initial exchange rate R_0, the current account is now negative. However, the savings less investment balance is even more negative, since the SI curve shifted to the left by more than the CA curve.[25] This puts upwards pressure on the interest rate which, in

[24]Note that a higher K level also induces an increase in savings as explained above in the context of equation (4.1). This reinforces the effect of a rise in K on the savings investment gap. Also note that, along the $dF/dt = 0$ curve, the trade account balance equals the interest payments on foreign debt, rF.

[25]This is due to the fact that only part of the change in consumption translates into a

turn, leads to capital inflows and a rise in R. The induced deterioration of the current account - indicated by a movement along the CA_1 curve to the upper left - is offset by net capital inflows.[26] The new medium-term equilibrium is given by point E_1 in Figure 4.2.

The described medium-term equilibrium point changes over time because the capital stock and the foreign debt do not remain unchanged. The evolvement of both variables can be seen in Figure 4.3. As capital inflows are associated with a current account deficit, the economy is located in a point such as H_1. Due to the current account deficit, the foreign debt increases while the $dK/dt = 0$ curve is not affected by this change. In Figure 4.3, this is expressed by a movement from H_1 to H_0. The higher debt level has two effects. First, it deteriorates the current account due to higher interest payments. Second, the higher debt level leads to a decline in wealth and, hence, to a decline in consumption. Therefore, savings rise and the negative savings investment difference is reduced. This, in turn, leads to a decline in capital inflows. In Figure 4.2, the SI curve that reflects this reduced gap lies to the right of SI_1. As long as the debt level rises, this process continues. A new equilibrium is reached once the savings-investment gap is closed. Because the increased debt level is associated with higher interest payments, the CA curve in Figure 4.2 shifts from CA_1 to CA_2. To reach a long-term equilibrium, the savings-investment gap has to be closed which requires F to rise sufficiently to shift the SI curve back to SI_0. The new long-term equilibrium is reached in E_2 with the new real exchange rate level R_2. The real exchange rate is now lower than in the initial equilibrium E_0, implying an improvement in the trade account. This improvement is needed to finance the interest payments on the higher foreign debt level.

Next, consider an increase in productivity. This leads to a rise in investment via a rise in the q-ratio. Starting again from E_0, the savings less investment balance turns negative so that the SI curve in Figure 4.2 shifts from SI_0 to the left to SI_1. The excess of investment over savings is financed by capital inflows from abroad. The new medium-term equilibrium is point E_4 indicating a real appreciation of the domestic currency to R_4.[27] The long-term effects of a productivity rise are displayed in Figure 4.3. Initially, the economy is in a point such as H_2. The productivity increase leads to a rise in q in H_2 and shifts the $dK/dt = 0$ curve to the right. At the same time, the

change in imports.

[26]Portfolio balance as indicated in equation (4.4) implies that the domestic interest rate only needs to rise marginally to trigger the required capital inflows.

[27]This analysis implies that additional investment goods are not associated with higher imports.

current account deficit associated with E_4 brings about a rise in net foreign debt. The economy moves along the trajectory H_2H'. In a longer-term perspective, the growing net debt induces a rise in savings which is fostered by the growth of the capital stock. The growing capital stock also induces - as explained above - a reduction in investment due to the decreasing productivity of capital. At some point, here H', savings and investment are equal and the debt remains constant. As the q-ratio is still above unity, investment is still positive and the capital stock is growing. This leads to a further rise in savings and a further decline in investment. The savings less investment balance becomes positive and capital outflows arise. The capital outflows, in turn, reduce the net foreign debt thereby partly offsetting the rise in savings. At some point, the positive impact on savings resulting from the growing capital stock and the negative effect on savings resulting from the declining net debt cancel out. Then, savings decline until both investment and savings become zero in the new equilibrium H_0. In Figure 4.2, the relevant SI curve is again SI_0. Compared to the initial situation, the capital stock is higher and the foreign debt level is lower in the new equilibrium. The lower debt goes hand in hand with lower interest payments and, hence, an improvement in the current account. At the same time, the higher wealth level (due to lower debt and a higher capital stock) implies higher imports so that the effect on the exchange rate is ambiguous. Starting from CA_0, the CA curve in Figure 4.2 can move to the right or to the left.

Finally, a rise in the world real interest rate r^* is considered. As shown in equation (4.4), this leads to an equal rise in the domestic real interest rate, r. This, in turn, induces a reduction in investment via a fall in the q-ratio. The impact of a rise in r on consumption and, thereby, savings is ambiguous. If $\partial C/\partial r < 0$ the SI curve shifts from SI_0 to the right to SI_2. If $\partial C/\partial r > 0$ the direction of the shift depends on whether $\partial C/\partial r < |\partial I/\partial r|$, in which case the SI curve shifts to the right to SI_2, or whether $\partial C/\partial r > |\partial I/\partial r|$, in which case it shifts to the left to SI_1.[28] The medium term effect on R depends on the direction of the shift of the SI curve. If it shifts to the right (left), the saving less investment balance becomes positive (negative) which

[28]The rise in the real interest rate also influences the current account. If the country is a net creditor its interest income rF rises, which leads to an improvement in the current account and, hence, to a rightward shift of the CA curve. In contrast, if the country is a net debtor the CA curve will shift to the left. However, as savings are affected by the same amount, there is an additional shift of the SI curve. As this shift exactly equals the shift of the CA curve, it does not affect the medium-term equilibrium value of R. Note that the rise in the real interest rate also affects the current account via its impact on the trade balance. However, this effect is supposed to be rather small and, for simplicity, it is assumed to be zero as discussed in section 4.1.1.

leads to net capital outflows (inflows) and, hence, a decline (rise) in the real exchange rate.

The long-term effects also depend on the direction of the SI curve shift. Two cases can be distinguished. In the first case, the SI curve shifts to the right, i.e., $S - I > 0$. Then, the net foreign debt declines. As the higher interest rate leads to disinvestment and, thereby, to a decline in the long-term capital stock, the economy moves in Figure 4.3 from a point such as H_3 to the lower left. During the adjustment process, savings decline as a result of the lower capital stock. This effect is partially offset by the decline in net foreign debt. Simultaneously, disinvestment is reduced as the capital stock reaches its lower steady-state level. In the new long-term equilibrium H_0, savings again equal investment and the SI curve in Figure 4.2 shifts back to SI_0. The impact of the declining capital stock and the declining net foreign debt on the long-term value of R is ambiguous as both have opposite effects on the wealth level and, hence, the trade balance. In the second case, which can be distinguished, the SI curve shifts to the left in the medium term, i.e., $S - I < 0$. Then, net debt rises which partially offsets the decline in savings induced by the shrinking capital stock. The economy moves along trajectory H_4H_0. In the new steady state H_0, the capital stock is lower and the net debt higher than before. The effect on R is again ambiguous. On the one hand, both the decline in K and the rise in F cause a reduction in the wealth level and, hence, an improvement in the current account via a reduction in imports. On the other hand, the rise in F leads to a deterioration in the current account via higher interest payments. This shows that, taken these effects together, a rise in the world interest rate reduces the capital stock, but exerts ambiguous effects on the foreign debt level and the equilibrium exchange rate.

To sum up, the medium-term equilibrium real exchange rate $\tilde{R}$ increases with a rise in the time preference rate or the productivity measure, while the impact of the foreign real interest rate is ambiguous. The long-term equilibrium exchange rate $\bar{R}$, by contrast, decreases with a rise in the time preference rate. The impact of both the productivity measure and the foreign real interest rate on $\bar{R}$ are ambiguous (see Table 4.1).

Table 4.1: Effects of Changes in Exogenous Factors

Factor	Medium-Term Effects	Long-Term Effects
ρ	$\frac{\partial R}{\partial \rho}=-\frac{\left(1+\frac{\partial B}{\partial C}\right)\frac{\partial C}{\partial \rho}}{\frac{\partial B}{\partial R}}>0$	$\frac{\partial \bar{R}}{\partial \rho}=\frac{\partial R}{\partial F}\frac{\partial \bar{F}}{\partial \rho}+\frac{\partial R}{\partial \rho}<0$ $\frac{\partial \bar{F}}{\partial \rho}=-\frac{\partial S}{\partial \rho}\Big/\frac{\partial S}{\partial F}>0$ $\frac{\partial \bar{K}}{\partial \rho}=0$
u	$\frac{\partial R}{\partial u}=-\frac{\frac{\partial Y}{\partial u}-\frac{\partial I}{\partial u}}{\frac{\partial B}{\partial R}}>0$	$\frac{\partial \bar{R}}{\partial u}=\frac{\partial R}{\partial K}\frac{\partial \bar{K}}{\partial u}+\frac{\partial R}{\partial F}\frac{\partial \bar{F}}{\partial u}+\frac{\partial R}{\partial u}\gtrless 0$ $\frac{\partial \bar{F}}{\partial u}=\frac{\frac{\partial S}{\partial K}\frac{\partial I}{\partial u}-\frac{\partial I}{\partial K}\frac{\partial S}{\partial u}}{\frac{\partial I}{\partial K}\frac{\partial S}{\partial F}}<0$ $\frac{\partial \bar{K}}{\partial u}=-\frac{\partial I}{\partial u}\Big/\frac{\partial I}{\partial K}>0$
r^*	$\frac{\partial R}{\partial r^*}=-\frac{\frac{\partial C}{\partial r}+\frac{\partial I}{\partial r}}{\frac{\partial B}{\partial R}}\gtrless 0$	$\frac{\partial \bar{R}}{\partial r^*}=\frac{\partial R}{\partial K}\frac{\partial \bar{K}}{\partial r^*}+\frac{\partial R}{\partial F}\frac{\partial \bar{F}}{\partial r^*}+\frac{\partial R}{\partial r^*}\gtrless 0$ $\frac{\partial \bar{F}}{\partial r^*}=\frac{\frac{\partial S}{\partial K}\frac{\partial I}{\partial r}-\frac{\partial I}{\partial K}\frac{\partial S}{\partial r}}{\frac{\partial I}{\partial K}\frac{\partial S}{\partial F}}\gtrless 0$ $\frac{\partial \bar{K}}{\partial r^*}=-\frac{\partial I}{\partial r}\Big/\frac{\partial I}{\partial K}<0$

4.2 Methodology and Data Set

For the purpose of the empirical analysis, it is useful to consider the evolution of the actual real exchange rate R as the sum of three components:

$$R_t = [R_t - \tilde{R}(K_t, F_t, u_t, \rho_t, r_t^*)] + [\tilde{R}(K_t, F_t, u_t, \rho_t, r_t^*) - \bar{R}(u_t, \rho_t, r_t^*)] + \bar{R}(u_t, \rho_t, r_t^*). \tag{4.7}$$

The first term on the right-hand side of identity (4.7) represents the deviation of the actual real exchange rate R from its medium-term equilibrium level, $\tilde{R}$. This deviation can be attributed to speculative and cyclical factors which are, on average, zero over time. The second term represents the deviation of the medium-term equilibrium exchange rate from its long-term value, $\bar{R}$, reflecting that the capital stock and the stock of foreign debt still change. The third term is the steady-state value of the real exchange rate, when capital and debt have reached their long-term equilibrium values.

To disentangle the long-term equilibrium relationship from the movement towards the equilibrium, the non-linear least squares estimation (NLS) suggested by Phillips and Loretan (1991) is applied to the following equation:

$$R_t = \mathcal{B}Z_t + a[R_{t-1} - \mathcal{B}Z_{t-1}] + b[Z_t - Z_{t-1}] + e_t, \tag{4.8}$$

where e_t are assumed to be i.i.d. $N(0, \sigma^2)$. The exogenous variables are subsumed in vector $Z = (\rho, \rho^*, u, u^*, r^*)$. The first term on the right-hand side of equation (4.8), BZ_t, is the steady state value of the real exchange rate. It corresponds to the last term in equation (4.7), i.e., $\bar{R}(u_t, \rho_t, r_t^*) = \mathcal{B}Z_t$. This is the sought-for cointegrating equation. The second term, $a[R_{t-1} - \mathcal{B}Z_{t-1}]$, is the error correction component. It corresponds to the adjustment term $[\tilde{R}(K_t, F_t, u_t, \rho_t, r_t^*) - \bar{R}(u_t, \rho_t, r_t^*)]$ in equation (4.7). The cointegrating vector $\mathcal{B}$ is constrained to be the same in both terms. While the term $\mathcal{B}Z_t$ represents the long-term NATREX $\bar{R}$, the term $\mathcal{B}Z_t + a[R_{t-1} - \mathcal{B}Z_{t-1}]$ represents the medium-term NATREX $\tilde{R}$. The third term, $b[Z_t - Z_{t-1}]$, is the reaction of the current real exchange rate to changes in the exogenous variables. Together with the residual term e_t it represents the deviation of the current real exchange rate from its medium-term equilibrium. Hence, it relates to the term $[R_t - \tilde{R}(K_t, F_t, u_t, \rho_t, r_t^*)]$ in equation (4.7). Normally, the term $[Z_t - Z_{t-1}]$ should be given by the changes in productivity, the time preference of the euro area and its trading partners, and the changes in the world real interest rate. However, these differences do not come out as significant at conventional significance levels in the estimation. Stein (1994) encountered the same problem in his empirical analysis of the US dollar exchange rate movements over the period 1975 to 1989. I adopt a remedy to this problem similar to the one chosen by Stein (1994) and replace the changes in the exogenous variables by the real interest differential between the euro area and the rest of the world. This is based on the consideration that fairly short term changes in the exogenous variables lead to temporary international real interest rate differentials. These induce portfolio adjustments which eventually eliminate such differentials. As the contemporaneous world real interest rate is already included in the estimated equation, the lagged interest rate differential is employed instead. In addition, two dummy variables are included, one for the German reunification in 1990 and one for the introduction of the euro in 1999.

Equation (4.8) is estimated based on quarterly data covering the sample period 1980Q1-2004Q4.[29] The real effective exchange rate of the euro based on GDP deflators, denoted REER, is employed as a measure of the real exchange rate of the euro where the foreign currencies and price indices are weighted according to their average trade share (exports plus imports) with the euro area during the period 2002-2004.[30] The countries whose currencies enter the calculation of the effective exchange rate are Australia, Canada, Denmark, Japan, Hong Kong, Korea, Norway, Singapore, Sweden, Switzerland, the United Kingdom, and the United States. These countries correspond to the "narrow" group countries as defined by the European Central Bank in its calculation of the effective exchange rate of the euro.[31] For the period prior to the launch of the euro in 1999, a synthetic effective exchange rate of the euro is calculated based on national exchange rates weighted by the four-year average (1996-1998) of the trade shares (exports plus imports) of each euro area country with the 13 most important trading partners outside the euro area. The data on exchange rates and on trade are taken from the International Financial Statistics (IFS) and the Direction of Trade Statistics of the International Monetary Fund, respectively.

Time preference is measured as the ratio of consumption (public and private) to GDP (both in nominal terms). Both consumption and GDP data

[29]Where quarterly data are not available, the data are interpolated from annual data following the method proposed by Gandolfo (1981).

[30]The choice of the GDP deflator in the calculation of the real exchange rate is motivated by the fact that it relies less heavily on nontradable goods than the consumer price index, and is more readily available than the producer price index and the wholesale price index. For simplicity, the weighing scheme is based on a fixed weight index rather than a time varying weight index. Given the slow moving nature of trade flows, the error should be negligible (Chinn, 2004).

[31]International trade of the euro area with these 12 countries accounted for 56 percent of the average annual total trade of the euro area between 2002 and 2004.

are taken from the IFS. The European variable is called NCGDP_EU and is calculated by aggregating the data from the individual euro area countries. The variable of the euro area trading partners, called NCGDP_TP, is calculated as a trade-weighted average of the corresponding consumption-to-GDP ratios of the individual countries.

Two alternative measures are employed to capture productivity developments.[32] First, following Lim and Stein (1997), productivity is measured as real GDP per employment. The GDP data are taken from the IFS, employment data are taken from the OECD Economic Outlook database if available or from the IFS, otherwise. The European productivity variable is called RGDPEMP_EU. The variable of the euro area trading partners is called RGDPEMP_TP and is calculated as a trade weighted average of the productivity variables of the individual countries. Measuring productivity as GDP per employment has the caveat that it does not capture the fact that productivity increases during the past two decades might have resulted in a reduction of hours worked. Moreover, it might vary with variations in the endogenously determined capital stock. Therefore, I employ total factor productivity as an alternative productivity measure. Total factor productivity is calculated as the Solow residual from a Cobb-Douglas production function with constant returns to scale:

$$Y = AK^{\theta}L^{1-\theta}. \tag{4.9}$$

A is the productivity parameter, Y is output, K is the capital stock, L is the total labor force, and θ is the share of capital's income in total income. Dividing equation (4.9) by L yields

$$\frac{Y}{L} = A\left(\frac{K}{L}\right)^{\theta}. \tag{4.10}$$

Given θ, the parameter A can be calculated as

$$A = \exp\left[\ln\left(\frac{Y}{L}\right) - \theta \ln\left(\frac{K}{L}\right)\right]. \tag{4.11}$$

In the calculations, Y is real GDP, K is the capital stock of the business sector, L is the number of hours worked calculated as average hours worked

[32]Empirical studies on the NATREX-model apply a wide variety of proxies for productivity: Stein (1997) uses a 12-quarter moving average of real GDP, and Stein and Sauernheimer (1996) use the ratio of industrial share prices to the producer price index which is closely related to the q-ratio.

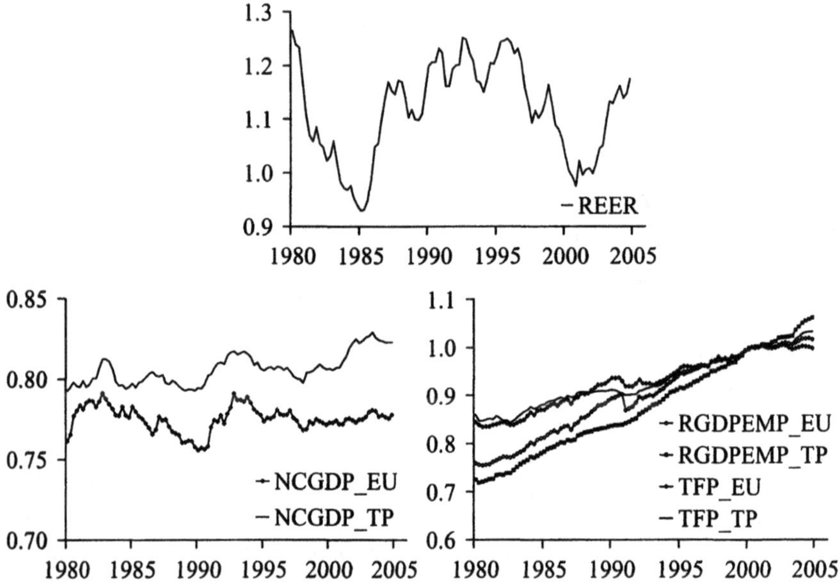

Figure 4.4: Development of Different Economic Indicators, Euro Area and Trading Partners, 1980-2005

per employee times total employment, and θ is one minus the share of labor income in national income. Labor income comprises the total income of dependent employees (wages plus private employers' contributions to social security and pension funds) and the total income of the self-employed (calculated as the total income per employee in the private sector times the number of self-employed). Data an real GDP and national income are taken from the IFS, all other data are taken from the OECD Economic Outlook database. Measuring productivity by the Solow residual has the advantage that this proxy is really exogenous to the model. However, as data on capital stocks and average hours worked are not available for all of the countries in the sample, some countries have to be excluded from the calculations. These are Austria, Luxembourg, Greece, Portugal, Singapore, Korea, and Hong Kong. As these countries only have a small share in total euro area trade, the error should be small. The European productivity variable is called TFP_EU and the variable of the euro area trading partners is called TFP_TP.

Figure 4.4 shows the developments of the real effective exchange rate of the euro (quantity quotation), the proxy for time preference, and the two

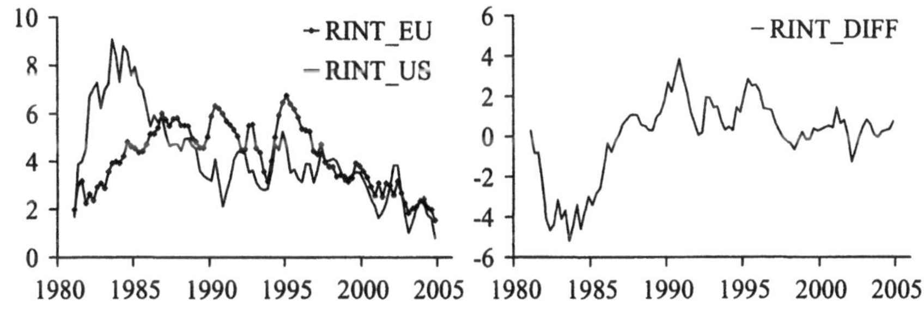

Figure 4.5: Real Interest Rates, Euro Area and United States

productivity measures in the euro area and in the trading partner countries of the euro area. While the real effective exchange rate of the euro fluctuated significantly during the period 1980-2004, the time preference increased slightly but steadily in both the euro area and in the group of trading partner countries as a whole. Productivity rose in both the euro area and its trading partner countries with the productivity gains being somewhat stronger in the trading partner countries. Comparing the two alternative proxies shows that real GDP per employment growth outpaced total factor productivity growth. This observation is to be expected as part of the rise in real GDP over the past 25 years was caused by capital deepening.

As it is assumed that the euro area cannot influence the real interest rate in the world capital market, the nominal yield on 10-year US government bonds less the US CPI inflation rate is employed as a measure for the exogenous world real interest rate.[33] This variable is denoted by RINT_US. It is plotted in Figure 4.5 together with the CPI based real interest rate of the euro area, RINT_EU, and the real interest rate differential between the euro area and the United States, RINT_DIFF.[34] The difference between both real interest rates is stationary at an expected value of zero, indicating real interest rate convergence.[35] Granger causality tests show evidence that the US real long-term rate of interest Granger causes the euro area rate, while

[33]It is assumed that economic agents have static expectations, implying that the real interest rate is an ex-post real interest rate.

[34]Prior to 1994Q1, no data for the euro area aggregates are available from Eurostat and, thus, the interest rate has to be calculated as a trade weighted average of the interest rates of each euro area country. As the price index for the euro area as of 1998, I employ the Harmonized Index of Consumer Prices (HICP) as published by the European Central Bank.

[35]The ADF is -2.055 (MacKinnon 5%-critical value: -1.944).

there is hardly any evidence of Granger causality running in the opposite direction. When using quarterly data, the probability that the real interest rate of the US does not Granger cause the real interest rate of the euro area equals 0.045 for 1 lag, 0.112 for 2 lags, and 0.054 for 3 lags, while the probability that the real interest rate of the euro area does not Granger cause the real interest rate of the US equals 0.181 for 1 lag, 0.624 for 2 lags, and 0.806 for 3 lags. This result supports the assumption that the US real interest rate is exogenous to the euro area.[36]

4.3 Estimation Results

As a first step, augmented Dickey-Fuller (ADF) tests are conducted to investigate the presence of unit roots in each of the series (see Table 4.2).[37] The tests suggest that the real interest rate differential RINT_DIFF is stationary, while all other series are I(1), as required by the estimation technique. In the case of NCGDP_EU, the conclusion is, however, not clear-cut, as there are some signs of stationarity at the 10 percent significance level.

The number of cointegrating vectors is determined using the trace and maximum eigenvalue tests proposed by Johansen (1988). The results are presented in Table 4.3 for two different specifications. In specification (1), productivity is proxied by real GDP per employment and in specification (2), it is proxied by the Solow residual.[38] For both specifications, the trace test and the maximum eigenvalue test indicate the existence of one single combination of the variables that produces stationary residuals. This suggests that, for both specifications, the use of the single-equation approach of Phillips and Loretan (1991) is appropriate to estimate the cointegrating relationship.

As a next step, equation (4.8) is estimated by applying non-linear least square estimates. The results are shown in Tables 4.4 and 4.5.[39] All of the

[36]My approach differs from, for instance, Duval (2002) who does not include the world real interest rate as an exogenous variable in his analysis of the euro exchange rate.

[37]To reduce the risk of misspecification concerning the deterministic regressors in the testing equations, I first estimate the general model including a constant and a trend and then drop the deterministic regressors successively if they do not prove to be significant at the 10% significance level.

[38]Two constants are included in the model, one in the cointegration space, and one in the VAR space. The lag length is set at five, as this lag length is required to obtain residuals that are free from autocorrelation and do not display any signs of heteroskedasticity.

[39]Since hardly any studies on the euro have been published in the literature, a comparison of the coefficients with those from similar studies is not possible.

Table 4.2: Augmented Dickey-Fuller Tests

Variable	Level	First difference
REER	−0.058	−6.989***
NCGDP_EU	−2.651* [c]	−8.770***
NCGDP_TP	0.907	−7.981***
RGDPEMP_EU	4.798	−9.942*** [c]
RGDPEMP_TP	−2.377 [t]	−10.575*** [c]
TFP_EU	3.469	−9.435*** [c]
TFP_TP	−2.555 [t]	−5.276*** [c]
RINT_US	−1.298	−6.719***
RINT_DIFF	−2.055**	–

Note: ***, ** and * denote rejection of the hypothesis of non-stationarity at the 1%, 5% and 10% significance level. The lag length is chosen according to the Schwarz information criterion. The symbols [c] and [t] indicate that the testing equation contains a constant and trend, respectively, that is significant at a significance level of 10 percent or higher.

estimated coefficients of the cointegrating vector have the signs as predicted by the NATREX model and are similar in magnitude across the two specifications. Looking at the standard errors reveals, however, that the coefficients on domestic and foreign productivity do not turn out as significant. Specification (1) performs somewhat better in this respect, since the coefficient on domestic productivity is at least marginally significant. The coefficient is negative, meaning that productivity growth within the euro area depreciates the real long-term value of the euro. The coefficient on the domestic time preference rate is insignificant in both specifications, while the foreign time preference turns out as significant, although only at the 10 percent significance level in specification (2). The coefficient is positive, meaning that a rise in the foreign time preference rate appreciates the long-term value of the euro. Finally, the coefficient on the US real interest rate RINT_US is highly significant and negative, implying that an increase in the US real interest rate depreciates the euro in the long term.

Figures 4.6 and 4.7 compare the actual real effective exchange rate REER with the medium-term and the long-term NATREX derived by using the estimated coefficients in Tables 4.4 and 4.5, respectively, and actual values of the fundamentals. Both figures show a very similar development of the medium and long-term NATREX respectively, suggesting that the evaluation of any real exchange rate misalignment is not sensitive to the choice of

Table 4.3: Johansen Maximum Likelihood Procedure

	trace$(r\|k)$			max$(r\|r+1)$	
H_0	(1)	(2)	H_0	(1)	(2)
$r=0$	136.351*	145.967**	$r=0\|1$	56.989*	56.957*
$r\leq 1$	79.362	89.010	$r=1\|2$	35.374	44.725
$r\leq 2$	43.988	44.285	$r=2\|3$	28.380	24.902
$r\leq 3$	15.608	19.383	$r=3\|4$	10.444	13.316
$r\leq 4$	5.164	6.067	$r=4\|5$	4.897	4.368
$r\leq 5$	0.267	1.699	$r=5\|6$	0.267	1.699

Note: ** and * denote rejection of the null hypothesis at the 1%, 5% and 10% significance level. The p-values are based on MacKinnon, Haug and Michelis (1999) and are adjusted for the sample size employing the methodology proposed by Cheung and Lai (1993b).

Table 4.4: NLS Estimation, Specification (1)

REER = C(1) + C(2)·RGDPEMP_EU + C(3)·RGDPEMP_TP + C(4)·NCGDP_EU + C(5)·NCGDP_TP + C(6)·RINT_US + C(7)·(REER(−1)− C(1) − C(2)·RGDPEMP_EU(−1) − C(3)·RGDPEMP_TP(−1) − C(4)·NCGDP_EU(−1) − C(5)·NCGDP_TP(−1) − C(6)·RINT_US(−1))+ C(8)·RINT_DIFF(−1) + C(9)·DUMMY_DEU + c(10)·DUMMY_EUR

	Coefficient	Standard error	t-statistic	Probability
C(1)	1.114	1.212	0.919	0.361
C(2)	−1.054	0.644	−1.637	0.105
C(3)	0.475	0.446	1.066	0.290
C(4)	−0.890	1.044	−0.852	0.397
C(5)	1.635	0.918	1.782	0.078
C(6)	−1.169	0.356	−3.288	0.002
C(7)	0.924	0.054	17.245	0.000
C(8)	0.303	0.239	1.268	0.208
C(9)	−0.045	0.012	−3.887	0.000
C(10)	−0.039	0.006	−6.902	0.000

Note: The standard-errors are calculated based on the Newey-West covariance matrix, which accounts for possible autocorrelation and heteroskedasticity in the residuals. Adjusted R-squared = 0.935; Durbin-Watson stat. = 1.507; Breusch-Godfrey LM test, 4 lags, prob. = 0.067; ARCH LM test, 4 lags, prob. = 0.627; White heteroskedasticity test, prob. = 0.638; Jarque-Bera test, prob. = 0.335., ADF test on residuals from entire equation: ADF = −7.617 ; ADF test on residuals from hypothesized cointegrating relationship: ADF = −2.126.

the productivity measure. Both figures indicate that the actual real effective exchange rate REER converges to the medium-term NATREX as well as to

Table 4.5: NLS Estimation, Specification (2)

REER = C(1) + C(2)·TFP_EU + C(3) TFP_TP + C(4)·NCGDP_EU
+ C(5)·NCGDP_TP + C(6)·RINT_US + C(7)·(REER(−1)− C(1)
− C(2)·TFP_EU(−1) − C(3)·TFP_TP(−1) − C(4)·NCGDP_EU(−1)
− C(5)·NCGDP_TP(−1) − C(6)·RINT_US(−1))+ C(8)·RINT_DIFF(−1)
+ C(9)·DUMMY_DEU + c(10)·DUMMY_EUR

	Coefficient	Standard error	*t*-statistic	Probability
C(1)	0.844	1.565	0.539	0.591
C(2)	−0.977	0.857	−1.140	0.258
C(3)	0.611	0.581	1.051	0.296
C(4)	−0.761	1.158	−0.658	0.513
C(5)	1.590	0.972	1.635	0.106
C(6)	−1.116	0.339	−3.293	0.001
C(7)	0.926	0.056	16.607	0.000
C(8)	0.252	0.235	1.070	0.288
C(9)	−0.030	0.013	−2.257	0.027
C(10)	−0.040	0.005	−7.949	0.000

Note: The standard-errors are calculated based on the Newey-West covariance matrix, which accounts for possible autocorrelation and heteroskedasticity in the residuals. Adjusted R-squared = 0.935; Durbin-Watson stat. = 1.517; Breusch-Godfrey LM test, 4 lags, prob. = 0.073; ARCH LM test, 4 lags, prob. = 0.603; White heteroskedasticity test, prob. = 0.673; Jarque-Bera test, prob. = 0.269.; ADF test on residuals from entire equation: ADF = −7.637 ; ADF test on residuals from hypothesized cointegrating relationship: ADF = −2.068.

the long-term NATREX. The first observation is confirmed by augmented Dickey-Fuller tests showing that the deviations of the actual real exchange rate from the medium-term NATREX are stationary.[40] While augmented Dickey-Fuller tests cannot reject the hypothesis of nonstationarity for the deviations of the actual real exchange rate from the long-term NATREX,[41] the Johansen maximum likelihood procedure suggests that there is cointegration between the real effective exchange rate and the fundamental variables.

Based on the estimates, I assess a possible misalignment of the euro during the more recent past and compare my results to previous research (see Table 4.6). More specifically, three different quarters of the sample are examined. The first quarter investigated is the first quarter after the euro was launched, i.e., the first quarter of 1999. The widely shared impression that the euro

[40]The ADF is −7.240 for specification (1) and −7.372 for specification (2).

[41]The ADF is = −2.126 for specification (1) and = −2.068 for specification (2).

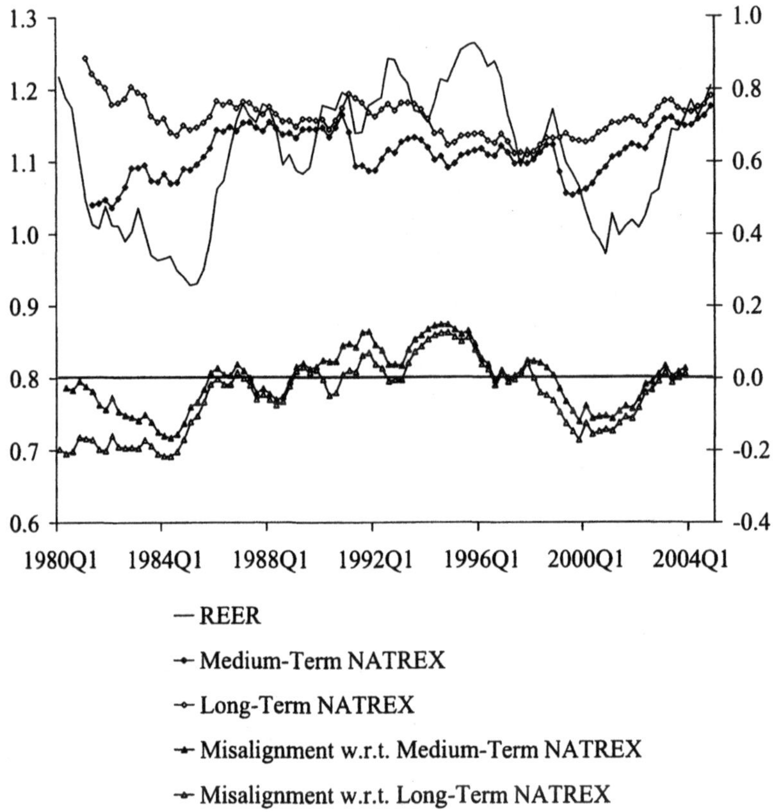

Figure 4.6: The Actual Real Exchange Rate compared to the Medium and Long-Term NATREX, Specification (1)

started at a fairly high level is only partly confirmed by empirical research. While Detken et al. (2002) find an overvaluation of the euro when employing a BEER approach, their structural NATREX estimation indicates an undervaluation of the euro in real effective terms. Detken and Marín Martínez (2001) and Duval (2002) also point to an undervaluation of the euro at the time of its launch. This is confirmed by the studies of Alberola et al. (1999) and Lorenzen and Thygesen (2000) who employ the BEER approach. Osbat, Rüffer, and Schnatz (2003) investigate the bilateral exchange rate of the euro vis-à-vis the Japanese yen within a BEER framework and find that the euro was fairly valued in 1998Q4/1999Q1. My own estimates reported above imply that the euro was fairly in line with the long-term NATREX in the first

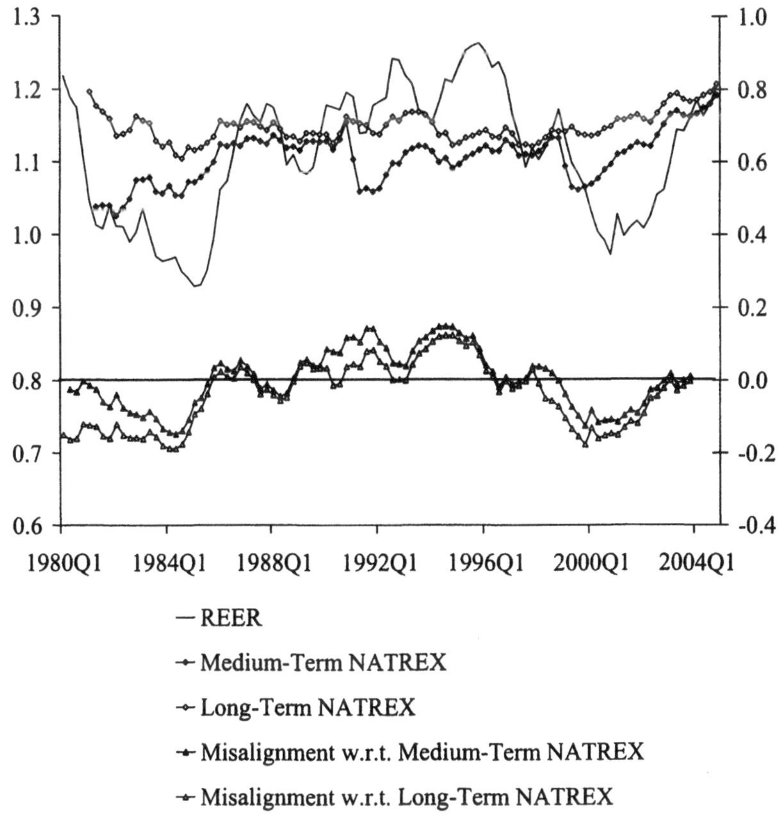

Figure 4.7: The Actual Real Exchange Rate compared to the Medium and Long-Term NATREX, Specification (2)

quarter of 1999, but slightly undervalued with respect to the medium-term NATREX (the degree of undervaluation is estimated at 3.2 percent in both specifications).

The second period that is examined is the third and the fourth quarter of 2000, when the European Central Bank intervened several times in foreign exchange markets. At the time, the European Central Bank stated that the euro was heavily undervalued against all major currencies. The results of this study tend to confirm this perception. While the euro is found to have been only slightly undervalued against the medium-term NATREX (the degree of undervaluation is estimated at 3 percent in both specifications), the calcula-

Table 4.6: Comparison of estimated Over- and Undervaluation of the Euro

Study	Exchange Rate	Approach	1999:Q1	2000:Q4	2004:Q4
Own analysis	Effective	NATREX	−0.4%	−15.2%	+0.5%
Alberola et al. (1999)	Effective	BEER	−4.5%[a]	–	–
Detken, Marín Martínez (2000)	Effective	NATREX	−10%	–	–
Lorenzen, Thygesen (2000)	EUR-USD	BEER	−24%[a]	–	–
Maseo-Fernandez et al. (2001)	Effective	BEER	−8% to +6%	−6% to −17%	–
Detken et al. (2002)	Effective	BEER	+11%	−10%	–
		NATREX	−6%	−28%	–
Duval (2002)	EUR-USD	BEER/NATREX	−3%	−25%[b]	–
Borowski, Couharde (2003)	EUR-USD	FEER	–	−20%[c]	–
Osbat, Rüffer, Schnatz (2003)	EUR-JPY	BEER	±0%	±0%	–

Notes: ' + ' and ' − ' indicate an undervaluation and overvaluation of the euro, respectively, defined as deviation of the actual exchange rate from the estimated long-term NATREX level or from other equilibrium exchange rate levels as indicated. [a] Value refers to 1998:Q4. [b] Value refers to 2000:Q3. [c] Value refers to 2001.

tions point to an average undervaluation of around 14 percent with respect to the long-term NATREX during the third and forth quarters of 2000. This estimate is fairly in line with previous research. Maseo-Fernandez, Osbat, and Schnatz (2001) find that the undervaluation of the euro ranged between 6 and 17 percent, depending on the model specification. Detken et al. (2002) estimate an undervaluation of 10 percent using the BEER model, and an undervaluation of almost 28 percent using the structural NATREX approach.

Finally, the last quarter investigated is the latest quarter of the data set, i.e., the fourth quarter of 2004. Over the period 2002 to 2004, the euro appreciated considerably, especially vis-à-vis the US dollar. The estimates suggest that the real effective exchange rate of the euro was almost in equilibrium at that time with respect to both the medium and the long-term NATREX. This suggests that the European Central Bank reacted appropriately when dismissing several demands by politicians to intervene in the foreign exchange market.

4.4 Out-of-Sample Forecast Quality

In order to examine further the goodness of fit of the NATREX model, its out-of-sample forecasting ability is compared with the simple random walk model. Hence, I use the same benchmark as in chapter 3 for assessing the forecasting performance of the monetary model. More specifically, the forecasting ability is evaluated by comparing the random walk prediction with the exchange rate prediction implied by the NATREX expression (4.8), which includes long-term, medium-term and short-term influences of the fundamentals. A rolling estimation strategy is employed in which both models are estimated with data from the first quarter of 1980 up to the fourth quarter of 1989 in a first step. Based on these estimates an initial set of k-quarter ahead predictions is formed, $k = 1, 2, \ldots, 12$, where the actual values of the fundamentals are employed in the case of the NATREX model. I then update the sample with observations from the first quarter of 1990, and repeat the forecast, continuing this way until the end of the data set.

The quality of the forecasts of the NATREX model relative to that of the random walk model is evaluated based on four different measures of forecasting accuracy: the root mean squared error (RMSE), the sign-test, Wilcoxon's signed rank test, and the Diebold-Mariono (DM) statistic as modified by

Table 4.7: Out-of-sample Forecasting Performance - Expanding Windows

	RMSE Ratio		Sign Statistic		Signed Rank Statistic		Modified DM-Statistic	
h	(1)	(2)	(1)	(2)	(1)	(2)	(1)	(2)
1	1.16	1.08	−0.77	0.00	−1.74*	−0.87	−2.15**	−1.27
2	1.21	1.13	−1.43	−0.65	−1.89*	−0.92	−1.77	−1.10
3	1.24	1.15	−1.05	−0.26	−1.96**	−0.47	−1.42	−0.84
4	1.23	1.14	0.13	1.19	−1.43	−0.20	−1.18	−0.72
5	1.22	1.14	−1.07	−0.53	−1.78*	−0.70	−1.01	−0.64
6	1.24	1.16	−1.21	−0.40	−1.88*	−0.94	−0.95	−0.62
7	1.25	1.16	−1.09	−1.09	−1.92*	−1.23	−0.88	−0.57
8	1.27	1.17	−0.41	0.14	−1.66*	−0.93	−0.83	−0.55
9	1.29	1.19	−1.39	−0.28	−1.85*	−0.96	−0.85	−0.57
10	1.31	1.20	−1.26	0.14	−2.04**	−1.09	−0.85	−0.58
11	1.33	1.21	−1.13	0.28	−2.25**	−1.33	−0.89	−0.64
12	1.35	1.23	−1.29	−0.43	−2.63**	−1.81*	−0.94	−0.71

Notes: ** and * denote rejection of the zero hypothesis of equal forecasting performance at the 5% and 10% significance level, respectively. A better forecasting performance of the NATREX model relative to the random walk is indicated by a RMSE ratio smaller than unity or a positive value of the other three test statistics.

Harvey, Leybourne, and Newbold (1997).[42] The results of the analysis are reported in Table 4.7.

The first two columns of Table 4.7 show the RMSE of the two alternative specifications of the NATREX model relative to that of the random walk. The calculations reveal that the RMSE ratio is larger than unity for all forecasting horizons, meaning that the random walk model provides more precise predictions than the two NATREX specifications. This result is confirmed by the other three test statistics which take on negative values in the overwhelming majority of the cases.

The sign test, the signed rank test, and the Diebold-Mariano test allow an assessment of the significance of the superiority of the random walk model. The sign test and the Diebold-Mariano test can, for the most part, not reject the hypothesis that both models yield equally precise forecasts. The only exception is the one-step ahead forecast of specification (1), which is shown to be significantly worse than that of the random walk by the modified Diebold-Mariano statistic. Wilcoxon's signed rank test generally confirms the results

[42]The precise computation of the test statistics as well as their merits and drawbacks are explained in section 3.4.3.

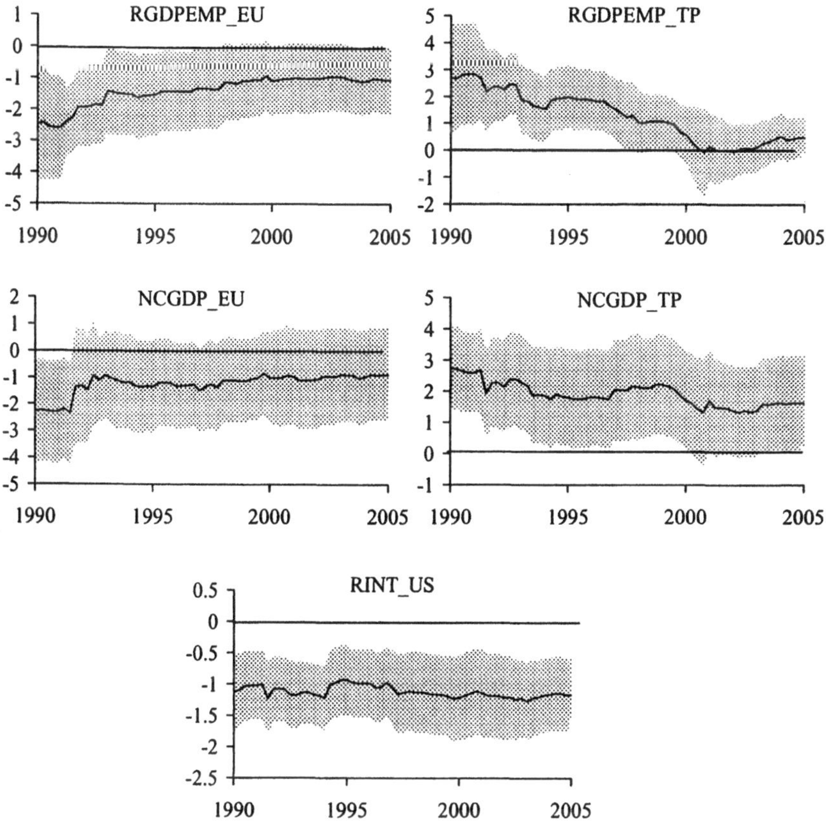

Figure 4.8: Rolling Regression, Specification (1)

of the other two statistics for specification (2). By contrast, the statistic indicates that the random walk model significantly outperforms specification (1) of the NATREX model at almost all forecasting horizons.

The poor predictive ability of the NATREX model might be explained by the fact that the impact of the fundamentals on the real effective exchange rate varies over time. Figures 4.8 and 4.9 show the coefficients obtained by estimating equation (4.8) for the period 1980Q1 up to 1989Q4 in a first step and then successively extending the end of the sample until it reaches the end of the data set. Both figures show that the estimated coefficients change over time as the data set is successively updated. The coefficients on domestic productivity and domestic time preference tend to increase over

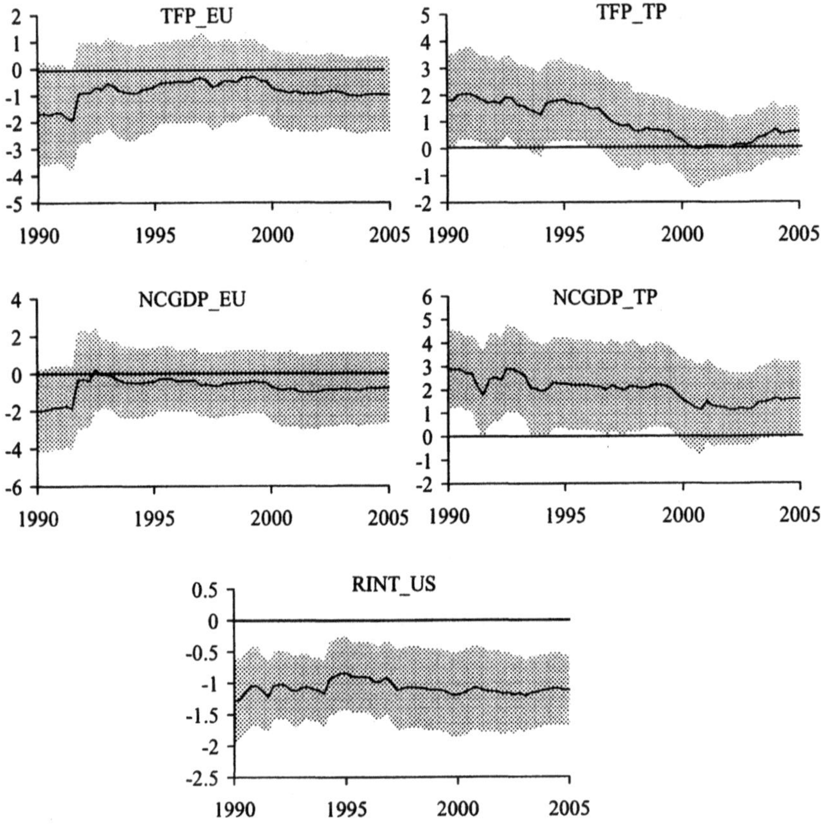

Figure 4.9: Rolling Regression, Specification (2)

time, while the coefficients on the two foreign counterparts tend to decrease. The coefficient on the US real interest rate seems to be fairly robust to variations in the estimation horizon.

The time-varying behavior of the estimated coefficients has important implications for the forecasting accuracy of the NATREX model. The further into future the exchange rate is predicted, the less the employed coefficients represent the relationship between the fundamentals and the exchange rate over the recent past. Though this is a natural limitation of all fundamental-based models, in the present case, the time-variation is so strong, that the prediction based on the outdated coefficients is even worse than the no-change prediction.

Table 4.8: Out-of-sample Forecasting Performance - Moving Windows

	RMSE Ratio		Sign Statistic		Signed Rank Statistic		Modified DM-Statistic	
h	(1)	(2)	(1)	(2)	(1)	(2)	(1)	(2)
1	1.13	1.12	−0.39	0.78	−1.05	−0.62	−1.30	−1.14
2	1.29	1.25	−1.00	−0.60	−1.65*	−1.20	−1.40	−1.19
3	1.37	1.33	−0.82	−0.82	−1.91*	−1.40	−1.20	−1.04
4	1.34	1.30	−1.04	−0.63	−1.73*	−1.64	−1.00	−0.88
5	1.32	1.27	−1.71*	−0.85	−2.00**	−1.54	−0.84	−0.71
6	1.29	1.24	−1.09	−0.65	−1.76*	−1.51	−0.71	−0.58
7	1.26	1.22	−0.89	−0.89	−1.64	−1.61	−0.59	−0.49
8	1.25	1.19	0.23	0.23	−1.37	−1.29	−0.51	−0.40
9	1.25	1.19	0.00	0.00	−1.37	−1.24	−0.46	−0.33
10	1.23	1.16	−0.24	−0.24	−1.21	−1.02	−0.41	−0.28
11	1.23	1.15	0.00	0.00	−1.45	−1.03	−0.42	−0.26
12	1.22	1.16	−0.26	−0.26	−1.36	−1.36	−0.39	−0.25

Notes: The forecasts of the NATREX model are based on 17-year rolling windows. ** and * denote rejection of the zero hypothesis of equal forecasting performance at the 5% and 10% significance level, respectively. A better forecasting performance of the NATREX model relative to the random walk is indicated by a RMSE ratio smaller than unity or a positive value of the other three test statistics.

If the poor predictive capacity of the NATREX model were indeed related to the time-varying behavior of the estimated coefficients, dropping the most outdated observations from the sample should improve the predictive capacity of the model. The analysis is therefore repeated, but this time employing rolling instead of expanding windows for estimating the NATREX model. When choosing the length of the moving window, a trade-off between the up-to-dateness of the data and the number of degrees of freedom has to be made: On the one hand, a shorter window entails the use of more up-to-date data for the estimation; but on the other hand, a shorter window makes it harder to capture the long-run relationship between the variables. For practicality, the length of the moving window is set to 17 years which is the average length of the windows used in the expanding window approach.

Table 4.8 summarizes the results of the analysis. The values of the test statistics are generally smaller in absolute value compared to those in Table 4.7, meaning that the moving-window approach leads to more accurate forecasts of the NATREX model than the expanding-window approach. However, the NATREX model is still unable to significantly outperform the random walk at any forecasting horizon and at several forecasting horizons there is still some evidence that the random walk produces significantly more accurate forecasts than the NATREX model.

4.5 A Summary of the Main Findings

Given the considerable fluctuations of the euro exchange rate since the beginning of EMU, this chapter investigated whether the developments of the real effective exchange rate of the euro can be described by the natural real exchange rate approach. A small country version of the NATREX model was employed in which the domestic economy is sufficiently specialized to be able to influence the world market price of its exports.

The results exhibit a good statistical fit suggesting that the euro exchange rate can be explained fairly well by the NATREX approach. However, comparing the forecasting quality of the estimated NATREX model with the predictions of the random walk model showed that, for all time horizons between one quarter and three years, the estimated NATREX model is unable to outperform the random walk.

To inspect the implications of the estimation results, the undervaluation and overvaluation of the euro at different points in time was calculated. The analysis suggests that the euro was fairly in line with fundamentals at the time of its launch, but was markedly undervalued at the end of 2001. The sharp nominal appreciation of the euro over the period 2002 to 2004 led to a correction of the real exchange rate misalignment and by the end of 2004 the euro was more or less back in equilibrium.

Chapter 5

Real Equilibrium Exchange Rates of the New EU Member Countries of 2004: A Reduced Form NATREX Estimation

This chapter takes a closer look at the currencies of the eight central and eastern European countries that joined the European Union on 1 May 2004. The aim of the chapter is to estimate equilibrium exchange rate paths for the new EU member countries in order to evaluate in how far these countries may encounter difficulties in complying with the convergence criteria laid down in the Maastricht Treaty. If the real exchange rates of the new EU member countries change over time either because of corresponding changes in the equilibrium rates or because of substantial misalignments that call for a corrective step, the countries might face difficulties in simultaneously participating in the ERM II and having an inflation rate that does not exceed the average inflation rate of the lowest three inflation countries in the euro area by more than 1.5 percentage points.

Though estimating equilibrium exchange rate paths for the new EU member countries is very interesting from a policy perspective, it is a very difficult task due to data availability and measurement problems. Furthermore, since 1990 the majority of these countries have gone through a transition process from a planned to a market-oriented economy so that the length of the time series that can be employed for empirical studies is somewhat limited. Several studies also indicate that particularly during the early years of transition, exchange rates in these countries were strongly affected by unconventional factors such as a sharp increase in the demand for foreign goods and a reorientation of external trade from countries of the former Soviet Union to Western Europe. In addition, authorities in the transition countries tended to set initial exchange rates at highly undervalued levels which led to rising exchange rates in the following years to correct for the initial undervaluation. This suggests that estimates of a long-run relationship between the exchange rate and economic fundamentals based on data from the transition period could be misleading, further complicating the task of determining an equilibrium exchange rate.

This chapter makes use of the NATREX approach in evaluating the real effective exchange rates of the new EU member countries. To take account of the above mentioned limitations in estimating equilibrium exchange rates for these countries, a two step methodology is employed. In a first step, the long-run relationship between the real effective exchange rate and economic fundamentals is estimated for a group of 21 OECD countries, which does not include any of the new EU member countries. In a second step, the equilibrium real exchange rates of the new EU member countries are derived by applying the estimated coefficients to data from these countries.[43] It is reasonable to assume that the new EU member countries will ultimately be fairly similar to the average OECD country (e.g., Maeso-Fernandez, Osbat, and Schnatz, 2004).

The outline of the rest of the chapter is as follows. Section 5.1 outlines the model, which is employed in the empirical analysis, and section 5.2 explains the estimation procedure. Section 5.3 presents the estimation results for the OECD countries and section 5.4 presents the derivation of equilibrium real exchange rates for the new EU member countries. Finally, section 5.5 comments on the policy implications.

5.1 A Small Country NATREX Model

In the analysis of the real effective exchange rates of the new EU member countries, it is assumed that these countries are small and can therefore nei-

[43]The two-step approach has recently been applied by Halpern and Wyplosz (1997) and Krajnyák and Zettelmeyer (1998) who use a sample of 85 industrial, developing, planned and transition economies in the first-step estimation and by Kim and Korhonen (2000) who employ data from 29 middle and high income countries in the first step. A thorough discussion of the merits of this methodology can also be found in Maeso-Fernandez, Osbat and Schnatz (2004).

ther influence the world real interest rate nor the world market prices of their products, so that both the world real interest rate and the terms of trade are exogenous. In addition, it is assumed that these countries face a limited foreign supply of capital implying that world asset markets impose a risk premium on the domestic real interest rate. To account for these characteristics, the empirical analysis is based on a small country version of the NATREX approach that is similar to the model Lim and Stein (1997) use in their analysis of the Australian dollar. Section 5.1.1 outlines the structure of this NATREX model and section 5.1.2 then discusses the adjustment of the endogenous variables to exogenous shocks.

5.1.1 The Model

In the model, a small open economy is considered which produces a tradable good 1 and a non-tradable good N. The tradable good 1 is used for both domestic purposes (consumption and investment) and for exports, while the non-tradable good N is solely used for domestic purposes. Additionally, the economy imports a tradable good 2 from the rest of the world which is used for both consumption and investment. The price indices of the domestic economy and the rest of the world, i.e., p and p^*, are then given by

$$P = P_N^{\varphi} P_1^{1-\varphi} \quad \text{and} \tag{5.1}$$

$$P^* = P_N^{*\varphi^*} P_2^{*1-\varphi^*}, \tag{5.2}$$

where φ is the weight of the non-tradable good in the GDP deflator and an asterisk denotes the rest of the world. It is assumed that the law of one price holds for tradable goods such that $P_j\mathcal{E} = P_j^*$ for $j = 1, 2$, where $\mathcal{E}$ is the nominal exchange rate. The country faces perfectly elastic world demand for its exports and perfectly elastic world supply of the importable good. Hence, the terms of trade TOT defined as $TOT = P_1/P_2$ are exogenous. Using equations (5.1) and (5.2), the real exchange rate R can be written as the weighted average of the relative prices of non-tradables to tradables in the domestic country and the rest of the world and of the domestic country's terms of trade:

$$R = \frac{P\mathcal{E}}{P^*} = \left(\frac{P_N}{P_1}\right)^{\varphi} \left(\frac{P_2^*}{P_N^*}\right)^{\varphi^*} TOT. \tag{5.3}$$

With P_1^*, P_2^* and P_N^* given by the world market, the only endogenous relative price is $R_N \equiv P_N/P_1$.

The structure of a NATREX model for such a country can be expressed by the following equations which are the small-country analogues to equations (4.1) to (4.4) in section 4.1.1:

$$(5.4)\quad Q_N(\overset{+}{R}_N, \overset{-}{K}, \overset{-}{u}_1, \overset{+}{u}_N) =$$

$$C_N(\overset{-}{R}_N, \overset{+}{K}, \overset{-}{F}, \overset{+}{\rho}, \overset{\pm}{r}, \overset{-}{TOT}) + I_N(\overset{-}{R}_N, \overset{-}{K}, \overset{-}{r}, \overset{+}{u}_1, \overset{+}{u}_N, \overset{+}{TOT});$$

$$(5.4a)\quad S(\overset{+}{K}, \overset{+}{F}, \overset{+}{u}_1, \overset{+}{u}_N, \overset{-}{\rho}, \overset{\pm}{r^*}) - I(\overset{-}{K}, \overset{-}{r}, \overset{+}{u}_1, \overset{+}{u}_N, \overset{+}{TOT}) = Q_1(\overset{-}{R}_N, \overset{+}{K}, \overset{+}{u}_1, \overset{-}{u}_N)$$

$$- I_1(\overset{+}{R}_N, \overset{-}{K}, \overset{-}{r}, \overset{+}{u}_1, \overset{+}{u}_N, \overset{+}{TOT}) - I_2(\overset{+}{R}_N, \overset{-}{K}, \overset{-}{r}, \overset{+}{u}_1, \overset{+}{u}_N, \overset{+}{TOT})$$

$$- C_2(\overset{+}{R}_N, \overset{+}{K}, \overset{-}{F}, \overset{+}{\rho}, \overset{\pm}{r}, \overset{+}{TOT}) - C_1(\overset{+}{R}_N, \overset{+}{K}, \overset{-}{F}, \overset{+}{\rho}, \overset{\pm}{r}, \overset{-}{TOT}) - r^*F,$$

$$\text{where } S(\overset{+}{K}, \overset{+}{F}, \overset{+}{u}_1, \overset{+}{u}_N, \overset{-}{\rho}, \overset{\pm}{r^*}) \equiv Q_N(\overset{+}{R}_N, \overset{-}{K}, \overset{-}{u}_1, \overset{+}{u}_N)$$

$$+ Q_1(\overset{-}{R}_N, \overset{+}{K}, \overset{+}{u}_1, \overset{-}{u}_N) - C_N(\overset{-}{R}_N, \overset{+}{K}, \overset{-}{F}, \overset{+}{\rho}, \overset{\pm}{r}, \overset{-}{TOT})$$

$$- C_2(\overset{+}{R}_N, \overset{+}{K}, \overset{-}{F}, \overset{+}{\rho}, \overset{\pm}{r}, \overset{+}{TOT}) - C_1(\overset{+}{R}_N, \overset{+}{K}, \overset{-}{F}, \overset{+}{\rho}, \overset{\pm}{r}, \overset{-}{TOT}) - r^*F;$$

$$(5.5)\quad \frac{dK}{dt} = I(\overset{-}{K}, \overset{-}{r}, \overset{+}{u}_1, \overset{+}{u}_N, \overset{+}{TOT});$$

$$(5.6)\quad \frac{dF}{dt} = I(\overset{-}{K}, \overset{-}{r}, \overset{+}{u}_1, \overset{+}{u}_N, \overset{+}{TOT}) - S(\overset{+}{K}, \overset{+}{F}, \overset{+}{u}_1, \overset{+}{u}_N, \overset{-}{\rho}, \overset{\pm}{r^*});$$

$$(5.7)\quad r = r^* + f(F).$$

Equation (5.4) reflects the condition for goods market equilibrium. Since the economy is small, the traded goods market will always be in equilibrium at the exogenous given world prices for traded goods. The world will purchase all of the export supply and provide all of the import demand of the country at prevailing world market prices. Goods market equilibrium therefore follows when the market for non-traded goods is in equilibrium. The left-hand side of equation (5.4) represents the supply of non-tradable goods Q_N, and the right-hand side represents the demand for non-tradable goods, which consists of consumption C_N and investment I_N. The signs over the different variables indicate the signs of the first derivatives of the respective functions. The supply of non-tradable goods depends positively on the relative price of non-tradable goods R_N and negatively on the capital stock K, since the non-tradable sector is assumed to be labor intensive. The supply of non-tradable goods is negatively related to productivity in the tradable sector u_1, but positively related to productivity in the non-tradable sector u_N. Consumption depends positively on the time preference rate ρ and negatively on the relative price of non-tradable goods and on the terms of trade TOT. The relation between consumption and the real interest rate r is ambiguous (indicated by a $\pm$ symbol). Consumption is positively related to real net wealth, which is the difference between capital K and real net foreign debt F.[44] Based on the idea of Tobin's q, investment I is assumed to be a negative function of the capital stock K and the real interest rate r and a positive function of productivity in the tradable and non-tradable sector and of the terms of trade (Lim and Stein, 1997, p. 119). Regarding the impact of R_N on investment, it is assumed that it does not affect overall investment, but merely allocates investment between the sectors, where $\partial I_N/\partial R_N < 0$, $\partial I_1/\partial R_N > 0$ and $\partial I_2/\partial R_N > 0$.

Market clearing in the non-tradable sector is equivalent to balance of payment equilibrium, which is given by equation (5.4a). The left-hand side of equation (5.4a) is the capital account balance, the right-hand side is the current account balance, where exports are equal to the supply of the tradable good Q_1 minus the domestic demand for the tradable good 1, consisting of consumption C_1 and investment I_1, and imports are equal to investment I_2 plus consumption C_2 of the importable good. Equation (5.4a) implies that savings S depend on capital K, foreign debt F, the world real interest rate r^*, and the exogenous factors ρ, u_1 and u_N. Assuming that a higher capital stock increases output by more than consumption, a higher capital stock has a positive impact on S, i.e., $\partial S/\partial K > 0$. The impact of foreign debt on savings is theoretically ambiguous. However, to ensure that the debt level converges to a steady state level, a positive relationship between savings and foreign debt is necessary, $\partial S/\partial F = -r^* - \partial C_N/\partial F - \partial C_N/\partial r \cdot \partial r/\partial F - \partial C_2/\partial F - \partial C_2/\partial r \cdot \partial r/\partial F > 0$. The reaction of S to a change in r^* depends on whether the country is a net debtor ($F > 0$) or a net creditor ($F < 0$).[45] The three remaining partial derivatives are unambiguous, i.e., $\partial S/\partial u_1 = \partial Q_1/\partial u_1 > 0$, $\partial S/\partial u_N = \partial Q_N/\partial u_N > 0$ and $\partial S/\partial \rho < 0$.

[44] As the domestic real rate of interest r is a function of the net foreign debt level, a change in F affects consumption via its impact on wealth and via its impact on r. As the impact of r on consumption is ambiguous, the two effects may work in different directions. For simplicity, it is assumed that the wealth effect dominates.

[45] For instance, if the country is a net debtor, and consumption depends positively on the real interest rate, then savings depend negatively on the real interest rate.

Equations (5.5) and (5.6) describe the evolution of the capital stock and the foreign debt over time, respectively. Equation (5.7) is the portfolio balance condition, which states that the domestic real interest rate is equal to the world real interest rate plus a risk premium, that the country has to pay when borrowing capital at the world capital market, which depends upon the net foreign debt of the country.

Akin to the NATREX version discussed in chapter 4, the version employed in this chapter distinguishes between a medium-term and a long-term equilibrium real exchange rate. The medium-term equilibrium real exchange rate, i.e., the medium-term NATREX, is $\tilde{R} = (\tilde{R}_N)^{\varphi}(P_N^*/P*_2)^{\varphi*}TOT$, where $\tilde{R}_N$ is the relative price of non-tradable goods that equates the left-hand side and the right-hand side of equation (5.4) with portfolio balance (5.7) prevailing. Over the medium-term horizon, R_N and r are the endogenous variables and ρ, u_N, u_1, r^*, TOT, K, and F are the exogenous variables. A central implication of the approach is that the medium-term equilibrium real exchange rate $\tilde{R}$ is positively related to the time preference rate, productivity in the tradable sector, and the capital stock, and is negatively related to productivity in the non-tradable sector and net foreign debt, while the impact of both the foreign real interest rate and the terms of trade is ambiguous:[46]

$$\tilde{R} = (\tilde{R}_N)^{\varphi}(P_N^*/P_2^*)^{\varphi^*}TOT = \tilde{R}(\overset{+}{\rho}, \overset{-}{u_N}, \overset{+}{u_1}, \overset{\pm}{r^*}, \overset{\pm}{TOT}, \overset{+}{K}, \overset{-}{F}). \tag{5.8}$$

The long-term equilibrium is reached, when both the capital stock and the net foreign debt level have reached their steady state levels so that equations (5.5) and (5.6) are equal to zero. The implied real equilibrium exchange rate is referred to as the long-term NATREX $\bar{R}$. The framework implies that this long-term NATREX is positively related to productivity in the tradable sector and negatively to the domestic time preference rate, while the impact of all other variables is ambiguous:[47]

$$\bar{R} = (\bar{R}_N)^{\varphi}(P_N^*/P_2^*)^{\varphi^*}TOT = \bar{R}(\overset{-}{\rho}, \overset{\pm}{u_N}, \overset{+}{u_1}, \overset{\pm}{r^*}, \overset{\pm}{TOT}). \tag{5.9}$$

The long-term real equilibrium exchange rate $\bar{R}$ is constant since, together with K and F, all variables in equation (5.4) are constant.

5.1.2 Adjustment to Exogenous Shocks

As discussed in the previous section, the exogenous factors are productivity in the non-tradable sector u_N, productivity in the tradable sector u_1, the

[46] See Appendix A1 for the derivation of equation 5.8.

[47] See Appendix A2 for the derivation of equation 5.9

time preference rate ρ, the terms of trade TOT, and the world real rate of interest r^*. Figures 5.1 and 5.2 illustrate the medium-term and long-term impacts of changes in these parameters upon the real exchange rate. Figure 5.1 shows the demand for and supply of non-tradable goods. The demand curve $D_N = C_N + I_N$ is downward sloping because a rise in R_N decreases the quantity demanded for both non-tradable consumption and non-tradable investment. The supply curve Q_N is upward sloping because a rise in R_N increases the quantity supplied. The intersection of the two curves determines the equilibrium real exchange rate in the medium term. Both the D_N curve and the Q_N curve are drawn for given values of the endogenous debt and capital stock levels. As capital and debt change, the demand and supply curves for non-tradable goods shift.

The trajectories of capital and debt to the steady state are depicted in Figure 5.2. The curve $dK/dt = 0$ is the set of capital and debt at which the rate of net investment is equal to zero so that the capital stock remains constant. This is identical to saying that the q-ratio equals unity along the curve. The curve is downward sloping because a rise in K lowers the marginal product on capital and thus makes net investment negative. A decline in F reduces the risk premium $f(F)$ and thus the interest rate r, thereby restoring net investment to zero. To the right (left) of the curve $dK/dt = 0$ net investment is negative (positive). The curve $dF/dt = 0$ represents combinations of F and K for which the difference between savings and investment is equal to zero so that the foreign debt level remains constant. The curve is downward sloping because a decline in F increases wealth and consumption so that savings decline. The condition $S = I$ only remains satisfied if investment also declines, which requires a higher capital stock.[48] Above (below) the $dF/dt = 0$ curve, the current account is in surplus (deficit). For stability, the $dK/dt = 0$ curve must have an algebraically greater slope than the $dF/dt = 0$ curve which is equivalent to the condition $(\partial I/\partial r)(\partial r/\partial F)(\partial S/\partial K - \partial I/\partial K) > \partial I/\partial K(\partial S/\partial F - (\partial I/\partial r)(\partial r/\partial F))$.

In the following, the effects of changes in the exogenous factors u_N, u_1, ρ, r^*, and TOT are discussed with the help of Figures 5.1 and 5.2. First, consider a rise in the time preference rate ρ. The rise in ρ leads to a rise in the demand for the non-tradable good N. Starting in point E_0 in Figure 5.1, this is depicted by a shift of the D_N curve to the right from D_{N0} to D_{N1}. The relative price of non-tradable goods rises from R_{N0} to R_{N1}. Higher consumption is associated with lower savings so that the economy is located

[48]Note that a higher K level also induces an increase in savings, which reinforces the effect of a rise in K on the savings investment gap.

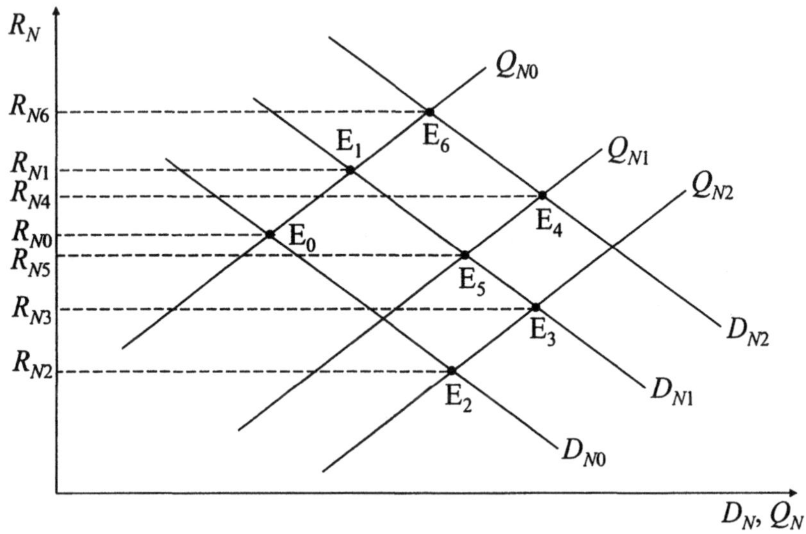

Figure 5.1: The Market for non-tradable Goods

in a point such as H_1 in Figure 5.2, which is characterized by a current account deficit. The net capital inflows are associated with a rise in F and hence, with a rise in the domestic real rate of interest due to the higher risk premium. As a result, investment becomes negative and the capital stock starts to decline. The economy moves along trajectory H_1H_0. The rise in F stimulates savings, thereby counteracting the initial decline in savings. This positive impact on savings is partially offset by the negative impact on savings stemming from the decline in the capital stock. The decline in the capital stock also offsets the decline in investment resulting from the growing debt level. In the new steady-state H_0, savings and investment are again equal to zero. The rise in the net debt level and the decline in the capital stock further affect the market for non-tradable goods. The decline in wealth reduces demand, while the decline in K causes a rise in the supply of non-tradable goods.[49] Thus, in Figure 5.1, the D_N curve shifts back to the left, say back to D_{N0}, and the supply curve shifts to the right to Q_{N2}. The relative price of non-tradable

[49] As the decline in K stimulates investment, it is theoretically ambiguous in which direction the D_N curve shifts. However, as the impact on output is assumed to exceed the impact on investment in absolute value (see the remark in Appendix A1) this does not affect the direction of the change in R_N and, hence, can be ignored in the discussion of the feedback effects.

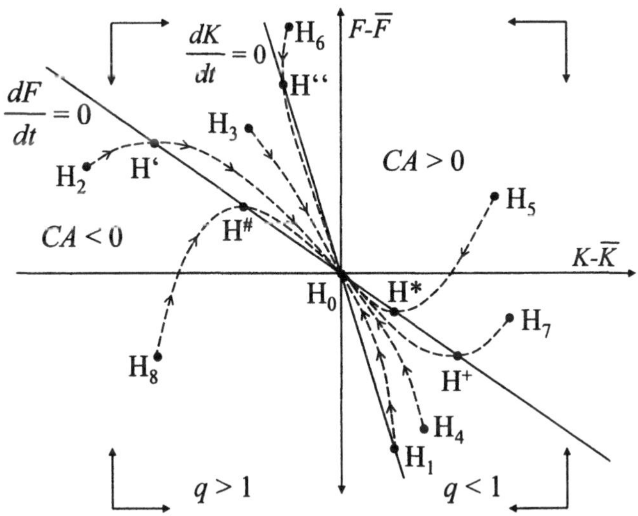

Figure 5.2: Net Foreign Assets and Capital Stock

goods declines to R_{N2} which is below the original level R_{N0}. The lower relative price of non-tradable goods is associated with an improvement in the trade account. This improvement is needed to finance the interest payments on the higher foreign debt level.

Next, consider a rise in productivity in the non-tradable goods sector. Starting again in point E_0 in Figure 5.1, the supply of and demand for non-tradable goods rise, implying a shift of the Q_N and D_N curves to the right from Q_{N0} to Q_{N2} and from D_{N0} to D_{N1}, respectively. As supply is assumed to rise by more than demand, the relative price of non-tradable goods declines from R_{N0} to R_{N3}. As resources are shifted from the tradable to the non-tradable sector, the supply of the tradable good 1 declines. Given that a higher share of the production of good 1 is used for domestic purposes ($\partial I_1/\partial u_N > 0$) exports decline. Moreover, imports of the tradable good 2 rise since $\partial I_2/\partial u_N > 0$. Hence, the trade balance deteriorates. The decline in the trade balance is associated with an equal decline in the current account balance so that the economy is located in a point such as H_2 in Figure 5.2 characterized by capital formation and a current account deficit. F and K rise as a result of net capital inflows and investment, respectively. The economy moves along trajectory H_2H'. The growing net debt stimulates savings which is fostered by the growth of the capital stock. As the capital stock grows, the marginal return on capital declines, leading to a reduction in investment. This effect is reinforced by a rise in the domestic interest rate resulting from the accumulation of net foreign debt. When the economy reaches point H', savings and investment are equal and the debt level remains constant. As investment is still positive, the capital stock continues to grow. Savings rise, while investment continues to decline. The savings less investment balance becomes positive and capital outflows arise. Along trajectory H'H_0, the capital stock rises and the net foreign debt declines. Eventually, the positive impact on savings resulting from the growing capital stock and the negative effect on savings resulting from the declining net debt cancel out. Then, savings decline until both investment and savings become zero in the new equilibrium H_0.[50] The rise in wealth $K - F$ increases the consumption demand for the non-tradable good N, while the rise in K reduces the investment demand back to zero. Starting from the demand curve D_{N1} in Figure 5.1, the demand curve may shift to the left or to the right, but will ultimately stay to the right of D_{N0}. The rise in the capital stock has a negative impact on Q_N. Yet, as the rise in K was caused by the rise in u_N, the new steady state must be characterized by a higher supply of non-tradable goods compared to the old steady state. In Figure 5.1, the new supply curve is Q_{N1}. Depending on the relative shifts of the demand and supply curves, the relative price of non-tradable goods may decline or rise relative to R_{N0}.

Now, consider an increase in productivity in the tradable goods sector 1. The rise in u_1 reduces the supply of and raises the demand for non-tradable goods. Starting in a point such as E_2 in Figure 5.1, this is depicted by a shift of the Q_N curve to the left, from Q_{N2} to Q_{N1}, and a shift of the D_N curve to the right, from D_{N0} to D_{N1}. The relative price of non-tradable goods rises from R_{N2} to R_{N5}. The rise in u_1 is associated with a rise in both the supply of and the demand for the tradable good 1. Assuming that the impact on supply is larger than the impact on demand, the economy faces a current account surplus. Hence, the economy is located in a point such as H_3 in Figure 5.2, which is characterized by capital formation and net capital outflows. The growth in the capital stock stimulates savings and reduces investment, thereby further widening the current account surplus. Eventually, net capital outflows will be so large that the impact of F on savings dominates so that savings start to decline. Then, both savings and investment decline until they are again equal to zero in the new steady state H_0. The feedback effects on the non-tradable goods market are an increase

[50] Note that along trajectory H'H_0, the negative impact on I resulting from the growth in the capital stock is partially offset by the positive impact on I resulting from the decline in the domestic real interest rate.

in consumption demand, resulting from the accumulation of wealth, and a decrease in investment demand (back to zero) and in supply, stemming from the growth in the capital stock. In Figure 5.1, the D_N curve may shift to the left or to the right, though it will certainly stay to the right of D_{N0}. The supply curve shifts further to the left, say to Q_{N0}. The relative price of non-tradable goods may rise or decline relative to R_{N5}, but will definitely end up at a higher level than the original relative price R_{N2}.

Next, a rise in the world real interest rate r^* is considered. As shown in equation (5.7), the rise in r^* leads to an equal rise in the domestic real interest rate r. The rise in r, in turn, reduces investment, while the impact on consumption is ambiguous. If $\partial C_N/\partial r < 0$ the demand for non-tradable goods is reduced and the D_N curve in Figures 5.1 shifts to the left, say from D_{N1} to D_{N0}. If $\partial C_N/\partial r > 0$ the direction of the shift depends on whether $\partial C_N/\partial r < |\partial I_N/\partial r|$, in which case the D_N curve shifts to the left to D_{N0}, or whether $\partial C_N/\partial r > |\partial I_N/\partial r|$, in which case it shifts to the right to D_{N2}. Starting in point E_1, the relative price of non-tradable goods may decrease from R_{N1} to R_{N0} or increase from R_{N1} to R_{N6}. In Figure 5.2, the economy is located in a point to the right of the $dK/dt = 0$ curve since investment is negative. Whether the economy is located to the right or to the left of the $dF/dt = 0$ curve depends on the direction of the shift of the D_N curve and on the net debtor/creditor position of the country.

Four cases can be distinguished. First, if the D_N curve shifts to the right and the country is a net debtor, the economy is located in a point such as H_4 which is characterized by net capital inflows and a shrinking capital stock. The rise in F and the decline in K have counteracting effects on savings and investment. However, eventually, both savings and investment will rise along trajectory H_4H_0 until they become zero in the new steady state. In Figure 5.1, the rise in F and the decline in K lead to a rightward shift of the Q_N curve and to a leftward shift of the D_N curve. Compared to the original level R_{N0}, the relative price of non-tradable goods may rise or decline.

Second, if the D_N curve shifts to the left and the country is a net creditor, the economy may be located in a point such as H_5, H_6, or H_7, all three of which are characterized by net capital outflows and a shrinking capital stock. Starting in point H_5, the rise in net foreign assets, i.e. the decline in F, reduces the risk premium and thus partially offsets the initial rise in the domestic interest rate. This positive impact on investment is further strengthened by the decline in the capital stock. Savings decline as a result of both the decline in the capital stock and the accumulation of net foreign assets. The economy moves along trajectory $H_5H^*H_0$. At some point, here

H*, savings and investment are equal and the debt remains constant.[51] As investment is still negative, the capital stock continues to decline, leading to a further reduction in savings and disinvestment. The current account balance turns negative and net capital inflows arise. Eventually, the negative impact on savings resulting from the declining capital stock will be dominated by the positive impact on savings resulting from the rise in F. Then, savings rise until both investment and savings become zero in the new equilibrium H_0. In the new steady state, the level of net foreign assets is higher and the capital stock is lower than in the old steady state.

Starting in point H_6, savings and disinvestment decline along trajectory H_6H". In point H" investment has been reduced to zero and the capital stock is constant. As the current account is still in surplus, net foreign asset accumulation continues, leading to a further decline in savings and to a rise in investment. As investment becomes positive, the capital stock increases. This fosters the decline in savings and counteracts the rise in investment stemming from the accumulation of net foreign assets. The economy moves along trajectory H"H_0. The new steady state H_0 is characterized by a higher level of net foreign assets and a lower capital stock compared to the old steady state.

Finally, starting in point H_7, the economy moves along trajectory $H_7H^+H_0$. The changes in S and I and, hence, the evolution of F and K are similar to those along trajectory $H_5H^*H_0$ with one important difference: The rise in F along the second part of the trajectory, i.e., along H^*H_0, more than offsets the initial decline in F, so that the new steady state is characterized by a lower level of net foreign assets compared to the old steady state. As the changes in F and K are ambiguous, the shifts of the supply and demand curves in Figure 5.1 are ambiguous as well. Hence,the relative price of non-tradable goods may rise or decline.

Third, if the D_N curve shifts to the left and the country is a net debtor, the economy may either be located in a point such as H_4, H_5, or H_7, and fourth, if the D_N curve shifts to the right and the country is a net creditor, the economy may be located in any of the four points H_4, H_5, H_6, and H_7. In all cases, the feedback effects upon the market for non-tradable goods are ambiguous and, hence, the relative price of non-tradable goods may rise or decline relative to its original level.

Finally, a rise in the terms of trade TOT is considered. The rise in TOT negatively affects C_N and positively affects I_N via a rise in the q-ratio. Hence,

[51] Note the special case of $H^* = H_0$ in which savings and investment directly equalize at a value of zero.

in Figure 5.1, the demand curve may shift to the right or to the left, leaving the reaction of the relative price of non-tradable goods undetermined. As overall investment increases while savings remain unchanged,[52] the medium-term equilibrium is represented by a point such as H_8 which is characterized by capital formation and net capital inflows. The economy moves along trajectory $H_8H^{\#}H_0$. The evolution of S and I and, hence, of F and K is similar to the one along trajectory $H_2H'H_0$ with the difference that the decline in F along the second part of the trajectory, i.e., along $H^{\#}H_0$, is smaller than the initial rise in F along the first part of the trajectory, i.e., along $H_8H^{\#}$, so that the new steady state is characterized by a higher level of net foreign debt compared to the old steady state. The rise in F and K further affect the market for non-tradable goods. While supply unambiguously rises, the impact on demand is ambiguous. As such, the impact on R_N is also ambiguous.

5.2 Estimation Methodology and Data Set

In order to estimate the model outlined in the previous section for the new EU member countries a two-step procedure is adopted. In a first step, the model is estimated for a group of 21 OECD countries.[53] In a second step, the equilibrium real exchange rates of the new EU member countries are derived by applying the estimated coefficients to data from these countries. This strategy has two advantages. First, it allows using time series starting in 1980 for the regression analysis, which makes it more likely that it captures the long-term relationship between the real exchange rate and economic fundamentals. For the majority of the new EU member countries, reliable data are not available for the early 1990s. Second, the influence of the transition effect present in the data of most of the new EU member countries is avoided.

---

[52]The change in the terms of trade does only affect the composition of consumption, but not its overall level.

[53]Recently, four central and eastern European countries, namely the Czech Republic, Hungary, Poland, and Slovakia also joined the OECD. In order to avoid the influence of the transition period on the regression results, these countries are excluded from the OECD sample. I also exclude Mexico, Switzerland and Turkey due to data availability problems as well as Japan and the United States, since these two countries cannot be considered as small in the sense that they are unable to influence the world market prices of their products and, therefore, do not fit into the model. Hence, 21 OECD countries remain. These are: Australia, Austria, Belgium, Canada, Denmark, Finland, France, Germany, Greece, Iceland, Ireland, Italy, Korea, Luxembourg, the Netherlands, New Zealand, Norway, Portugal, Spain, Sweden, and the United Kingdom.

Since unit root tests indicate that the data series are non-stationary, the long-run relationship between the real exchange rate and economic fundamentals is analyzed in a panel cointegration framework. For simplicity, the model is estimated in reduced form by relating the real effective exchange rate (REER) to the following five variables: productivity in industry (PROD_IND) and services (PROD_SER); the ratio of nominal consumption (public and private) to nominal GDP (NCGDP) as a measure of the time preference rate; the terms of trade (TOT), defined as the ratio of export prices to import prices; and the nominal yield on 10-year US government bonds less the US CPI inflation rate (RINT_US) as a proxy for the world real interest rate. PROD_IND, PROD_SER, and NCGPD are measured relative to the trading partner countries.

The reduced form relationship is estimated employing the pooled mean group estimator (PMGE) proposed by Pesaran, Shin, and Smith (1999) which estimates both the long-run relationship and the short-run dynamics. The procedure has the advantage that it only constrains the long-run coefficients to be the same across countries, while short-run coefficients and error variances are allowed to differ. Applied to the estimation of the real effective exchange rate REER, the pooled mean group estimator is based on the following autoregressive distributed lag (ARDL) model:

$$\begin{aligned}(5.10)\qquad \Delta\text{REER}_{jt} =\ & \phi_j\text{REER}_{jt-1} + \psi_j' X_{jt} \\ & + \sum_{k=1}^{\iota_k-1} \sigma_{jk}\Delta\text{REER}_{jt-k} + \sum_{k=0}^{\kappa_k-1} \zeta_{jk}'\Delta X_{jt-k} + \mu_j + \varepsilon_{jt},\end{aligned}$$

where j represents the different groups (in this analysis: countries), ϕ_j is the error correction parameter, σ_{jk} is a scalar of short-term dynamics, X_{jt} is the matrix of fundamental variables, i.e., X_{jt} = (PROD_IND$_{jt}$, PROD_SER$_{jt}$, NCGDP$_{jt}$, TOT$_{jt}$, RINT_US$_{jt}$), and all other variables are already defined above. Equation (5.10) is estimated using maximum likelihood. Cross-section demeaned data are employed to deal with the common factor problem. If the parameter ϕ_j is significantly negative, there exists a long-run relationship between the real exchange rate and economic fundamentals X. This relationship is then captured by the coefficient vector ψ_j. The pooled mean group estimator is obtained by constraining ψ_j to be the same for all countries, i.e., $\psi_j = \psi$ for all $j = 1, ..., 21$, while the short-run coefficients ϕ_j, σ_{jk}, and ζ_{jk}' and error variances are allowed to differ across countries.

The strategy of estimating the relationship between the real exchange rate and economic fundamentals for a sample that does not include any of the new EU member countries and then extrapolating the results to these countries requires slope homogeneity between both samples. Since slope homogeneity between both samples cannot be tested for, I at least require slope homogeneity for the OECD sample. In order to test for slope homogeneity within the OECD panel, equation (5.10) is also estimated with individual specific effects ψ_j which are then averaged across countries to obtain the mean group estimator. Pesaran, Smith and Im (1996) show that the mean group estimator is always consistent, while the pooled mean group estimator is consistent only if slopes are homogeneous. Hence, it is possible to test for slope homogeneity within the OECD panel by constructing a Hausman test.

Equation (5.10) is estimated for annual data covering the period 1980 to 2004. The obtained coefficients are then applied to annual data from the new EU member countries covering the period 1995 to 2004. Real effective exchange rates are based on GDP deflators, where the currencies and the price indices of the trading partner countries are weighted according to their average trade share (exports plus imports) with the respective country during the period 2002-2004. The trading partners of a country are defined as the countries, whose trade with the respective country accounts for at least two percent of the total trade of this country during the period 2002-2004. Data on exchange rates and on trade are taken from the International Financial Statistics and the Direction of Trade Statistics of the International Monetary Fund, respectively. For countries of the euro area, the exchange rate series are extrapolated by multiplying the euro exchange rates with the fixed conversion rates.

Productivity in the tradable sector is proxied by labor productivity in the industrial sector, measured as gross value added per employment. As a proxy for productivity in the non-tradable sector I use gross value added per employment in the service sector. Both variables are measured relative to trading partners. For the 21 OECD countries, data on gross value added are taken from the OECD Annual National Accounts database and employment data are taken from the OECD Labor Force Statistics. For the new EU member countries, all data are taken from Eurostat.

Data on GDP and public and private consumption to construct proxies for the time preference rates, and data on export and import prices to construct the terms of trade are taken from the OECD Economic Outlook database for the 21 OECD countries and from Eurostat for the new EU member countries.

Finally, data on the US consumer price index are taken from the OECD Economic Outlook database, and data on the nominal yield on 10-year US government bonds are taken from the IFS.[54]

[54]Assuming rational expectations, expected inflation rates are measured by future in-

5.3 Estimation Results for the OECD Panel

As a preliminary step of the econometric analysis, I test whether the variables used in the estimation are non-stationary. The unit root properties of the series REER, PROD_IND, PROD_SER, NCGDP, and TOT can be examined by employing panel unit root tests. This has the advantage of increasing the power of the test by exploiting cross-section information and time-series information simultaneously. I perform three types of panel unit root tests, proposed by Breitung (2000), Maddala and Wu (1999) and Hadri (1999). The main differences between the three tests lie in the selection of the null hypothesis and in whether there are restrictions on the autoregressive process across cross sections. The first two tests employ a null hypothesis of a unit root, while the test by Hadri (1999) uses a null hypothesis of no unit root. The tests by Breitung (2000) and Hadri (1999) assume that there is a common unit root process in all series so that the autoregressive coefficients are identical across cross sections. By contrast, the test suggested by Maddala and Wu (1999) allows for individual unit root processes so that the autoregressive coefficients vary across cross sections. It is important to note that under the alternative hypothesis of this test, not necessarily all series in the panel must be stationary.

The results of the panel unit root tests are shown in the upper part of Table 5.1. The test by Hadri (1999) consistently rejects the null hypothesis of no unit root for all series. This finding is in line with the results of the test by Breitung (2000) which is unable to reject the unit root null at conventional significance levels for all five series. The unit root test by Maddala and Wu (1999) confirms the other two tests for all series but NCGDP, for which the tests indicates stationarity when including a time trend in the regression. Overall, on the basis of the unit root test results and particularly in view of the strong rejection of the null hypothesis of no unit root by the Hadri (1999) test, it seems reasonable to conclude that all five series follow a unit root process.

Since the measure of the world real interest rate, i.e., the real interest rate of the United States (RINT_US), is the same for all countries, univariate unit root tests have to be used to examine its unit root properties. Two unit root tests are chosen, the Augmented Dickey Fuller (ADF) test and the KPSS test proposed by Kwiatkowski et al. (1992) which is in the spirit of the Hadri (1999) test in that it has a reverse null hypothesis. The lower part of Table 5.1

flation rates. Measuring expected inflation rates by past inflation rates and thus assuming static expectations barely affects the results.

Table 5.1: Unit Root Tests

Variable	Breitung t-statistic	Maddala and Wu p_λ-statistic	Hadri z-statistic
REER	−1.242	44.530	10.469***
PROD_IND	0.595	42.886	14.614***
PROD_SER	−0.443	39.420	12.663***
NCGDP	−0.076	58.810**	13.658***
TOT	−0.969	29.840	8.656***
	ADF	KPSS	
RINT_US	−2.301	0.578**	

Note: ***, ** and * denote rejection of the null hypothesis of a unit root in the case of the Breitung test and the Maddala and Wu test and of stationarity in the case of the Hadri test at the 10%, 5% and 1% significance level, respectively. All regression equations contain a constant. The lag length for the Breitung t-test and the DF-GLS-test is selected according to the Schwarz information criterion. The kernel estimator used in the Maddala and Wu p_λ-test, the Hadri z-test and the KPSS-test is the Bartlett kernel and the bandwidth is selected according to the Newey-West methodology.

shows the results of the unit root tests for the real interest rate of the United States. The ADF test is unable to reject the unit root null at conventional significance levels, implying that the series follows a unit root process. This result is confirmed by the KPSS tests which rejects the null of stationarity at the five percent significance level.

Given the unit root characteristics of the time series, cointegration analysis is applied to examine whether, for the countries in the panel, there indeed exists a cointegrating relationship between the real effective exchange rate and economic fundamentals. Specifically, the DF_ρ and the DF_ρ^* statistics proposed by Kao (1999) as well as the parametric and nonparametric panel-t and group-t statistics proposed by Pedroni (1999) are employed. These statistics have reasonable power even for samples with a small time dimension. All tests are based on the residuals from the proposed long-term relationship. While the tests by Kao (1999) assume homogenous cointegrating vectors, the tests by Pedroni (1999) allow both the dynamics and the cointegrating vectors themselves to differ across countries. Table 5.2 shows the results of the six tests. The parametric and nonparametric panel t-statistics and the nonparametric group t-statistic by Pedroni (1999) are unable to reject the null hypothesis of no cointegration at conventional significance levels, whereas the remaining three tests indicate the presence of a cointegrating relationship. In light of the strong rejection of the null hypothesis of no cointegration by the

Table 5.2: Panel Cointegration Tests

	Test statistic (p-value)
DF_ρ	0.000
DF^*_ρ	0.000
Panel t-statistic (nonparametric)	0.223
Panel t-statistic (parametric)	0.179
Group t-statistic (nonparametric)	0.293
Group t-statistic (parametric)	0.066

Note: The panel t-statistics pool along the 'within' dimension of the panel, while the group t-statistics pool along the 'between' dimension.

Table 5.3: PMGE Estimates

Variable	Coefficient	Standard error	t-statistic	p-value
PROD_IND	0.156	0.034	4.542	0.000
PROD_SER	0.272	0.048	5.611	0.000
NCGDP	−0.141	0.040	−3.523	0.001
TOT	0.864	0.052	16.757	0.000
RINT_US	−0.010	0.001	−7.466	0.000

DF_ρ and the DF^*_ρ statistics by Kao (1999), I conclude that the real effective exchange rate is cointegrated with the NATREX fundamentals, despite the failure of the panel t-statistics and the nonparametric group t-statistic to reject the no-cointegration null hypothesis.

The existence of a cointegrating relationship between the real exchange effective rate and economic fundamentals suggests that the estimation methodology discussed in the previous section can be used to estimate the long-run coefficients. Table 5.3 contains the estimation results. All coefficients are highly significant and in line with the predictions of the NATREX model. As claimed by the model, relative labor productivity in the industrial sector (PROD_IND) is positively related to the real effective exchange rate whereas the relative time preference rate (NCGDP) is negatively related to it. Both the coefficients on relative labor productivity in services (PROD_SER) and the terms of trade (TOT) come out positive, while the coefficient on the world interest rate (RINT_US) comes out negative.

The model is additionally estimated using the mean group estimator. Based on these estimates and the pooled mean group estimates reported in Table 5.3, a Hausman test is constructed to test for slope homogeneity between the countries in the panel. The obtained p-value of the Hausman test is 0.28, meaning that the null hypothesis of homogeneous slopes cannot be rejected. This evidence in favor of slope homogeneity is fairly important for the viability of the two-step estimation procedure. Although slope homogeneity within the OECD panel does not guarantee slope homogeneity between this panel and the new EU member countries, evidence of heterogeneous slopes would clearly make the two-step procedure unsustainable.

5.4 Derivation of Equilibrium Real Exchange Rates for the New EU Member Countries

In this section, the estimation results obtained for the OECD panel are used to calculate real effective equilibrium exchange rates for the new EU member countries. Since the necessary data are not available for Cyprus and Malta, these two countries have to be excluded from the analysis and, hence, the second step focuses on the eight new EU member countries from central and eastern Europe: the Czech Republic, Estonia, Hungary, Latvia, Lithuania, Poland, Slovakia, and Slovenia.

An important issue in extrapolating the real effective equilibrium exchange rates of the new EU member countries from the relationship estimated for the OECD countries is the choice of the intercept terms. When estimating the NATREX model for the panel of OECD countries, the pooled mean group estimator provides country-specific estimates of such intercepts for each OECD country. However, as the new EU member countries are not included in this estimation, no such intercepts are available for these countries and, hence, they have to be inferred indirectly. Following the suggestions by Maseo-Fernandez, Osbat and Schnatz (2004), three alternative strategies for choosing the intercept terms are pursued. First, the sample average of the constants of all 21 OECD countries is employed. Second, the sample average of the constants of Spain, Portugal, and Greece is employed, since these countries can be considered as being most similar to the new EU member countries in terms of economic development. Third, a year where the real exchange rates of the new EU member countries were broadly in line with fundamentals is identified and the intercept terms are chosen such that the estimates also point to real exchange rate equilibrium for this year.

Identifying a year in which the real exchange rates of the new EU member countries were in line with fundamentals is a difficult task. This study deals with this issue in such way that it complies with the findings of previous studies on equilibrium exchange rates in these countries. For the currencies of Estonia and Hungary, several studies suggest that the currencies were broadly in line with fundamentals in 1996 (e.g., Begg, Halpern and Wyplosz, 1999; Rahn, 2003; and, for the Estonian kroon, Filipozzi, 2000). Regarding the Czech koruna, the studies by Halpern and Wyplosz (1997) and Rahn (2003) also point to an equilibrium in 1996, although Begg, Halpern and Wyplosz (1999) and Égert and Lahrèche-Révil (2003) argue that the Czech koruna was still somewhat undervalued at that time. The only study examining the equilibrium exchange rate of the Latvian lats is Begg, Halpern and Wyplosz (1999). They find that the currency was close to its equilibrium in 1996. For the Lithuanian litas, Alonso-Gamo et al. (2002) find that the currency changed from undervaluation to overvaluation in the first quarter of 1995, suggesting that 1995 might serve as a reference year. Begg, Halpern and Wyplosz (1999) find, however, that the currency was undervalued at least until 1996. For the Polish zloty, 1997 can be identified as a year in which the currency was roughly in line with fundamentals (e.g., Begg, Halpern and Wyplosz, 1999; Égert and Lahrèche-Révil, 2003; and Rahn, 2003). For the Slovakian koruna, the studies by Égert and Lahrèche-Révil (2003) and Lamdany et al. (1998) both suggest that the currency was close to equilibrium from 1994 to 1996 or 1997, respectively, although Begg, Halpern and Wyplosz (1999) find that the currency was undervalued throughout this period. For the Slovenian tolar, the studies by Halpern and Wyplosz (1997), Rahn (2003), and Égert and Lahrèche-Révil (2003) all point to equilibrium in 1996. Based on the findings discussed above, 1996 is chosen as reference year for all currencies under examination except for the Polish zloty, where the reference year is set to 1997.

The results of the calculations are displayed in Figures 5.3 to 5.5. The equilibrium real exchange rates displayed in Figure 5.3 are derived by employing the average of the constants of all 21 OECD countries. The calculations reveal that the real effective exchange rates of all eight countries were close to equilibrium in 1995 which is in line with prior research as discussed in the previous paragraph. The real exchange rate appreciations observed in the Czech Republic, Hungary, Poland and the three Baltic countries in the second half of the 1990s led to a rising overvaluation of the currencies of these six countries as the equilibrium real exchange rate, though appreciating as well, did not follow suit. In 2000, the currencies of the Czech Republic, Hungary, Poland, Estonia, Latvia, and Lithuania were overvalued by 13 percent, 11 percent, 24 percent, 16 percent, 33 percent, and 39 percent, respectively.

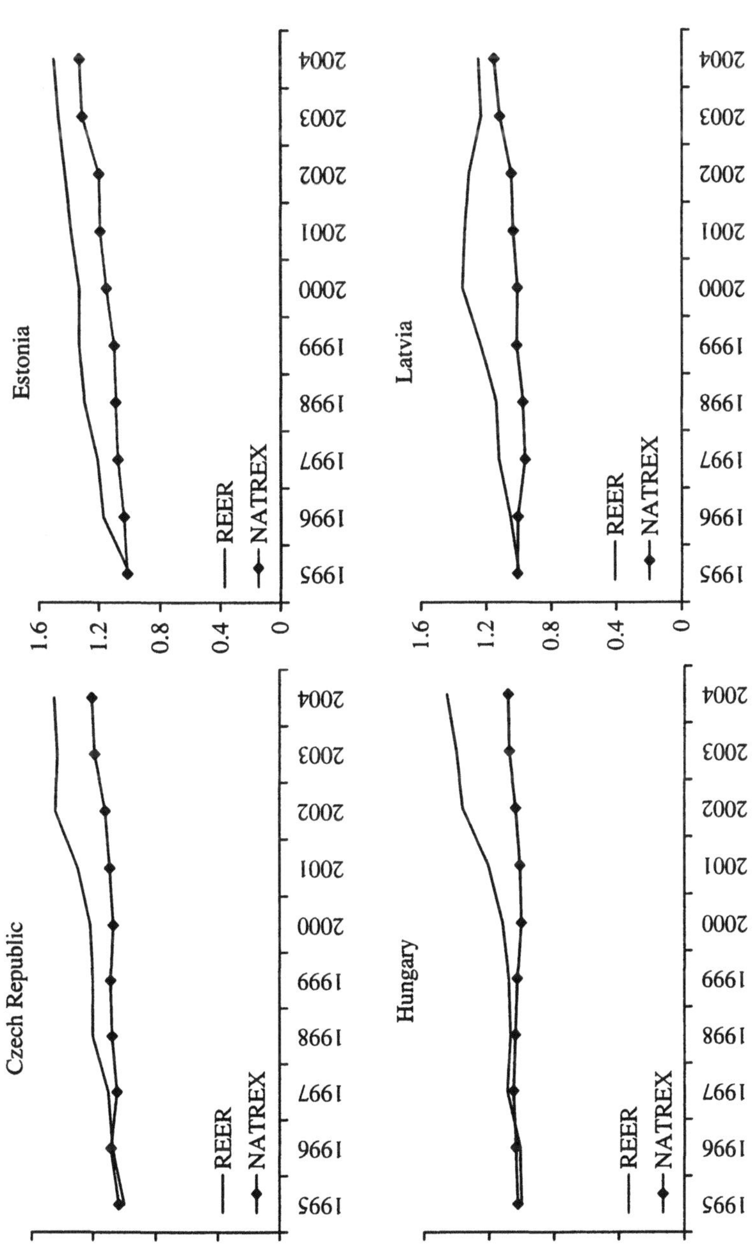

Figure 5.3: Actual and Equilibrium Real Effective Exchange Rates - Common Constant based on all 21 OECD Countries

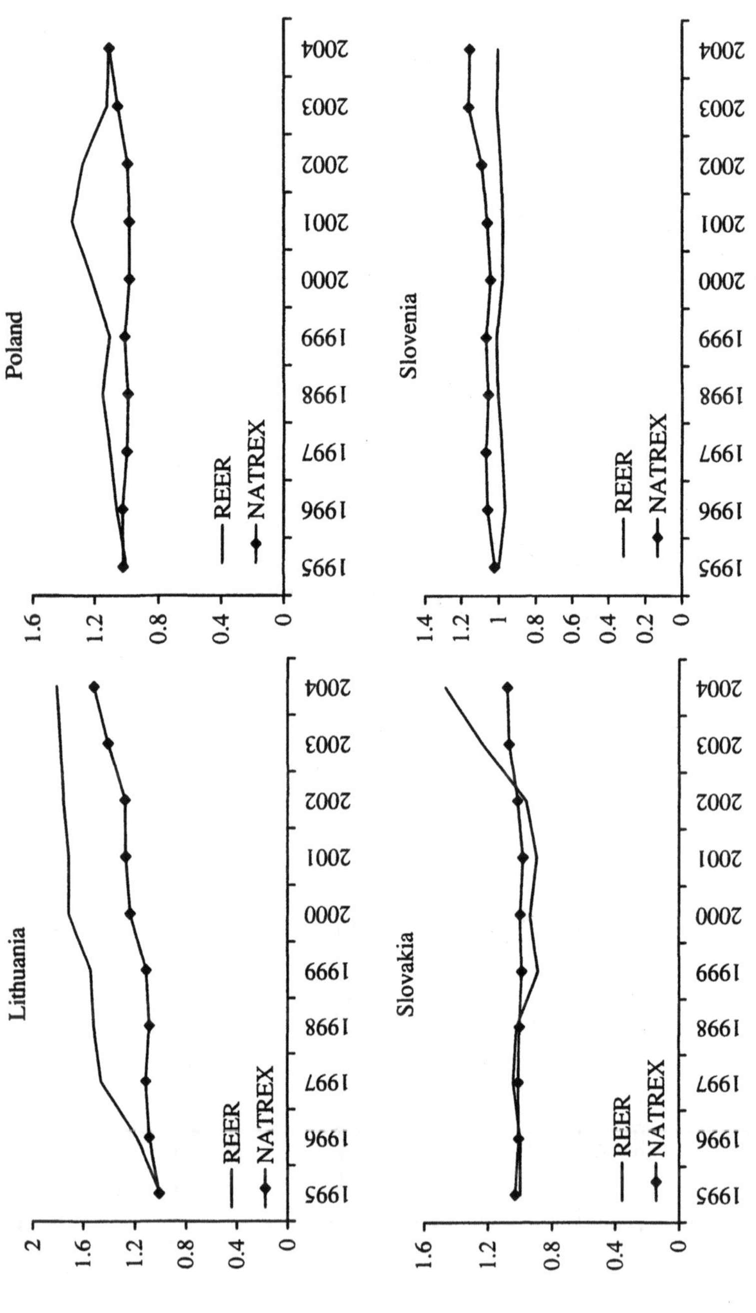

Figure 5.3: Actual and Equilibrium Real Effective Exchange Rates - Common Constant based on all 21 OECD Countries (cont.)

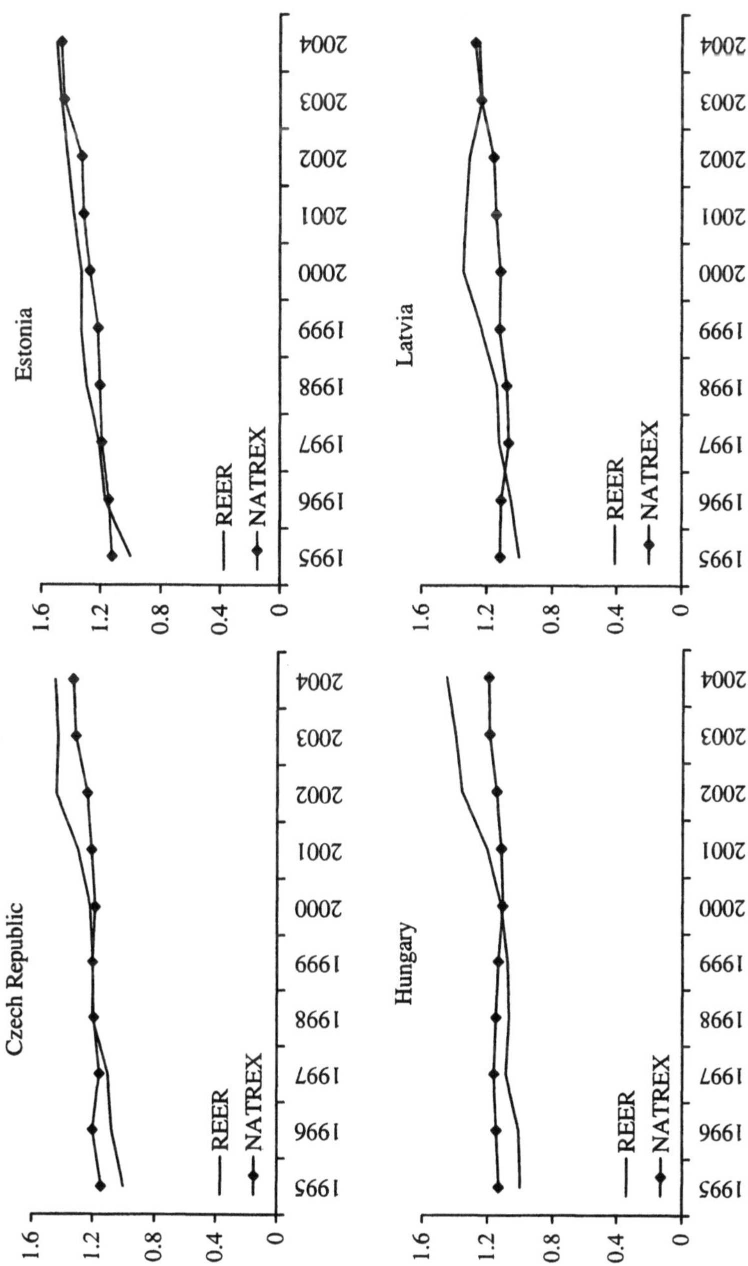

Figure 5.4: Actual and Equilibrium Real Effective Exchange Rates - Common Constant based on Spain, Portugal, and Greece

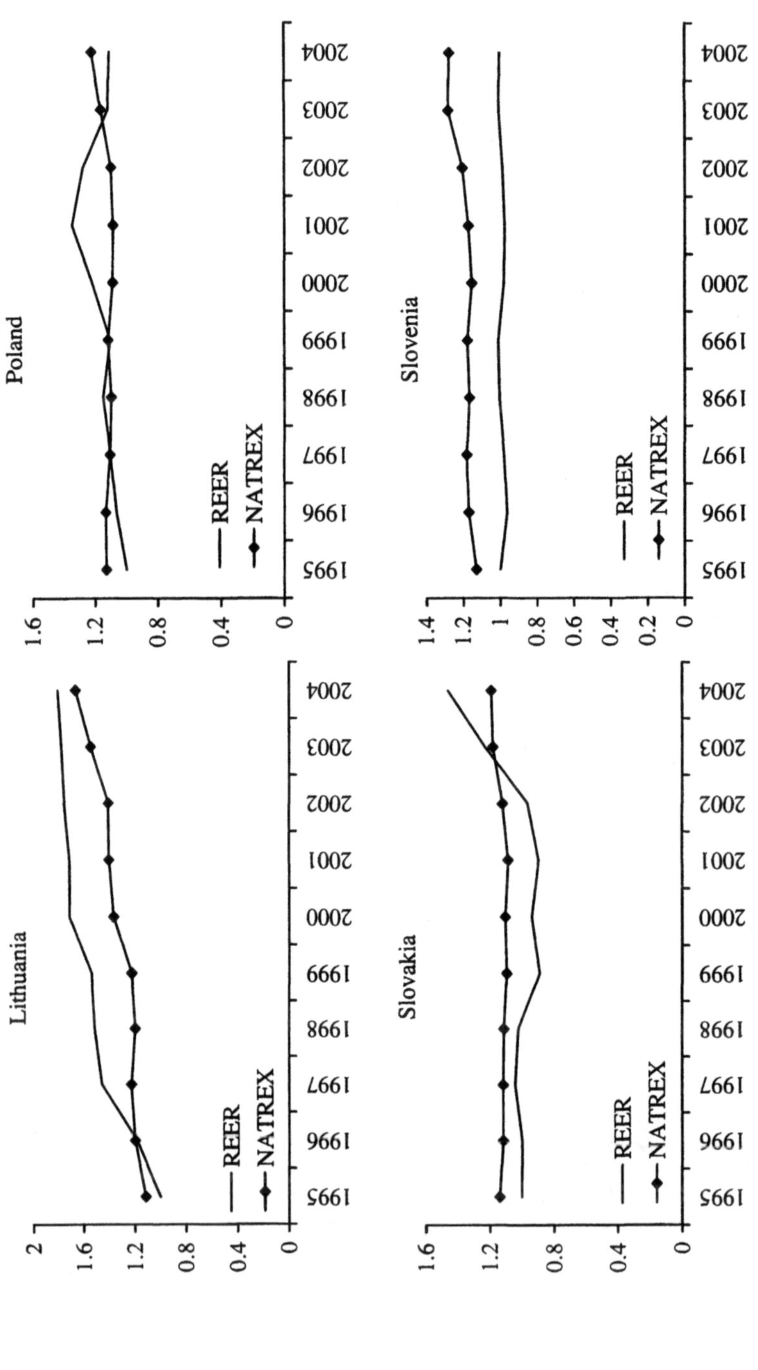

Figure 5.4: Actual and Equilibrium Real Effective Exchange Rates - Common Constant based on Spain, Portugal, and Greece (cont.)

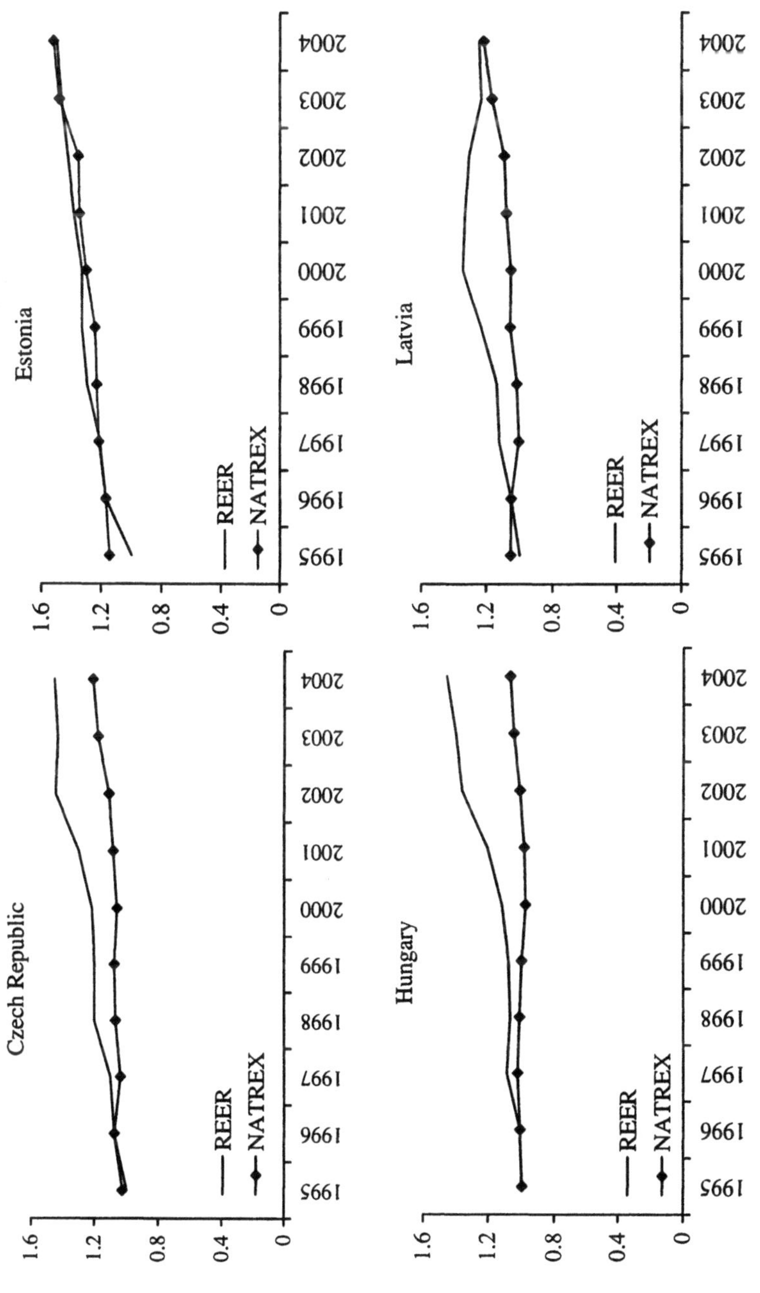

Figure 5.5: Actual and Equilibrium Real Effective Exchange Rates - Country-Specific Constants

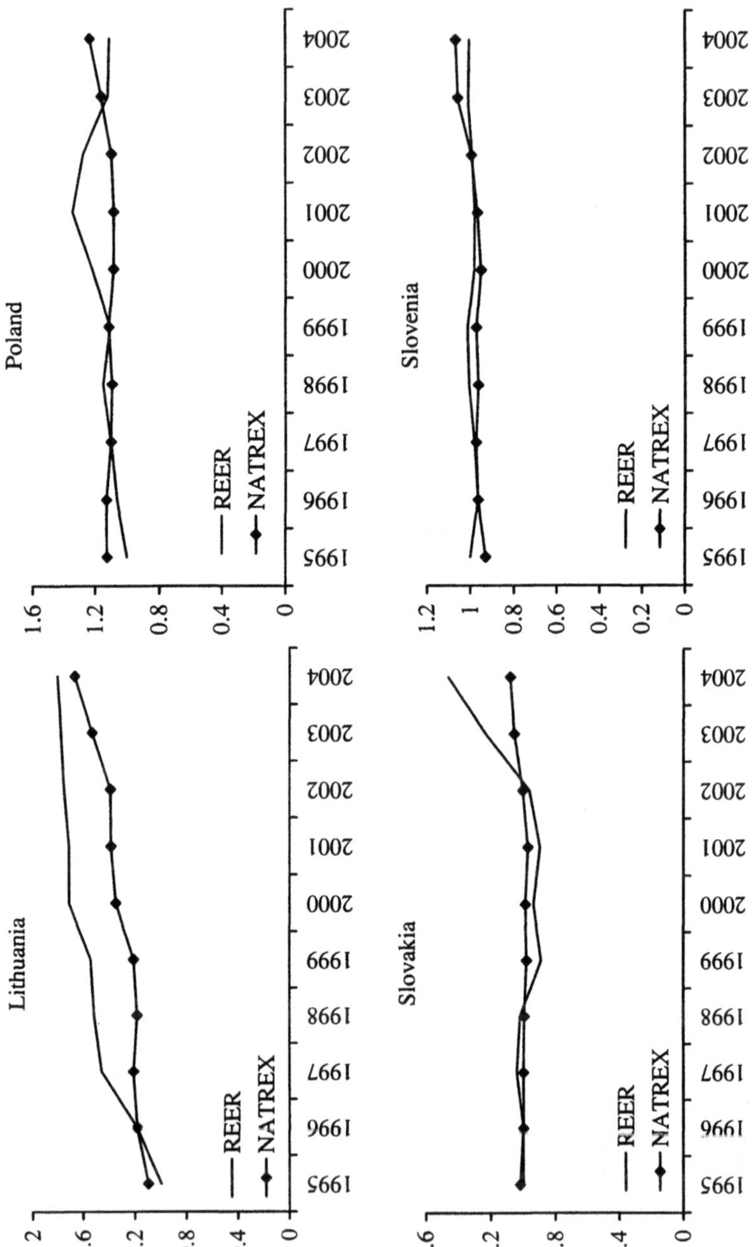

Figure 5.5: Actual and Equilibrium Real Effective Exchange Rates - Country-Specific Constants (cont.)

While the appreciation slowed down in Lithuania and even reversed in Latvia, the currencies of the Czech Republic, Hungary, and Poland continued to appreciate at a fast pace. In 2002, when the trend appreciation finally also slowed down in the Czech Republic and in Hungary, the two currencies were overvalued by 28 and 31 percent, respectively. In Poland, the appreciation began to reverse in 2001 and until 2004 the zloty depreciated by 18 percent in real effective terms. The depreciation of the Latvian lats and the Polish zloty can be interpreted as an equilibrium phenomenon as it brought the two currencies closer to their equilibrium path. By 2004, the overvaluation had been reduced to 8 percent in Latvia, while in Poland, it was fully eliminated. By contrast, the Czech koruna, the Hungarian forint, and the Lithuanian litas were still heavily overvalued in 2004, with the degree of overvaluation estimated at 20 percent, 34 percent, and 20 percent, respectively. In Estonia, where the actual real exchange rate appreciated by roughly the same amount as the equilibrium rate, the overvaluation still amounted to 12 percent in 2004.

The Slovenian tolar and the Slovak koruna showed a somewhat different development than the other six currencies in that their real effective exchange rates remained rather stable during the second half of the 1990s and during the first years of the new millennium. While the real exchange rate of the Slovenian tolar also remained rather stable in recent years, the Slovak koruna began to heavily appreciate in 2002. Between 2002 and 2003, the currency appreciated by 27 percent, followed by another 17 percent between 2003 and 2004. The equilibrium real exchange rates of the two currencies slightly appreciated over the observation period, leading to an undervaluation of the Slovenian tolar from 1996 onwards and to an undervaluation of the Slovak koruna from 1999 onwards. The recent appreciation of the Slovak koruna is not supported by fundamentals and the currency became heavily overvalued in 2003. The overvaluation amounted to 15 percent in 2003 and to 35 percent in 2004.

Figure 5.4 compares the actual real effective exchange rates to the equilibrium rates derived by employing the average of the constants of Spain, Portugal, and Greece. The obtained average is higher than the average of the constants of all 21 countries, implying that all countries started at an undervalued level in 1995. However, in the Czech Republic, Hungary, Poland, and the three Baltic countries, this initial undervaluation was quickly eliminated by the strong appreciation of the actual real effective exchange rate. The Czech koruna, the Hungarian forint, and the Lithuanian lats became overvalued in 2000, 2001, and 1996, respectively, and stayed at an overvalued level until the end of the observation horizon. With values of 9 percent, 22 percent, and 8 percent, respectively, the overvaluation observed in 2004 is notable lower compared to the previous case, where the constant was based on all 21 OECD countries.

The Polish zloty and the Latvian lats both became overvalued in 1997, though the overvaluation has subsequently been reversed by the recent depreciation of both currencies. For 2004, the calculations point to an undervaluation of 9 percent for the Polish zloty and 2 percent for the Latvian lats and, hence, lead to rather different conclusions compared to the previous case. The conclusions that can be drawn for the Estonian kroon also differ markedly from those in the previous case. While the Estonian kroon was shown to have been undervalued from 1996 onwards based on the average of all 21 constants, the currency is shown to have been fairly valued based on the average of the constants of Spain, Portugal, and Greece.

In the case of the Slovak koruna, the results differ from the previous case in so far as the heavy appreciation in 2003 and 2004 can at least partially be considered as an equilibrium phenomenon when employing the average of the constants of Spain, Portugal, and Greece. The Slovak koruna is found to have been undervalued by over 14 percent in 2002. However, the actual real effective exchange rate appreciated by 52 percent between 2002 and 2004, resulting in an overvaluation of 23 percent by 2004. In the case of Slovenia, the estimated undervaluation is notably higher when employing the average of the constants of Spain, Portugal, and Greece as opposed to the average of all 21 constants. For 2004, the undervaluation is estimated at 21 percent in real effective terms.

Figure 5.5 shows the equilibrium real exchange rates derived by applying country specific constants that are compatible with real exchange rate equilibrium in the reference years specified above. For the Czech Republic, Hungary, and Slovakia the results are very similar to those of the first approach, where the constants were set equal to the average of the constants of all 21 OECD countries. By contrast, for Estonia, Latvia, Lithuania, and Poland the obtained equilibrium real exchange rates mirror those obtained under the second approach, where Spain, Portugal, and Greece where used as reference countries. Finally, in the case of the Slovenian tolar, the calculations point to a slight undervaluation of the currency, which is markedly lower than the undervaluation found with the other two approaches.

5.5 Conclusions

Given that the central and eastern European countries that joined the European Union in May 2004 have to adopt the euro as soon as they fulfill the convergence criteria laid down in the Maastricht Treaty, this chapter examined recent exchange rate movements in these countries. As one of the Maastricht criteria requires the new EU member countries to participate in the European exchange rate mechanism for at least two years, the question arises whether the exchange rates of these countries are already roughly in line with economic fundamentals. To address this question, a small-country version of the NATREX approach was applied, which assumes that the terms of trade are exogenous and the domestic interest rate diverges from the world interest rate by a risk premium.

The analysis revealed that the equilibrium real exchange rates of all eight countries appreciated over the past ten years. In some countries, most notably in the Czech Republic, Hungary, Lithuania, and, for the more recent period, in Slovakia actual real exchange rates appreciated by even more than the equilibrium rate, leading to an overvaluation of these countries' currencies. Hence, for these countries' currencies, there seems to be some scope for depreciation over the coming years. While the Polish zloty and the Latvian lats also became heavily overvalued in the second half of the 1990s, the corrective step back towards equilibrium seems to have already taken place as both currencies depreciated in recent years and were back in line with fundamentals or even slightly undervalued in 2004. The observed real appreciation of the Estonian kroon was roughly supported by economic fundamentals since the equilibrium rate appreciated by roughly the same amount. In the case of the Slovenian tolar, the appreciation of the actual real exchange rate did not keep up with the appreciation of the equilibrium rate, leading to an undervaluation of the currency with respect to the NATREX.

Appendix A1

Equation (5.8) is derived by first taking the total derivative of equation (5.4):

$$\begin{aligned}&\frac{\partial Q_N}{\partial R_N}dR_N+\frac{\partial Q_N}{\partial K}dK+\frac{\partial Q_N}{\partial u_1}du_1+\frac{\partial Q_N}{\partial u_N}du_N=\\&\quad\frac{\partial C_N}{\partial R_N}dR_N+\frac{\partial C_N}{\partial K}dK+\frac{\partial C_N}{\partial F}dF+\frac{\partial C_N}{\partial \rho}d\rho+\frac{\partial C_N}{\partial r}\left(dr^*+\frac{\partial r}{\partial F}dF\right)\\&\quad+\frac{\partial C_N}{\partial TOT}dTOT+\frac{\partial I_N}{\partial R_N}dR_N+\frac{\partial I_N}{\partial K}dK+\frac{\partial I_N}{\partial r}\left(dr^*+\frac{\partial r}{\partial F}dF\right)\\&\quad+\frac{\partial I_N}{\partial u_N}du_N+\frac{\partial I_N}{\partial u_1}du_1+\frac{\partial I_N}{\partial TOT}dTOT.\end{aligned}$$

Solving this equation for dR_N and assuming that $\partial Q_N/\partial z > \partial I_N/\partial z$ in absolute value for any exogenous variable z yields the following partial derivatives:

$$\frac{dR_N}{dK}=\frac{\frac{\partial C_N}{\partial K}-\frac{\partial Q_N}{\partial K}+\frac{\partial I_N}{\partial K}}{\frac{\partial Q_N}{\partial R_N}-\frac{\partial C_N}{\partial R_N}-\frac{\partial I_N}{\partial R_N}}>0;\quad \frac{dR_N}{dF}=\frac{\frac{\partial C_N}{\partial F}+\frac{\partial C_N}{\partial r}\frac{\partial r}{\partial F}}{\frac{\partial Q_N}{\partial R_N}-\frac{\partial C_N}{\partial R_N}-\frac{\partial I_N}{\partial R_N}}<0;$$

$$\frac{dR_N}{d\rho}=\frac{\frac{\partial C_N}{\partial \rho}}{\frac{\partial Q_N}{\partial R_N}-\frac{\partial C_N}{\partial R_N}-\frac{\partial I_N}{\partial R_N}}>0;\quad \frac{dR_N}{du_N}=\frac{\frac{\partial I_N}{\partial u_N}-\frac{\partial Q_N}{\partial u_N}}{\frac{\partial Q_N}{\partial R_N}-\frac{\partial C_N}{\partial R_N}-\frac{\partial I_N}{\partial R_N}}<0;$$

$$\frac{dR_N}{du_1}=\frac{\frac{\partial I_N}{\partial u_1}-\frac{\partial Q_N}{\partial u_1}}{\frac{\partial Q_N}{\partial R_N}-\frac{\partial C_N}{\partial R_N}-\frac{\partial I_N}{\partial R_N}}>0;\quad \frac{dR_N}{dr^*}=\frac{\frac{\partial C_N}{\partial r}+\frac{\partial I_N}{\partial r}}{\frac{\partial Q_N}{\partial R_N}-\frac{\partial C_N}{\partial R_N}-\frac{\partial I_N}{\partial R_N}}\gtrless 0;$$

$$\frac{dR_N}{dTOT}=\frac{\frac{\partial C_N}{\partial TOT}+\frac{\partial I_N}{\partial TOT}}{\frac{\partial Q_N}{\partial R_N}-\frac{\partial C_N}{\partial R_N}-\frac{\partial I_N}{\partial R_N}}\gtrless 0.$$

Appendix A2

Equation (5.9) can be derived by writing equations (5.5) and (5.6) in matrix notation:

$$\begin{bmatrix} dK/dt \\ dF/dt \end{bmatrix} = \begin{bmatrix} I \\ I-S \end{bmatrix}$$

Applying a first order Taylor approximation gives

$$\begin{bmatrix} I \\ I-S \end{bmatrix} = \begin{bmatrix} \bar{I} \\ \bar{I}-\bar{S} \end{bmatrix} + \left.\begin{bmatrix} \frac{\partial I}{\partial K} & \frac{\partial I}{\partial r}\frac{\partial r}{\partial F} \\ \frac{\partial I}{\partial K} - \frac{\partial S}{\partial K} & \frac{\partial I}{\partial r}\frac{\partial r}{\partial F} - \frac{\partial S}{\partial F} \end{bmatrix}\right|_{-} \begin{bmatrix} K-\bar{K} \\ F-\bar{F} \end{bmatrix},$$

where the bar denotes the long-term equilibrium. Considering a change in only one exogenous variable x at a time,

$$\begin{bmatrix} \frac{\partial I}{\partial x} \\ \frac{\partial I}{\partial x} - \frac{\partial S}{\partial x} \end{bmatrix} = \left.\begin{bmatrix} \frac{\partial I}{\partial K} & \frac{\partial I}{\partial r}\frac{\partial r}{\partial F} \\ \frac{\partial I}{\partial K} - \frac{\partial S}{\partial K} & \frac{\partial I}{\partial r}\frac{\partial r}{\partial F} - \frac{\partial S}{\partial F} \end{bmatrix}\right|_{-} \begin{bmatrix} -\frac{\partial \bar{K}}{\partial x} \\ -\frac{\partial \bar{F}}{\partial x} \end{bmatrix}.$$

Applying Cramer's rule gives

$$\frac{\partial \bar{K}}{\partial \rho} = \frac{-\frac{\partial I}{\partial r}\frac{\partial r}{\partial F}\frac{\partial S}{\partial \rho}}{\frac{\partial I}{\partial r}\frac{\partial r}{\partial F}\frac{\partial S}{\partial K} - \frac{\partial I}{\partial K}\frac{\partial S}{\partial F}} < 0; \quad \frac{\partial \bar{K}}{\partial u_N} = \frac{\frac{\partial S}{\partial F}\frac{\partial I}{\partial u_N} - \frac{\partial I}{\partial r}\frac{\partial r}{\partial F}\frac{\partial S}{\partial u_N}}{\frac{\partial I}{\partial r}\frac{\partial r}{\partial F}\frac{\partial S}{\partial K} - \frac{\partial I}{\partial K}\frac{\partial S}{\partial F}} > 0;$$

$$\frac{\partial \bar{K}}{\partial u_1} = \frac{\frac{\partial S}{\partial F}\frac{\partial I}{\partial u_1} - \frac{\partial I}{\partial r}\frac{\partial r}{\partial F}\frac{\partial S}{\partial u_1}}{\frac{\partial I}{\partial r}\frac{\partial r}{\partial F}\frac{\partial S}{\partial K} - \frac{\partial I}{\partial K}\frac{\partial S}{\partial F}} > 0; \quad \frac{\partial \bar{K}}{\partial TOT} = \frac{\frac{\partial I}{\partial TOT}\frac{\partial S}{\partial F}}{\frac{\partial I}{\partial r}\frac{\partial r}{\partial F}\frac{\partial S}{\partial K} - \frac{\partial I}{\partial K}\frac{\partial S}{\partial F}} > 0;$$

$$\frac{\partial \bar{K}}{\partial r^*} = \frac{\frac{\partial I}{\partial r}\frac{\partial S}{\partial F} - \frac{\partial I}{\partial r}\frac{\partial r}{\partial F}\frac{\partial S}{\partial r^*}}{\frac{\partial I}{\partial r}\frac{\partial r}{\partial F}\frac{\partial S}{\partial K} - \frac{\partial I}{\partial K}\frac{\partial S}{\partial F}} \gtrless 0; \quad \frac{\partial \bar{F}}{\partial \rho} = \frac{\frac{\partial I}{\partial K}\frac{\partial S}{\partial \rho}}{\frac{\partial I}{\partial r}\frac{\partial r}{\partial F}\frac{\partial S}{\partial K} - \frac{\partial I}{\partial K}\frac{\partial S}{\partial F}} > 0;$$

$$\frac{\partial \bar{F}}{\partial u_N} = \frac{\frac{\partial I}{\partial K}\frac{\partial S}{\partial u_N} - \frac{\partial S}{\partial K}\frac{\partial I}{\partial u_N}}{\frac{\partial I}{\partial r}\frac{\partial r}{\partial F}\frac{\partial S}{\partial K} - \frac{\partial I}{\partial K}\frac{\partial S}{\partial F}} < 0; \quad \frac{\partial \bar{F}}{\partial r^*} = \frac{\frac{\partial I}{\partial K}\frac{\partial S}{\partial r^*} - \frac{\partial I}{\partial r}\frac{\partial S}{\partial K}}{\frac{\partial I}{\partial r}\frac{\partial r}{\partial F}\frac{\partial S}{\partial K} - \frac{\partial I}{\partial K}\frac{\partial S}{\partial F}} \gtrless 0;$$

$$\frac{\partial \bar{F}}{\partial u_1}=\frac{\dfrac{\partial I}{\partial K}\dfrac{\partial S}{\partial u_1}-\dfrac{\partial S}{\partial K}\dfrac{\partial I}{\partial u_1}}{\dfrac{\partial I}{\partial r}\dfrac{\partial r}{\partial F}\dfrac{\partial S}{\partial K}-\dfrac{\partial I}{\partial K}\dfrac{\partial S}{\partial F}}<0;\ \frac{\partial \bar{F}}{\partial TOT}=\frac{-\dfrac{\partial I}{\partial TOT}\dfrac{\partial S}{\partial K}}{\dfrac{\partial I}{\partial r}\dfrac{\partial r}{\partial F}\dfrac{\partial S}{\partial K}-\dfrac{\partial I}{\partial K}\dfrac{\partial S}{\partial F}}>0.$$

Considering the effect of a change in any exogenous variable z on the long-term equilibrium exchange rate $\bar{R}$ as the sum of the direct medium-term effect and the indirect long-term effect that works through changes in K and F, i.e.,

$$\frac{\partial \bar{R}}{\partial z}=\frac{\partial \tilde{R}}{\partial z}+\frac{\partial \tilde{R}}{\partial K}\frac{\partial \bar{K}}{\partial z}+\frac{\partial \tilde{R}}{\partial F}\frac{\partial \bar{F}}{\partial z},$$

yields equation (5.9).

Chapter 6

A Structural NATREX Estimation

In Chapter 5, a small country version of the NATREX approach was estimated in reduced form in order to assess whether recent real exchange rate developments in the the new EU member countries were consistent with economic fundamentals. While the simplifications that reduced-form estimations impose on the theoretical complexity of models allow an intuitive interpretation of the results, they make it impossible to verify whether the analytical conditions for equilibrium are met. A viable alternative can therefore be found in the so-called structural approach that explicitly accounts for the underlying behavioral relationships. In this chapter, the small country version of the NATREX approach, outlined in section 5.1, is therefore estimated in structural form. This guarantees that the analytical conditions for equilibrium are met and, additionally, allows verifying whether the underlying behavioral relationships are in line with the predictions of the structural model. The derived equilibrium real exchange rates can therefore be interpreted as equilibrium values not only from an empirical point of view but, more importantly, also from a theoretical point of view.

A small country version of the NATREX has not yet been estimated within an integrated structural approach. So far, only four studies have estimated the NATREX approach in structural form. These are Verrue and Colpaert (1998) for the Belgian franc, Gandolfo and Felettigh (1998) for the Italian lira, Detken et al. (2002) for the euro, and Karádi (2003) for the Hungarian forint. All four studies employ the large country version of the NATREX model originally formulated by Stein (1994).

Estimating the small country version of the NATREX model in structural form for the new EU member countries is difficult in terms of data availability. Since the underlying behavioral relationships are expected to be country-specific, estimating them in a panel framework is not feasible. Instead, they have to be estimated on a country-by-country basis. As realiable data on most of the new EU member countries is not available prior to the mid 1990s, a country-by-country estimation requires at least quarterly data. The only country, for which disaggregated data on output, consumption and investment (which is essential in order to discriminate between tradable and non-tradable goods) are available at quarterly frequency is Lithuania. The empirical analysis therefore has to be restricted to the Lithuanian economy.

The outline of the rest of the chapter is as follows. In section 6.1 the behavioral equations of the NATREX model that need to be estimated in the empirical analysis are presented. Subsequently, these equations are solved for the medium and long-term equilibrium values of the relative price of non-tradable goods. Section 6.2 then presents the data set and section 6.3 discusses the estimation results. Finally, section 6.4 summarizes the main findings and concludes.

6.1 A Structural Solution to the Small Country NATREX Model

In order to estimate the model outlined in section 5.1 in structural form several modifications are necessary. First, all level variables are expressed as ratio to total output Q. Second, as it is not possible to obtain data on the composition of consumption and investment with respect to the tradable good 1 produced by the domestic economy and the tradable good 2 imported from the rest of the world the two goods are considered as one single good, which is simply called the tradable good T. Third, following Detken et al. (2002), time preference is measured by the nominal interest rate. As the country is small, the nominal interest rate is endogenous, implying that an equation has to be added to the model that describes the behavior of the nominal interest rate.[55] The resulting model is defined by the following set of equations:

[55]Time preference cannot be proxied by the ratio of consumption to GDP as commonly done in NATREX studies as this would lead to linear dependencies in the model.

Non-tradable goods market equilibrium:

$$(6.1) \quad \frac{Q_N}{Q} = \frac{C_N}{Q} + \frac{I_N}{Q}.$$

Behavioral equations:

$$(6.2) \; \frac{Q_N}{Q} = a_1 + a_2 R_N - a_3 \frac{K^r}{Q^r} - a_4 u_T + a_5 u_N;$$

$$(6.3) \; \frac{C_N}{Q} = a_6 - a_7 R_N + a_8 \frac{K^r}{Q^r} - a_9 \frac{F}{Q} + a_{10} i \pm a_{11} r - a_{12} TOT;$$

$$(6.4) \; \frac{I_N}{Q} = a_{13} - a_{14} R_N - a_{15} \frac{K^r}{Q^r} - a_{16} r + a_{17} u_T + a_{18} u_N + a_{19} TOT;$$

$$(6.5) \; \frac{C_T}{Q} = a_{20} + a_{21} R_N + a_{22} \frac{K^r}{Q^r} - a_{23} \frac{F}{Q} + a_{24} i \pm a_{25} r + a_{26} TOT;$$

$$(6.6) \; \frac{I_T}{Q} = a_{27} + a_{28} R_N - a_{29} \frac{K^r}{Q^r} - a_{30} r + a_{31} u_T + a_{32} u_N + a_{33} TOT.$$

Nominal and real interest rates:

$$(6.7) \quad r = r^* + a_{34} + a_{35} \frac{F}{Q};$$

$$(6.8) \quad i = i^* + (\pi - \pi^*) + (r - r^*).$$

Stock accumulation:

$$(6.9) \quad K_t^r = (1 - \delta) K_{t-1}^r + I_t / P^I;$$

$$(6.10) \quad F_t = F_{t-1} + I_t - S_t.$$

Steady state capital stock and net foreign debt:

$$(6.11) \; \overline{\frac{K^r}{Q^r}} = \frac{1+g}{\delta+g} \frac{\overline{I}}{Q} \frac{P^Q}{P^I};$$

$$(6.12) \; \overline{\frac{F}{Q}} = \frac{1+\varpi}{\varpi} \left(\overline{\frac{I}{Q}} - \overline{\frac{S}{Q}} \right).$$

Equation (6.1) reflects the condition for equilibrium in the market for non-tradable goods and corresponds to equation (5.4) in section 5.1.1. Equations (6.2) to (6.4) describe the behavior of the supply of and the demand for the non-tradable good N and the tradable good T in terms of their underlying fundamentals. The superscript r signifies the real value of the respective variable. Equations (6.7) and (6.8) describe the behavior of nominal and real interest rates. Equation (6.7) corresponds to the portfolio balance equation (5.7) in section 5.1.1 where the risk premium $f(F)$ is assumed to be a linear function in F and equation (6.8) is the Fisher open (Fisher, 1930). Equations (6.9) and (6.10) describe the evolution of capital and net foreign debt over time t and correspond to equations (5.5) and (5.6) in section 5.1.1. Solving equations (6.9) and (6.10) for the steady state yields equations (6.11) and (6.12), where g is the growth rate of Q^r, ϖ is the growth rate of Q, P^Q and P^I are the output and investment deflators, δ is the rate of depreciation, total investment is $I = I_N + I_T$, $S = Q - C_N - C_T - r^*F$, and a bar denotes the steady state value of the respective variable.[56]

The medium-term equilibrium relative price of non-tradable goods $\tilde{R}_N$ is obtained by inserting equations (6.2) to (6.4), (6.7), and (6.8) into equation (6.1) and then solving for the relative price of non-tradable goods:

$$(6.13)\ \tilde{R}_N = (a_2 + a_7 - a_{14})^{-1} \Big[a_6 + a_{13} - a_1 + (a_{18} - a_5)u_N + (a_{17} + a_4)u_T + a_{10}(i^* + \pi - \pi^* + a_{34}) - (a_{16} \mp a_{11})(r^* + a_{34}) + (a_{19} - a_{12})TOT + (a_3 + a_8 - a_{15})\frac{K^r}{Q^r} - (a_9 + (a_{16} - a_{10} \mp a_{11})a_{35})\frac{F}{Q} \Big]$$

The long-term equilibrium relative price of non-tradable goods $\bar{R}_N$ is obtained by using the full model. In a first step, the steady state levels of K^r/Q^r and F/Q are derived by inserting the behavioral equations (6.2) to (6.6) into equations (6.11) and (6.12) and then solving the resulting equation system for $\overline{K^r/Q^r}$ and $\overline{F/Q}$ under the assumption that the portfolio balance

[56]Dividing both sides of equations (6.9) and (6.10) by Q_t^r and Q_t, respectively, gives

$$\frac{K_t^r}{Q_t^r} = \frac{(1-\delta)K_{t-1}^r}{(1+g)Q_{t-1}^r} + \frac{I_t}{Q_t}\frac{P^Q}{P^I} \quad \text{and} \quad \frac{F_t}{Q_t} = \frac{F_{t-1}}{(1+\varpi)Q_{t-1}} + \frac{I_t}{Q_t} - \frac{S_t}{Q_t}.$$

In the steady state, $K_t^r/Q_t^r = K_{t-1}^r/Q_{t-1}^r = \overline{K^r/Q^r}$, $F_t/Q_t = F_{t-1}/Q_{t-1} = \overline{F/Q}$, $I_t/Q_t = \overline{I/Q}$, and $S_t/Q_t = \overline{S/Q}$, implying

$$\frac{\overline{K^r}}{\overline{Q^r}} = \frac{1-\delta}{1+g}\frac{\overline{K^r}}{\overline{Q^r}} + \frac{\overline{I}}{\overline{Q}}\frac{P^Q}{P^I} \quad \text{and} \quad \frac{\overline{F}}{\overline{Q}} = \frac{1}{1+\varpi}\frac{\overline{F}}{\overline{Q}} + \frac{\overline{I}}{\overline{Q}} - \frac{\overline{S}}{\overline{Q}}.$$

Solving these two equations for $\overline{K^r/Q^r}$ and $\overline{F/Q}$, respectively, yields equations (6.11) and (6.12).

equation (6.7) and the Fisher relation (6.8) hold:

$$
\begin{aligned}
(6.14)\ \overline{\frac{K^r}{Q^r}} = {} & \gamma_1(\gamma_2(a_{13}+a_{27}) + \gamma_3(1-a_6-a_{20}) + \gamma_2(a_{17}+a_{31})u_T \\
& + \gamma_2(a_{18}+a_{32})u_N + (\gamma_2(a_{28}-a_{14}) + \gamma_3(a_7-a_{21}))R_N \\
& - \gamma_3(a_{24}+a_{10})(i+\pi-\pi^*+a_{34}) \\
& - \gamma_2(a_{16}+a_{30}) \pm \gamma_3(a_{11}+a_{25}))(r^*+a_{34}) \\
& + ((\gamma_2(a_{19}+a_{33}) + \gamma_3(a_{12}-a_{26}))TOT);
\end{aligned}
$$

$$
\begin{aligned}
(6.15)\ \overline{\frac{F}{Q}} = {} & \gamma_4((a_{13}+a_{27})(1+\gamma_5) - 1 + a_6 + a_{20} + (a_{31}+a_{17})(1+\gamma_5)u_T \\
& + (a_{18}+a_{32})(1+\gamma_5)u_N + ((a_{28}-a_{14})(1+\gamma_5) - a_7 + a_{21})R_N \\
& + (a_{24}+a_{10})(i+\pi-\pi^*+a_{34}) \\
& - ((a_{16}+a_{30})(1+\gamma_5) \mp a_{11} \mp a_{25})(r^*+a_{34}) \\
& + ((a_{19}+a_{33})(1+\gamma_5) - a_{12} + a_{26})TOT);
\end{aligned}
$$

where

$$
\begin{aligned}
\gamma_1 &= (1+g)/((\delta+g)P^I/P^Q + (1+g)(a_{29}+a_{15})); \\
\gamma_2 &= 1-\gamma_3(1+\gamma_5); \\
\gamma_3 &= a_{35}\gamma_4(a_{16}+a_{30}); \\
\gamma_4 &= (1+\varpi)/(\varpi + (1+\varpi)(-r^* + a_9 + a_{23} + a_{35}((a_{16}+a_{30})(1+\gamma_5) \\
&\quad - a_{10} - a_{24} \mp a_{11} \mp a_{25}))); \\
\gamma_5 &= \gamma_1(a_8 + a_{22} - a_{15} - a_{29}).
\end{aligned}
$$

In a second step, equations (6.14) and (6.15) are inserted into equation (6.13) and the resulting expression is then solved for the relative price of non-tradable goods to give $\bar{R}_N$:

$$
\begin{aligned}
(6.16)\ \bar{R}_N = {} & (a_2 + a_7 - a_{14} - \gamma_6(a_{28}-a_{14}) - \gamma_7(a_7-a_{21}))^{-1}[(a_{13}+a_{27})\gamma_6 \\
& + a_6 + a_{13} - a_1 + (1-a_6-a_{20})\gamma_7 + (a_{18} - a_5 + (a_{18}+a_{32})\gamma_6)u_N \\
& + (a_{17} + a_4 + (a_{17}+a_{31})\gamma_6)u_T \\
& + (a_{10} - (a_{10}+a_{24})\gamma_7)(i+\pi-\pi^*+a_{34}) \\
& - (a_{16} \mp a_{11} + (a_{16}+a_{30})\gamma_6 \pm (a_{11}+a_{25})\gamma_7)(r^*+a_{34}) \\
& + (a_{19} - a_{12} + (a_{19}+a_{33})\gamma_6 + (a_{12}-a_{26})\gamma_7)TOT];
\end{aligned}
$$

where

$$\gamma_6 = \gamma_1\gamma_2(a_3 + a_8 - a_{15}) - \gamma_4(1 + \gamma_5)(a_9 + a_{35}(a_{16} - a_{10} \mp a_{11}));$$
$$\gamma_7 = \gamma_1\gamma_3(a_3 + a_8 - a_{15}) + \gamma_4(a_9 + a_{35}(a_{16} - a_{10} \mp a_{11})).$$

The calculation of the medium and long-term equilibrium level of the relative price of non-tradable goods requires estimates of the parameters a_1 through a_{35}. As the results may depend on the estimation technique used to estimate equations (6.2) through (6.7) (Égert and Halpern, 2006), two alternative estimation techniques are employed. The first one is the full information maximum likelihood (FIML) technique proposed by Johansen (1995) and the second one is the dynamic OLS (DOLS) estimator advocated by Stock and Watson (1993). The latter technique involves adding leads and lags of changes in all explanatory variables to the equation. The number of leads and lags is initially set at one. The model is then simplified by successively eliminating insignificant leads and lags.

6.2 The Data Set

The data set consists of quarterly observations covering the period 1995:Q1 to 2005:Q4. The choice of the sample period is motivated by data availability concerns. Prior to the mid 1990s, no reliable data on the Lithuania economy exist. The primary source for the data is Eurostat. In cases where other data sources are used, this is explicitly specified.

The relative price of non-tradable to tradable goods R_N is calculated from sectoral price indices which are disaggregated at the NACE6 level. The sectors that are classified as tradable are agriculture, hunting, forestry, and fishing (AB); and total industry (CDE). The sectors that are classified as non-tradable are construction (F); wholesale and retail trade, repair of motor vehicles, motorcycles and personal and household goods, hotels and restaurants, transport, storage and communication (GHI); financial intermediation, real estate, renting and business activities (JK); and public administration and defence, compulsory social security, education, health and social work, other community, social and personal service activities, and private households with employed persons (LMNOP). The relative price of non-tradable to tradable goods is obtained as the ratio of the price index of non-tradable goods to the price index of tradable goods, where the two price indices are calculated as weighted averages of the price indices of the respective sectors.

The output of non-tradable goods Q_N is proxied by the total gross value added in the four non-tradable sectors F, GHI, JK, and LMNOP. Investment of non-tradable goods I_N is proxied by gross fixed investment in housing and other construction work. Investment in tradable goods is calculated as total investment minus investment in non-tradable goods and comprises investment in products of agriculture, forestry, fisheries, and aquaculture; metal products and machinery; transport equipment; and other products. Consumption of non-tradable goods C_N has to be inferred indirectly since the data are not available at quarterly frequency. C_N is therefore calculated by subtracting the investment of non-tradable goods from the total output of non-tradable goods, i.e., $C_N = Q_N - I_N$.[57] Consumption of tradable goods C_T is calculated by subtracting consumption of non-tradable goods from total consumption, i.e., $C_T = C - C_N$.

Data on the Lithuanian capital stock are not readily available, implying that the data have to be inferred indirectly as well. The capital stock at the end of 2000 is calculated by assuming that the ratio of the capital intensity to the wage rate in Lithuania equals the average of the corresponding ratios in Canada, Finland, France, Germany, Italy, Japan, the United Kingdom, and the United States (these are the only countries for which data on the total capital stock, i.e., business and residential housing, are available). For all eight countries, data on wage rates, employment and the capital stock are obtained from the OECD Economic Outlook database. Capital stock data for the remaining quarters are derived by employing the perpetual inventory method. The average annual rate of depreciation is calculated as the weighted average of the depreciation rates of the different investment categories. For simplicity, the rate of depreciation is set equal to 2 percent for housing and other construction work and equal to 10 percent for products of agriculture, forestry, fisheries, and aquaculture; metal products and machinery; transport equipment; and other products.

Time series data on net foreign debt is obtained by setting the net foreign debt level at the end of 2000 equal to the difference between foreign assets and foreign liabilities as provided by the International Financial Statistics database. For the remaining periods, the data are constructed assuming that the change in the net foreign asset position equals the current account balance.

As a measure for productivity in the non-tradable goods sector u_N labor productivity in the four non-tradable sectors F, GHI, JK, and LMNOP is

[57]Note that this strategy rests upon the assumption that non-tradable goods are not put on stock.

employed. The data are calculated by dividing the total gross value added in the four sectors by total employment in these sectors. Productivity in the tradable goods sector u_T is measured by labor productivity in the two remaining sectors AB and CDE.

The domestic and foreign nominal interest rates i and i^* are measured by the Lithuanian money market rate and the US treasury bill rate, respectively. Real interest rates are calculated as the difference between nominal interest rates and CPI inflation rates.[58] Data on interest rates and CPI inflation rates are obtained from the International Financial Statistics database. The terms of trade are calculated as the ratio between export and import prices.

The developments of the various variables are displayed in Figure 6.1. The relative price of non-tradable goods R_N rose rapidly over the second half of the 1990s, but then remained rather stable over recent years. The output of non-tradable goods as a share of total output, Q_N/Q, increased slightly over the past ten years and reached a level of 0.62 at the end of 2005. The ratio of non-tradable consumption to GDP, C_N/Q, increased during the first half of the observation period, although the development was characterized by several markable disruptions. During the second half of the sample, the ratio decreased steadily and reached 0.48 percent at the end of 2005. The ratio of tradable consumption to GDP, C_T/Q, decreased until mid 2002 and then remained rather stable at a level of around 0.33 percent. The developments of the shares of non-tradable and tradable investment in GDP, I_N/Q and I_T/Q were characterized by sizable fluctuations during the second half of the 1990s, though the average levels were pretty stable at around 0.13 and 0.09, respectively. During recent years, both ratios evolved relatively smoothly.

The capital coefficient K^r/Q^r decreased steadily over the past ten years and reached a level of 2.2 at the end of the sample period. By contrast, the net foreign debt to GDP ratio increased over the past ten years, with the growth rate slowing down markedly at the beginning of the new millennium. The two productivity indices u_T and u_N rose steadily over the past ten years, with the average growth rate being markedly higher in the tradable goods sector than in the non-tradable goods sector. This is to be expected as the potential for a productivity catch-up with respect to more advanced countries is higher in the tradable goods sector. The terms of trade also rose over the entire observation horizon. Overall, the rise in the terms of trade amounted to 35 percent between the first quarter of 1995 and the last quarter of 2005.

[58]It is assumed that economic agents have static expectations, implying that the real interest rate is an ex-post real interest rate.

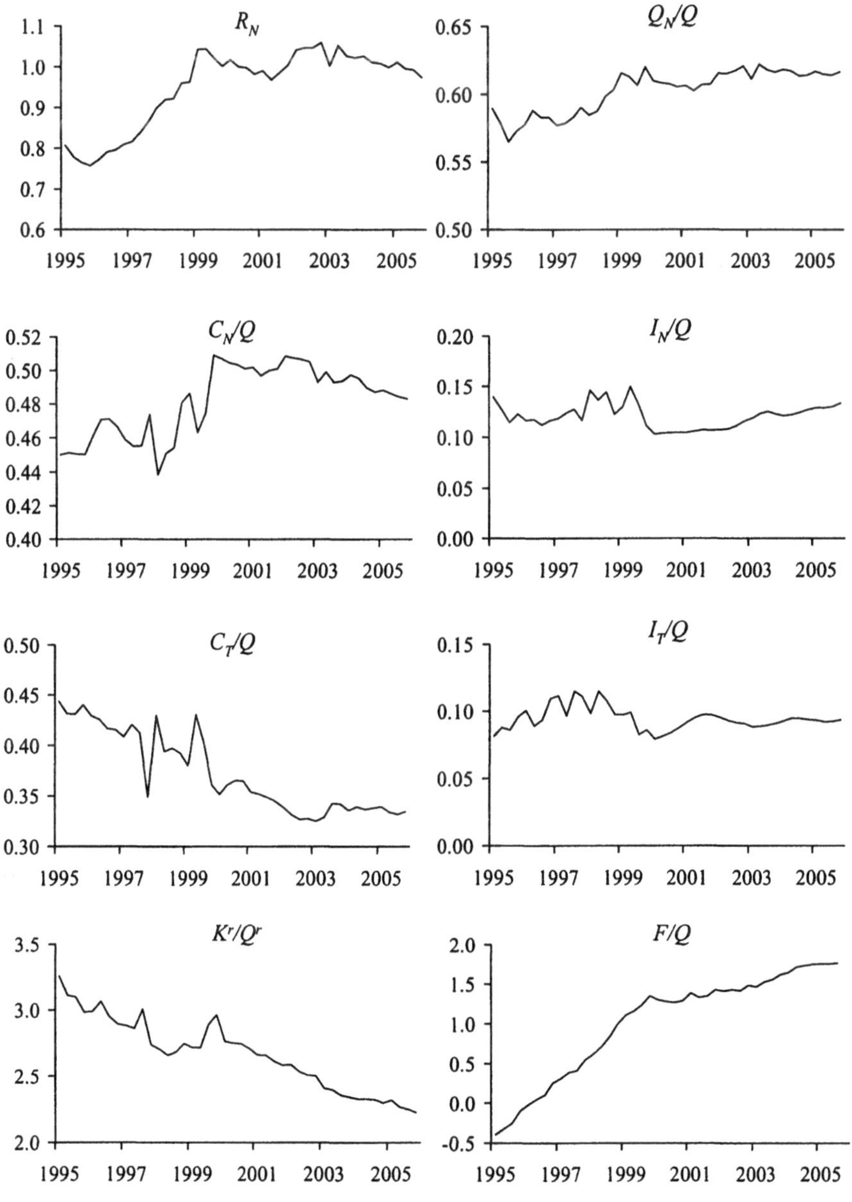

Figure 6.1: Development of Variables

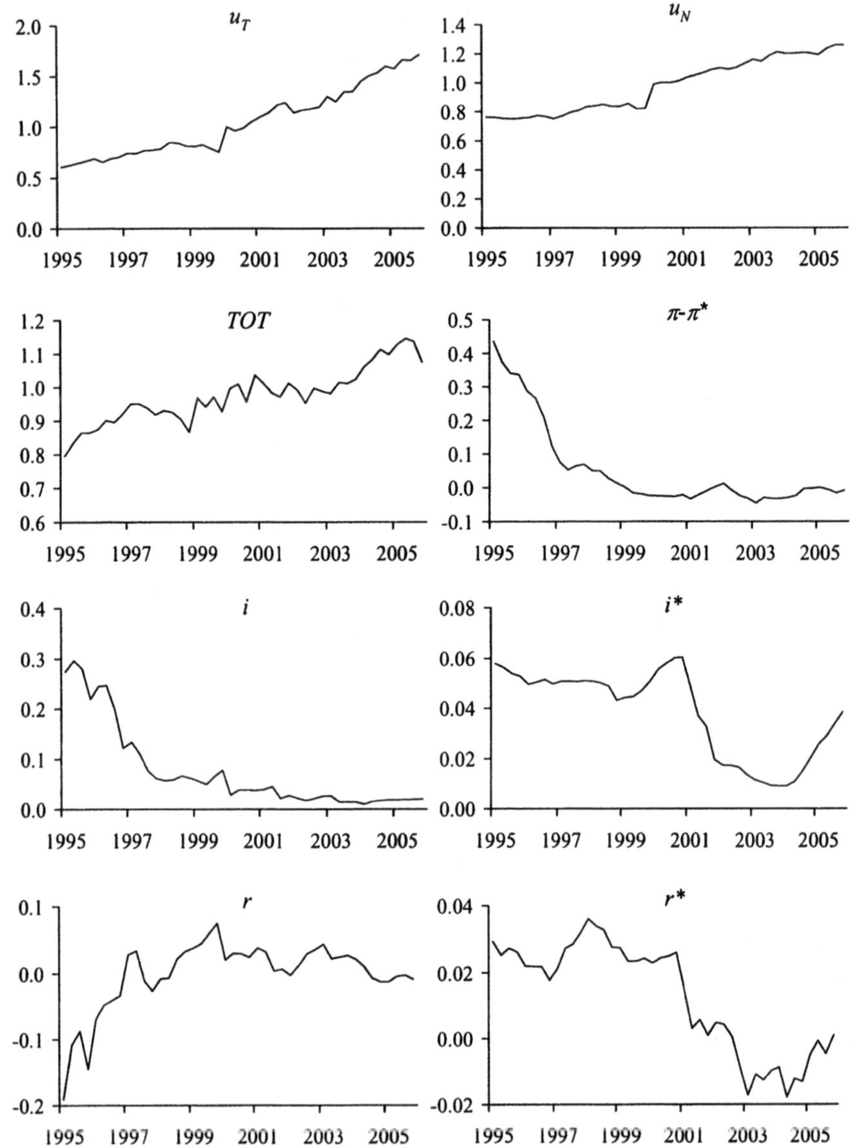

Figure 6.1: Development of Variables (cont.)

The inflation differential between Lithuania and the United States declined markedly during the first years of the sample as a result of the strong decline in the Lithuanian inflation rate from over 40 percent at the beginning of 1995 to below ten percent at the end of 1997. The inflation differential declined further during subsequent quarters and turned slightly negative in mid 1999.

Following the sharp decline in inflation, the Lithuanian nominal interest rate declined rapidly over the first years of the sample from around 27 percent in the first quarter of 1995 to around 6 percent in the fourth quarter of 1998. The interest rate continued to decline over subsequent years, albeit at a lower pace. The nominal interest rate of the United States slightly decreased over the first four years of the sample. During the new economy hype of the late 1990s, the nominal interest rate rose markedly and reached a level of 6 percent at the end of 2000. With the onset of the 2001 recession, the nominal interest rate started to decline and reached a level of just below one percent by the end of 2003. Since then, the nominal interest rate has risen again and reached almost four percent in the fourth quarter of 2005.

The real interest rate of Lithuania rose during the first years of the sample as the decline in the inflation rate outpaced the decline in the nominal interest rate. At the end of 1998, the real interest rate became positive for the first time and stayed positive until the end of 2004. During the year 2005, the real interest rate was slightly negative at around 0.9 percent. The real interest rate of the United States fluctuated around a level of three percent during the second half of the 1990s. During the 2001 recession, the real interest rate declined and became negative by the end of 2002. The real interest rate stayed negative until the fourth quarter of 2005, when it reached a level of slightly more than 1 percent.

6.3 Estimation Results

This section presents the empirical results of the analysis. Section 6.3.1 first discusses the results of the unit root and cointegration tests that serve as the basis for the estimation of the behavioral equations (6.2) through (6.6) and the portfolio balance equation (6.7). Section 6.3.2 then presents the estimated long-run relationships and derives the equilibrium relative price of non-tradable goods.

6.3.1 Unit Root and Cointegration Tests

As a preliminary step, the time series employed in the regressions are examined for the presence of a unit root. Two types of unit root tests are conducted, the ADF test by Dickey and Fuller (1979) which tests the null hypothesis of a unit root against the alternative hypothesis of stationarity and the KPSS test by Kwiatkowski et al. (1992) which has a reverse null hypothesis. The results of the tests are shown in Table 6.1. For several series, both the ADF test and the KPSS test indicate the presence of a unit root. These are the output of non-tradable goods, the consumption of tradable and non-tradable goods, the real capital stock (all as ratio to GDP), the relative price of non-tradable goods, productivity in the tradable and non-tradable goods sector, and the terms of trade. For the net foreign debt to GDP ratio, the nominal and real interest rate, and the real interest differential, the tests yield contradicting results. The KPSS test rejects the null hypothesis of no unit root, while the ADF test is unable to reject the null hypothesis of stationarity. Finally, for non-tradable and tradable investment as ratio to GDP, both tests suggest that the series are stationary. As there is evidence of a unit root in all series except for non-tradable and tradable investment, I conclude that the interrelationships between the series have to be analyzed within a cointegration framework.

The cointegration properties of the data are investigated by means of the trace and maximum eigenvalue tests proposed by Johansen (1988). The results of the tests are reported in Table 6.2. All systems contain a constant in the cointegration space and a separate constant in the error correction space. Given the small sample size, the lag length is set equal to unity in all behavioral equations. Diagnostic tests indicate that this lag length is sufficient to obtain residuals that are normally distributed and free from autocorrelation and heteroskedasticity (see the lower part of Table 6.4). In the portfolio balance equation, the number of endogenous variables is sufficiently small to select the lag length based on lag exclusion tests. The tests suggest that a lag length of six is appropriate for the model.

Table 6.2 shows that for the ratios of non-tradable and tradable consumption to GDP, both the trace test and the maximum eigenvalue test indicate the presence of a single cointegrating relationship at the one percent significance level. At the five percent significance level, the trace test finds a second cointegrating relationship for both non-tradable and tradeable consumption. However, this is not confirmed by the maximum eigenvalue test which indicates a second cointegrating relationship only for tradable consumption and

Table 6.1: Unit Root Tests

	ADF statistic	KPSS statistic
Q_N/Q	−1.395	0.701**
C_N/Q	−2.110	0.569**
I_N/Q	−2.843*	0.130
C_T/Q	−1.353	0.791***
I_T/Q	−2.860**	0.160
R_N	−1.511	0.615**
K^r/Q^r	−1.537	0.814***
F/Q	−4.050***	0.768***
u_T	−0.047	0.817***
u_N	1.075	0.820***
i	−2.624*	0.646**
r	−4.370***	0.396*
TOT	−1.468	0.780***
$r - r^*$	−4.212***	0.579**

Note: ***, ** and * denote rejection of the null hypothesis of a unit root in the case of the ADF test and of stationarity in the case of the KPSS test at the 10%, 5% and 1% significance level, respectively.

only at the ten percent significance level. I therefore conclude that a single cointegrating relationship exists between the ratios of non-tradable and tradable consumption to GDP and the underlying economic fundamentals.

For the ratio of non-tradable investment to GDP, both tests point towards a single cointegrating relationship at the five percent significance level. For tradable investment, by contrast, the maximum eigenvalue test is unable to detect a cointegrating relationship, while the trace test finds a cointegrating relationship at the ten percent significance level. Despite this rather weak evidence in favor of cointegration, the remaining part of the analysis assumes that the ratio of tradable investment to GDP is cointegrated with the set of fundamentals specified in equation (6.6). This decision is supported by the fact that the error correction coefficient in the investment equation is significantly negative (see Table 6.4).

As regards the ratio of non-tradable output to GDP, both tests are unable to detect a cointegrating relationship. As setting the lag length in the VECM equal to two leaves the estimated coefficients virtually unchanged, but leads to a rejection of the hypothesis of no cointegration in favor of a

Table 6.2: Cointegration Tests

$x' = \left[\frac{C_N}{Q}, R_N, \frac{K^r}{Q^r}, \frac{F}{Q}, i, r, TOT\right]$				$x' = \left[\frac{I_N}{Q}, R_N, \frac{K^r}{Q^r}, r, u_T, u_N, TOT\right]$				$x' = \left[\frac{Q_N}{Q}, R_N, \frac{K^r}{Q^r}, u_T, u_N\right]$			
trace$(r\|k)$-test		max$(r, r+1)$-test		trace$(r\|k)$-test		max$(r, r+1)$-test		trace$(r\|k)$-test		max$(r, r+1)$-test	
H_0	statistic	H_0	statistic	H_0	statistic	H_0	statistic	H_0	statistic	H_0	statistic
$r = 0$	192.950***	$r = 0\|1$	77.030***	$r = 0$	150.191**	$r = 0\|1$	58.494**	$r = 0$	62.253	$r = 0\|1$	27.709
$r \leq 1$	115.920**	$r = 1\|2$	40.308	$r \leq 1$	91.698	$r = 1\|2$	36.374	$r \leq 1$	34.544	$r = 1\|2$	17.006
$r \leq 2$	75.612	$r = 2\|3$	32.388	$r \leq 2$	55.324	$r = 2\|3$	22.780	$r \leq 2$	17.539	$r = 2\|3$	11.454
$r \leq 3$	43.224	$r = 3\|4$	22.508	$r \leq 3$	32.544	$r = 3\|4$	18.571	$r \leq 3$	6.085	$r = 3\|4$	6.028
$r \leq 4$	20.716	$r = 4\|5$	13.719	$r \leq 4$	13.973	$r = 4\|5$	8.649	$r \leq 4$	0.057	$r = 4\|5$	0.057
$r \leq 5$	6.997	$r = 5\|6$	6.245	$r \leq 5$	5.324	$r = 5\|6$	4.592				
$r \leq 6$	0.752	$r = 6\|7$	0.752	$r \leq 6$	0.732	$r = 6\|7$	0.732				

$x' = \left[\frac{C_T}{Q}, R_N, \frac{K^r}{Q^r}, \frac{F}{Q}, i, r, TOT\right]$				$x' = \left[\frac{I_T}{Q}, R_N, \frac{K^r}{Q^r}, r, u_T, u_N, TOT\right]$				$x' = \left[r - r^*, \frac{F}{Q}\right]$			
trace$(r\|k)$-test		max$(r, r+1)$-test		trace$(r\|k)$-test		max$(r, r+1)$-test		trace$(r\|k)$-test		max$(r, r+1)$-test	
H_0	statistic	H_0	statistic	H_0	statistic	H_0	statistic	H_0	statistic	H_0	statistic
$r = 0$	201.833***	$r = 0\|1$	77.493***	$r = 0$	144.933*	$r = 0\|1$	45.396	$r = 0$	26.470**	$r = 0\|1$	15.040
$r \leq 1$	124.340**	$r = 1\|2$	45.990*	$r \leq 1$	99.537	$r = 1\|2$	34.685	$r \leq 1$	11.430***	$r = 1\|2$	11.430***
$r \leq 2$	78.350	$r = 2\|3$	29.582	$r \leq 2$	64.852	$r = 2\|3$	24.466				
$r \leq 3$	48.767	$r = 3\|4$	26.187	$r \leq 3$	40.386	$r = 3\|4$	21.590				
$r \leq 4$	22.581	$r = 4\|5$	13.602	$r \leq 4$	18.796	$r = 4\|5$	13.110				
$r \leq 5$	8.979	$r = 5\|6$	7.528	$r \leq 5$	5.686	$r = 5\|6$	5.615				
$r \leq 6$	1.451	$r = 6\|7$	1.451	$r \leq 6$	0.071	$r = 6\|7$	0.071				

Notes: ***, ** and * denote rejection of H_0 at the 10%, 5% and 1% significance level, respectively. The critical values are adjusted for the sample size employing the method by Cheung and Lai (1993).

single cointegrating relationship, I conclude that the ratio of non-tradable output to GDP is indeed cointegrated with economic fundamentals.

Finally, in the case of the real interest differential between Lithuania and the United States and the net foreign debt to GDP ratio, the trace test indicates the existence of a cointegrating relationship, while the maximum eigenvalue test does not. As the errors are somewhat platykurtic relative to the normal distribution and the trace test is more robust to violations of the normality assumption than the maximum eigenvalue test (Cheung and Lai, 1993b), I conclude that the real interest differential and the net foreign debt to GDP ratio are cointegrated.

6.3.2 Derivation of the Equilibrium Relative Price of non-tradable Goods

The estimation results for the five behavioral equations (6.2) to (6.6) and the portfolio balance equation (6.7) are reported in Tables 6.3 and 6.4. Table 6.3 refers to the dynamic OLS procedure of Stock and Watson (1993) and Table 6.4 refers to the full information maximum likelihood procedure of Johansen (1995). The lower parts of the two tables summarize several diagnostic statistics. As can be seen in Table 6.3, the residuals from the DOLS equations display some signs of serial correlation and heteroskedasticity. The standard errors are therefore calculated based on the Newey and West covariance matrix (Newey and West, 1987). The residuals are generally normally distributed except for relationship (6.4), where the distribution of the residuals is skewed to the right and leptokurtic relative to the normal distribution. Augmented Dickey-Fuller unit root tests reveal that the residuals from the entire equations are all stationary. However, when applying the tests to the residuals from the hypothesized cointegrating relationships, the tests are only able to reject the null hypothesis of a unit root for equation (6.4). Looking at the diagnostic tests of the FIML estimates reported in the lower part of Table 6.4 shows that the residuals are generally normally distributed and free from serial correlation and heteroskedasticity.

The estimated equilibrium relationships are reported in the upper parts of Tables 6.3 and 6.4, respectively. Likelihood ratio tests of exclusion restrictions on the left-hand-side variables of the behavioral equations clearly reject the hypothesis that these variables are not part of the cointegrating vector. Hence, the estimated relationships are meaningful to interpret in the context of the NATREX model. Yet, looking at the estimates of the portfolio balance relationship shows that the real interest rate differential is only marginally significant with a p-value of 0.18.

Looking at the estimated coefficients on the left-hand-side variables shows that the signs and magnitudes of these coefficients are very similar across the two estimation techniques for the first three behavioral equations, i.e., equations (6.2) through (6.4). The ratio of the output of non-tradable goods to GDP, Q_N/Q, is positively related to the relative price of non-tradable goods R_N and to productivity in the non-tradable goods sector u_N, but negatively related to the capital coefficient K^r/Q^r and to productivity in the tradable goods sector u_T. These results are consistent with the predictions of the NATREX model. However, in the DOLS estimation, the relative price of non-tradable goods and the productivity in the non-tradable goods sector are only marginally significant with p-values of 0.156 and 0.197, respectively. In the FIML estimation, likelihood ratio tests of exclusions restrictions on the various coefficients reveal that the ratio of the capital coefficient may be excluded from the cointegrating vector. The corresponding p-value is 0.226.

The ratio of non-tradable consumption to GDP, C_N/Q, turns out to be negatively related to the relative price of non-tradable goods R_N, to the nominal interest rate i, and to the real interest rate r. It is positively related to the ratios of the capital stock and the net foreign debt level to GDP, K^r/Q^r and F/Q, and to the terms of trade TOT. Unfortunately, the signs of the coefficients on the nominal interest rate and the net foreign debt to GDP ratio do not comply with the predictions of the model. Moreover, the coefficient on K^r/Q^r does not come out as insignificant in the FIML estimation.

The ratio of non-tradable investment to GDP, I_N/Q, is negatively related to the capital stock to GDP ratio K^r/Q^r, the real interest rate r, and the terms of trade TOT. While the coefficient on K^r/Q^r is highly significant in both specifications, the coefficient on r is not significant in the FIML specification and the coefficient on TOT is not significant in the DOLS specification. Regarding the impact of productivity developments, the ratio of non-tradable investment to GDP turns out to be positively affected by productivity increases in the tradable goods sector (though the impact is not significant in the DOLS specification), but negatively affected by productivity increases in the non-tradable goods sector. The latter result is not in line with expectations, as productivity increases are expected to stimulate investment activities, irrespective of the sectoral composition. For the relative price of non-tradable goods R_N, the DOLS estimates point to a positive impact which is not in line with the model's predictions whereas the FIML estimates indicate that the variable may be excluded from the cointegrating vector at a p-value of 0.378.

Table 6.3: DOLS Estimates

Implied long-run relationships						
Equation	(6.2)	(6.3)	(6.4)	(6.5)	(6.6)	(6.7)
LHS variable	Q_N/Q	C_N/Q	I_N/Q	C_T/Q	I_T/Q	$r - r^*$
R_N	0.102 (0.000)	−0.293 (0.003)	0.064 (0.001)	−0.081 (0.297)	−0.033 (0.034)	
K^r/Q^r	−0.010 (0.226)	0.016 (0.037)	−0.136 (0.000)	0.102 (0.000)	−0.031 (0.003)	
F/Q		0.099 (0.000)		−0.021 (0.187)		0.069 (0.000)
u_T	−0.018 (0.036)		0.005 (0.821)		0.000 (0.999)	
u_N	0.048 (0.005)		−0.213 (0.000)		−0.040 (0.157)	
i		−0.102 (0.051)		−0.058 (0.537)		
r		−0.120 (0.010)	−0.194 (0.000)	−0.016 (0.821)	0.045 (0.200)	
TOT		−0.449 (0.000)	−0.025 (0.452)	0.183 (0.004)	0.000 (0.998)	
C	0.504 (0.000)	1.077 (0.000)	0.650 (0.000)	0.007 (0.947)	0.245 (0.000)	−0.088 (0.000)
Diagnostic statistics						
Adjusted R^2	0.946	0.914	0.794	0.953	0.759	0.759
Jarque-Bera	0.266 (0.875)	0.387 (0.842)	20.645 (0.000)	1.713 (0.425)	0.593 (0.743)	3.825 (0.148)
White heteroskedasticity	23.649 (0.167)	25.649 (0.693)	32.670 (0.067)	29.521 (0.687)	31.935 (0.371)	6.942 (0.139)
Breusch-Godfrey LM1	5.893 (0.015)	0.324 (0.569)	0.665 (0.415)	3.453 (0.063)	2.154 (0.142)	15.036 (0.000)
Breusch-Godfrey LM4	8.182 (0.085)	8.188 (0.085)	6.370 (0.173)	5.839 (0.211)	9.458 (0.051)	16.588 (0.002)
ARCH LM1	0.656 (0.418)	0.805 (0.369)	7.376 (0.007)	1.563 (0.211)	1.334 (0.248)	0.577 (0.448)
ARCH LM4	22.367 (0.000)	7.002 (0.136)	1.718 (0.787)	8.152 (0.086)	1.735 (0.784)	11.049 (0.026)
ADF, entire equation	−4.587	−5.633	−8.510	−8.075	−7.910	−3.003
ADF, cointegrating equation	−4.500	−2.149	−5.781	−3.012	−1.972	−4.164

Notes: LM1 and LM4 refer to Lagrange multiplier tests at lag 1 and at lags 1 to 4, respectively. p-values in parentheses. LHS = left-hand-side

Table 6.4: FIML Estimates

	(6.2)		(6.3)		(6.4)		(6.5)		(6.6)		(6.7)	
	β	α	β	α	β	α	β	α	β	α	β	α
LHS variable	−1.000 (0.003)	−0.634 (0.004)	−1.000 (0.020)	−0.132 (0.002)	−1.000 (0.000)	−0.525 (0.003)	−1.000 (0.036)	−0.103 (0.029)	−1.000 (0.014)	−0.423 (0.049)	−1.000 (0.180)	0.009 (0.981)
R_N	0.073 (0.156)	−1.453 (0.083)	−0.624 (0.003)	−0.436 (0.000)	0.026 (0.378)	−2.147 (0.001)	0.499 (0.030)	0.309 (0.001)	−0.008 (0.837)	2.647 (0.003)		
K^{τ}/Q^{τ}	−0.037 (0.062)	−1.714 (0.527)	0.039 (0.298)	0.081 (0.821)	−0.133 (0.000)	−2.206 (0.177)	0.073 (0.235)	0.155 (0.627)	−0.038 (0.058)	−0.229 (0.909)		
F/Q			0.107 (0.110)	−0.865 (0.002)			−0.042 (0.467)	0.757 (0.001)			0.105 (0.072)	1.339 (0.106)
u_T	−0.035 (0.106)	1.807 (0.265)			0.067 (0.090)	1.167 (0.355)			−0.070 (0.617)	−2.915 (0.085)		
u_N	0.055 (0.197)	1.646 (0.033)			−0.279 (0.000)	−0.424 (0.521)			0.029 (0.175)	−0.178 (0.866)		
i			−0.012 (0.000)	−0.220 (0.027)			0.016 (0.000)	0.226 (0.004)				
r			−0.009 (0.000)	−0.243 (0.035)	−0.024 (0.713)	−0.089 (0.877)	0.011 (0.000)	0.260 (0.004)	−0.102 (0.279)	−6.986 (0.926)		
TOT			−0.882 (0.000)	−0.026 (0.868)	−0.109 (0.113)	−0.495 (0.502)	0.908 (0.000)	−0.043 (0.745)	0.134 (0.120)	−0.322 (0.771)		
C	0.614		1.812		0.758		−1.260		0.118		−0.120	
Jarque-Bera	14.495 (0.152)		16.512 (0.283)		13.617 (0.479)		14.198 (0.435)		10.917 (0.693)		6.864 (0.143)	
Autocorrel. LM1	25.552 (0.432)		45.958 (0.597)		52.970 (0.324)		50.929 (0.398)		59.792 (0.139)		2.534 (0.639)	
Autocorrel. LM4	19.092 (0.793)		52.666 (0.334)		48.706 (0.485)		62.566 (0.092)		49.715 (0.445)		2.174 (0.704)	
Heteroskedasticity	201.165 (0.134)		504.828 (0.033)		497.601 (0.052)		482.206 (0.128)		463.889 (0.292)		86.077 (0.249)	

Notes: LM1 and LM4 refer to Lagrange multiplier tests of serial correlation at lag 1 and at lag 4, respectively. The numbers in parentheses denote the p-values of likelihood ratio tests on exclusion restrictions on the coefficients and the p-values of the diagnostic tests, respectively.

Turning to the two equations that relate to consumption and investment of the tradable good T, Tables 6.3 and 6.4 show that the estimation results differ markedly across the two different estimation procedures. When estimating the relationship between the ratio of tradable consumption to GDP and economic fundamentals with the Johansen procedure, the coefficients on all fundamentals are correctly signed, although likelihood ratio tests indicate that the capital stock and the net foreign debt to GDP ratios may be excluded from the cointegrating vector. When estimating the same relationship with DOLS, all coefficients come out as insignificant, except for the capital stock to GDP ratio and the terms of trade. The two significant coefficients have the expected positive sign.

When estimating the relationship between the GDP share of the investment of tradable goods and economic fundamentals, most of the coefficients come out as insignificant. The DOLS estimation shows that I_T/Q is negatively affected by the capital stock to GDP ratio and the relative price of non-tradable goods - the latter result not being in line with the model. All remaining coefficients are not significant at conventional significance levels. Johansen's FIML procedure suggests that I_T/Q is influenced by the capital stock to GDP ratio and the terms of trade. The direction of the impact complies with expectations in both cases.

For the relationship between the real interest rate differential and the net foreign debt to GDP ratio, the two estimation procedures yield again very similar results. The real interest differential is positively related to the net foreign debt to GDP ratio, meaning that a higher net foreign debt level raises the risk perception of investors who, in turn, demand a higher risk premium.

Table 6.4 also shows the adjustment coefficients of the vector error correction models. The adjustment coefficients on the right-hand-side variables of the five behavioral equations are significantly negative, implying that these variables respond to any misalignment in order to correct this misalignment. The ratio of the capital stock to GDP is weakly exogenous in all cases as indicated by the insignificant error correction parameter. The same holds true for the terms of trade, a finding that is perfectly in line with the model assumption that Lithuania is small in the sense that it can not influence the prices of its imports and exports. Moreover, productivity in the non-tradable goods sector and the real interest rate are weakly exogenous in the two investment equations, and productivity in the tradable goods sector is weakly exogenous in the equations on non-tradable output and investment. In the portfolio balance equation, the real interest rate differential turns out to be weakly exogenous. This is rather surprising, as one would usually expect

Table 6.5: The Impact of Fundamentals on $\tilde{R}_N$ and $\bar{R}_N$

	$\tilde{R}_N$		$\bar{R}_N$	
	DOLS	FIML	DOLS	FIML
K^r/Q^r	−	−	NA	NA
F/Q	+	−	NA	NA
u_T	+	+	+	+
u_N	−	−	−	−
$i^* + \pi - \pi^*$	−	−	−	−
r^*	−	−	−	−
TOT	−	−	−	+

Note: '+' ('−') indicates that $\tilde{R}_N$ and $\bar{R}_N$ are positively (negatively) affected by a change in the underlying fundamental variable.

the domestic real interest rate to respond to deviations from equilibrium. Imposing weak exogeneity restrictions on the VECMs hardly affects any of the remaining coefficients. The following discussion therefore focuses on the unrestricted estimates.

Figures 6.2 and 6.3 display the actual values of Q_N/Q, C_N/Q, I_N/Q, C_T/Q, I_T/Q, and r together with the medium-run values implied by the DOLS and FIML estimates, respectively.[59] Although the actual values deviated markedly from their medium-run levels in several quarters, these deviations where usually eliminated very quickly. Two exceptions are the GDP shares of non-tradable and tradable consumption. For the first half of the sample, the DOLS estimates suggest that the actual values of the two ratios were consistently above and below their medium-run value, respectively.

The estimated coefficients can be inserted into equations (6.13) and (6.16) in order to calculate how the medium and long-run equilibrium levels of the relative price of non-tradable goods are affected by changes in the underlying fundamentals. As shown in Table 6.5, the medium-run equilibrium relative price of non-tradable goods $\tilde{R}_N$ is positively related to productivity in the tradable goods sector u_T, and negatively related to the capital stock to GDP ratio K^r/Q^r, productivity in the non-tradable goods sector u_N, the foreign nominal interest rate less the CPI inflation differential $i^* + \pi - \pi^*$, the foreign

[59]Note that in the terminology of the NATREX model, the calculated equilibrium paths represent medium-run equilibria as the actual values of K^r/Q^r and F/Q are employed in the calculations.

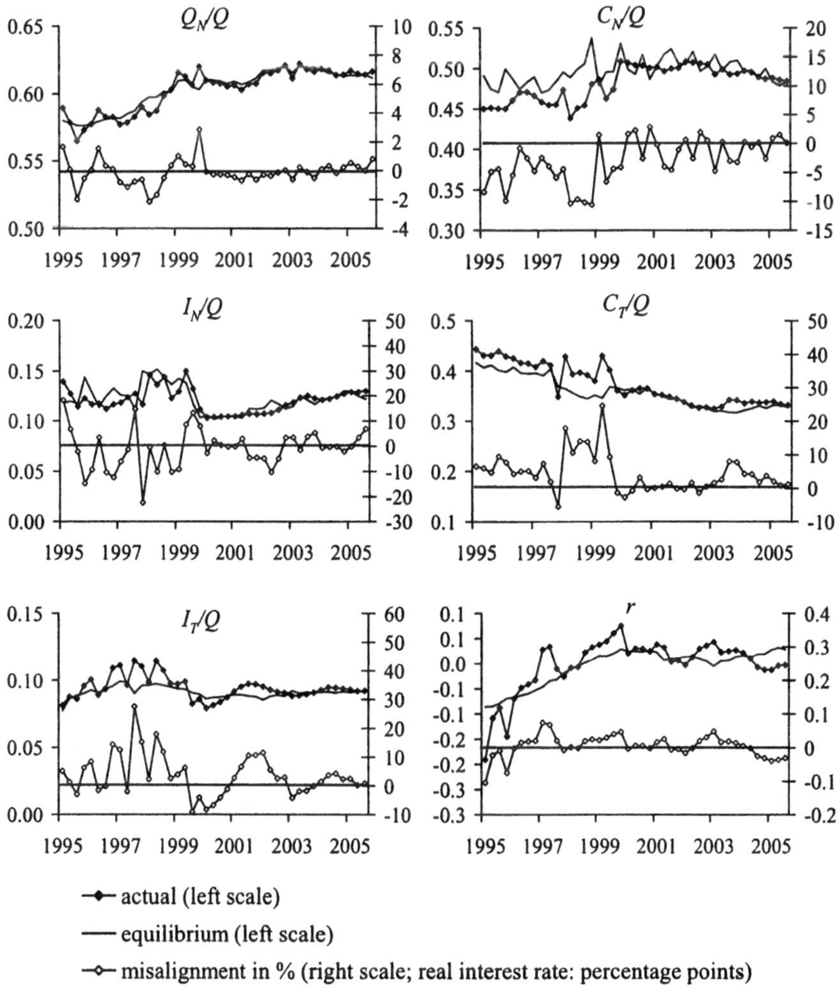

Figure 6.2: Actual and Implied Medium-run Levels of Output, Consumption, Investment, and the Real Interest Rate - DOLS

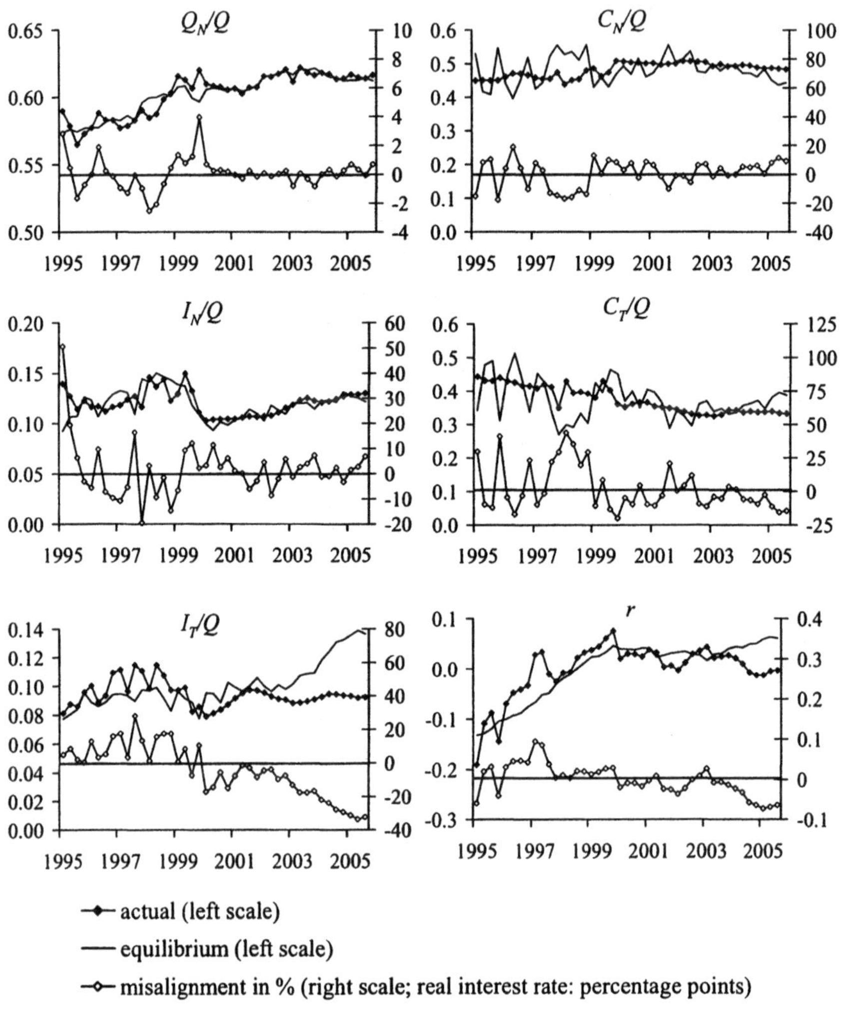

Figure 6.3: Actual and Implied Medium-run Levels of Output, Consumption, Investment, and the Real Interest Rate - FIML

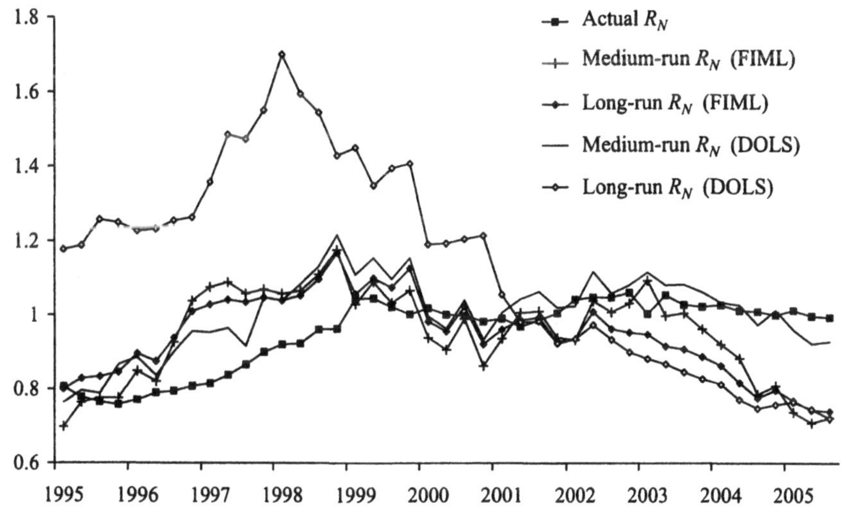

Figure 6.4: Actual and Equilibrium Paths of the Relative Price of non-tradable Goods

real interest rate, and the terms of trade. Among these variables, only K^r/Q^r and $i^* + \pi - \pi^*$ influence the medium-term equilibrium exchange rate in a way that does not comply with the NATREX model (see Appendix A1 in chapter 5). The impact of the net foreign debt to GDP ratio F/Q differs across the two estimation procedures. The DOLS estimates imply a positive relationship between F/Q and $\tilde{R}_N$, whereas the FIML estimates imply a negative relationship. The latter result is in line with the implications of the NATREX model.

In the long-run, K^r/Q^r and F/Q are endogenous to the model, so that $\bar{R}_N$ is ultimately only influenced by u_T, u_N, $i^* + \pi - \pi^*$, r^*, and TOT. The FIML estimates suggest that $\bar{R}_N$ increases with a rise in u_T, while the DOLS estiamtes suggest that $\bar{R}_N$ increases with a rise in u_T and TOT, but decreases with a rise in u_N, $i^* + \pi - \pi^*$, and r^*. All of these findings are in line with the predictions of the model (see Appendix A2 in chapter 5).

Based on equations (6.13) and (6.16) the medium and long-run equilibrium paths of the relative price of non-tradable goods can be derived from the estimated coefficients.[60] The results of the calculations are displayed in

[60]Note that the results of this analysis are not directly comparable to the results obtained in chapter 5 due to the diverging definitions of the real exchange rate. The analysis in

Figure 6.4 together with the actual relative price of non-tradable goods. The calculations reveal that the relative price of non-tradable goods was slightly undervalued with respect to its medium-term equilibrium at the beginning of the sample in 1995, but more or less in line with respect to the long-term equilibrium level derived from the FIML estimates. The DOLS estimates point to a much higher long-term equilibrium relative price of non-tradable goods, suggesting that the actual relative price of non-tradable goods was heavily undervalued at the beginning of 1995.

During the period 1995-1998, the medium- and long-run levels of the relative price of non-tradable goods rose by approximately 15 percent per annum. While the actual relative price of non-tradable goods also increased during this period, the rate of growth was notably lower compared to the growth rate of the equilibrium levels, so that the relative price fell below all calculated equilibrium levels in mid 1995. In 1998, all four equilibrium levels started to decline. While the long-run equilibrium level calculated from the DOLS estimates started to decline already at the beginning of 1998, the other three equilibrium levels did not follow before the third quarter of 1998. The decline in the equilibrium levels brought the actual relative price of non-tradable goods back in line with fundamentals. From the first quarter of 1999 onwards, the actual relative price of non-tradable goods was essentially in equilibrium with respect to the two medium-term levels and also with respect to the long-term level calculated from the FIML estimates.

Since 1999, the actual relative price of non-tradable goods has remained rather stable as did the medium-term equilibrium level derived from the DOLS estimates. As the medium-term equilibrium level derived from the FIML estimates started to decline in mid 2002, the actual relative price became undervalued with respect to this measure. Regarding the long-run equilibrium level, both the DOLS and the FIML estimates point towards a decline in the equilibrium level, meaning that the actual relative price became undervalued with respect to its long-term equilibrium path. Towards the end of the sample, the undervaluation amounted to 19 percent for the DOLS estimates and to 25 percent for the FIML estimates.

---

chapter 5 concentrated on the external real exchange rate, while this chapter focuses on the internal real exchange rate.

6.4 Summing up

This chapter investigated recent developments in the internal real exchange rate of Lithuania using a small country version of the NATREX approach. The model was estimated in structural form which guaranteed that the analytical conditions for equilibrium were met and, additionally, made it possible to verify whether the underlying behavioral relationships were in line with the predictions of the structural model.

The structural relationships were estimated using two alternative estimation techniques, the DOLS estimator advocated by Stock and Watson (1993) and Johansen's (1995) FIML procedure. For the three behavioral equations that relate to the non-tradable goods market and for the portfolio balance equations, the two estimation methodologies yielded very similar results. The overwhelming majority of the estimated coefficients was significant at conventional significant levels and correctly signed in terms of the underlying model. For the two behavioral equations that relate to the tradable goods market, the estimation results differed markedly across the two estimation procedures. Moreover, the hypothesis that the estimated coefficients are equal to zero could not be rejected in many cases.

Based on the estimated relationships, the medium and long-term equilibrium paths of the relative price of non-tradable goods were derived. The calculations showed that the relative price was below its medium and long-term levels from the mid-1990s onwards until about 1998. The decline in the equilibrium levels that set in in the course of 1998 brought the actual relative price of non-tradable goods back in line with fundamentals. In recent years, the actual relative price of non-tradable goods has remained rather stable, while the long-term equilibrium level has declined further, thus leading to an undervaluation from about 2003 onwards. Whether the actual relative price has also been undervalued with respect to its medium-term equilibrium depends on the employed estimation technique. While the FIML estimates pointed to an undervaluation, the DOLS estimates suggested that the relative price has been fairly valued in recent years.

Chapter 7

Implications of the Empirical Analyses

Since the beginning of the European Economic and Monetary Union in early 1999, the euro has gained considerable importance in international financial markets and has become the second most important currency after the US dollar. As a consequence, the evolution of the external value of the euro became the focus of a large body of research. This severe interest was even more fostered by the large fluctuations in the euro exchange rate that could be observed since the time of its launch. Moreover, the recent accession of ten countries from central and eastern Europe and the Mediterranean to the European Economic and Monetary Union raises the question how costly the adoption of the euro will be for these countries in terms of inflation differentials. If the real exchange rates of the new member countries change over time either because of corresponding changes in the equilibrium rates or because of substantial misalignments that call for a corrective step, tying these countries' nominal exchange rate to the euro means that any adjustment has to come through a higher inflation rate compared to the euro area.

This study addressed these questions by estimating equilibrium exchange rate paths for the euro and for the currencies of the new EU member countries. Chapters 3 and 4 first took a closer look at the nominal and real exchange rates of the euro. Specifically, chapter 3 investigated in how far variations in the nominal exchange rate of the euro vis-à-vis the U.S. dollar, the Canadian dollar, the British pound, the Norwegian krone, the Japanese yen, the Swiss franc, and the Australian dollar can be explained by the traditional monetary approach to the exchange rate. Four different versions of the monetary approach were taken into consideration, the flexible price versions of

Frenkel (1976) and Bilson (1978), and the sticky price versions of Dornbusch (1976) and Frankel (1979). Overall, the monetary approach was supported for only four out of seven bilateral exchange rates examined. These are the Australian dollar, the Canadian dollar, the Norwegian krone, and the US dollar. Moreover, a comparison of the out-of-sample forecasting performance of the monetary model to that of the simple random walk model revealed that the monetary model is unable to beat the random walk at any forecasting horizon. Hence, while there seems to be some scope for the monetary approach to explain the developments of the euro during the recent past, the model should not be used as the exclusive tool for evaluating exchange rate movements.

One obvious shortcoming of the monetary approach is the underlying assumption of a constant real exchange rate which is not reconcilable with the empirical evidence on the euro. Chapter 4 therefore made use of the natural real exchange rate approach advocated by Stein (1994) and Stein and Allen (1997), which explicitly focuses on movements in the real exchange rate. Compared to alternative real exchange rate models, the natural real exchange rate approach has the advantage that it builds on a structural model that explicitly distinguishes between the medium-term and the long-term equilibrium exchange rate. The estimates were used to evaluate in how far the large changes in the real effective exchange rate of the euro, that could be observed in recent years, represented movements in the underlying fundamentals. The calculations revealed that the euro was fairly in line with fundamentals at the time of its launch, though the sharp depreciation of the euro during the years 1999 to 2001 was not supported by fundamentals, so that the currency became heavily undervalued. The subsequent strong real appreciation of the euro over the period 2002 to 2004 led to a correction of the misalignment and by the end of 2004 the euro was more or less back in equilibrium. This suggests that the European Central Bank reacted appropriately when dismissing several demands by politicians to intervene in the foreign exchange market.

Chapters 5 and 6 of this study then took a closer look at the currencies of the central and eastern European countries that joined the European Union in May 2005. Both chapters employed a small country version of the natural real exchange rate approach in deriving equilibrium real exchange rate paths for these currencies. In chapter 5, a two step estimation strategy was used, where the long-run relationship between the real effective exchange rate and economic fundamentals was estimated for a group of 21 OECD countries in a first step, and the equilibrium real exchange rates of the new EU member countries were then derived in a second step by applying the estimated coefficients to data from these countries. This two-step estimation strategy had two important advantages. First, time series starting in 1980 could be used for the regression analysis, which made it more likely to capture the long-term relationship between the real exchange rate and economic fundamentals. Second, the influence of the transition effect present in the data of most of the new member countries could be avoided.

The calculations revealed that the equilibrium real exchange rates of all eight new EU member countries from central and eastern Europe appreciated over the past ten years. In the Czech Republic, Hungary, Lithuania, and, in recent years, Slovakia actual real exchange rates appreciated by even more, so that the currencies of these countries became undervalued in real effective terms. While the currencies of Poland and Latvia also became heavily overvalued in the second half of the 1990s, the recent depreciation of the Polish zloty and the Latvian lats brought these currencies back in line with fundamentals. Hence, the depreciation of these two currencies can be interpreted as a corrective step towards equilibrium. The observed real appreciation of the Estonian kroon over the past ten years was for the most part supported by economic fundamentals as the equilibrium rate appreciated by a similar amount. In the case of the Slovenian tolar, the appreciation of the actual real exchange rate did not keep up with the appreciation of the equilibrium rate, so that the currency became undervalued with respect to its long-term equilibrium path.

The findings obtained in the analysis have important implications for the countries' ability to comply with the convergence criteria laid down in the Maastricht Treaty. If the trend appreciation of the equilibrium real exchange rates is to continue over the coming years, tying the nominal exchange rates to the euro within the ERM II means that the adjustment has to come through inflation rates that exceed the inflation rate in the trading partner countries. As the set of trading partner countries consists to a large extend of euro area countries, the new EU member countries that participate in the ERM II might face higher inflation rates than the euro area, thus violating the Maastricht inflation criterion. Moreover, the substantial real exchange rate misalignments observed for a number of currencies means that some corrective steps might be required in the near future, further exacerbating the problem of simultaneously fulfilling the Maastricht inflation and exchange rate criteria.

Chapter 6 also made use of the small country NATREX model, though the analysis differed from the one in chapter 5 in several respects. First, while the analysis carried out in chapter 5 relied on the reduced form of the model, chapter 6 estimated the underlying behavioral relationships in structural form. As a structural estimation is very difficult to implement in terms of data availability, the model could only be estimated for the Lithuanian economy. Second, the definition of the real exchange rate differed between the two analyses. Chapter 5 focused on the external real exchange rate, defined as the price of the domestic currency in terms of the foreign currency, while chapter 6 focused on the internal real exchange rate, defined as the relative price of non-tradable to tradable goods. Due to this diverging definition of the real exchange rate, the results of the two chapters were not directly comparable. Overall, the analysis in chapter 6 revealed that the NATREX model is supported quite well by the Lithuanian data. Most of the estimated coefficients were in line with the predictions of the model, though in several cases the coefficients did not come out as significant in the estimations. Based on the estimated relationships, the medium and long-term equilibrium paths of the relative price of non-tradable goods were derived. The calculations revealed that the internal real exchange rate was undervalued with respect its medium and long-term equilibrium levels during the first years of the sample. Then, from 1999 onwards, it was fairly valued, though from mid-2002 onwards there have been signs of an overvaluation of the internal real exchange rate due to a decline in the equilibrium levels. Hence, a corrective adjustment of the actual internal real exchange rate may be warranted in the near future.

Bibliography

Abuaf, Niso and Philippe Jorion (1990): Purchasing power parity in the long run, *Journal of Finance*, Vol. 45, pp. 157-174.

Adler, Michael and Bruce Lehmann (1993): Deviations from purchasing power parity in the long run, *Journal of Finance*, Vol. 38, pp. 1471-1487.

Alberola, Enrique; Cervero, Susana G.; Lopez, J. Humberto and Angel Ubide (1999): Global equilibrium exchange rates: Euro, dollar, 'Ins', 'Outs', and other major currencies in a panel cointegration framework, IMF Working Paper No. 99/175.

Allen, Polly R. (1997): The economic and policy implications of the NATREX approach, in: Stein, Jerome L. and Polly R. Allen (eds.): *Fundamental determinants of exchange rates*, Oxford University Press, Oxford.

Alonso-Gamo, Patricia; Fabrizio, Stefania; Kramarenko, Vitali and Qing Wang (2002): Lithuania: History and future of the currency board arrangement, IMF Working Paper No. 02/127.

Alquist, Ron and Menzie D. Chinn (2002): Productivity and the euro-dollar exchange rate puzzle, NBER Working Paper No. 8824.

Amano, Robert B. and Tony S. Wirjanto (2000): On the stability of long-run M2 demand in Japan, *The Japanese Economic Review*, Vol. 51, No. 4, pp. 536-543.

Artis, Michael J. and Mark P. Taylor (1995): The effect of misalignment on desired equilibrium exchange rates: Some analytical results, in: Bordes, Christian; Girardin, Eric and Jacques Mélitz (eds.): *European currency crisis and after*, Manchester University Press, Manchester.

Artus, Jacques (1978): Methods of assessing the long-run equilibrium value of an exchange rate, *Journal of International Economics*, Vol. 8, pp. 277-299.

Artus, Jacques and Malcolm Knight (1984): Issues in the assessment of the exchange rates of the industrial countries: A study by the research department, IMF Occasional Paper No. 29.

Asano, Hirokatsu (1999): Financial deregulation and stability of money demand: The Australian case, *Australian Economic Papers*, Vol. 38, No. 4, pp. 407-421.

Backé, Peter; Fidrmuc, Jarko; Reininger, Thomas and Franz Schardax (2003): Price dynamics in central and eastern European EU accession countries, *Emerging Markets Finance and Trade*, Vol. 39, No. 3, pp. 42-78.

Backus, David (1984): Empirical models of the exchange rate: Separating the wheat from the chaff, *Canadian Journal of Economics* , Vol. 17, pp. 824-846.

Bahmani-Oskooee, Mohsen (2001): How stable is M2 money demand function Japan?, *Japan and the World Economy*, Vol. 13, pp. 455-461.

Balassa, Bela (1964): The purchasing-power-parity doctrine: A reappraisal, *Journal of Political Economy*, Vol. 72, No. 6, pp. 584-596.

Bårdsen, Gunnar (1992): Dynamic modelling of the demand for narrow money in Norway, *Journal of Policy Modelling*, Vol. 14, No. 3, pp. 363-393.

Barrell, Ray and Simon Wren-Lewis (1989): Fundamental equilibrium exchange rates for the G7, CEPR Discussion Paper No. 323.

Bayoumi, Tamim; Clark, Peter; Symansky, Steve and Mark P. Taylor (1994): The robustness of equilibrium exchange rate calculations of alternative assumptions and methodologies, in: Williamson, John (ed.): *Estimating equilibrium exchange rates*, Institute for International Economics, Washington D.C.,

Begg, David; Halpern, László and Charles Wyplosz (1999): Monetary exchange rate policies, EMU and central and eastern Europe, Fifth Forum Report of the Economic Policy Initiative, CEPR, London, and East-West Institute, New York.

Beveridge, Stephen and Charles R. Nelson (1981): A new approach to decomposition of economic time series into permanent and transitory components with particular attention to measurement of the business cycle, *Journal of Monetary Economics*, Vol. 7, pp. 151-174.

Bilson, John F. O. (1978): Rational expectations and the exchange rate, in: Frenkel, Jacob A. and Harry G. Johnson (eds.): *The economics of exchange rates: Selected studies*, Addison-Wesley, Reading, Massachusetts.

Borowski, Didier and Cécile Couharde (2003): The exchange rate macroeconomic balance approach: New methodology and results for the euro, the dollar, the yen and the pound sterling, *Open Economies Review*, Vol. 14, pp. 169-190.

Bulíř, Aleš and Katařina Šmídková (2005): Exchange rates in the new EU accession countries: What have we learned from the forerunners?, *Economic Systems*, Vol. 29, No. 2, pp. 163-186.

Brand, Claus and Nuno Cassola (2000): A money demand system for euro area M3, ECB Working Paper No. 39.

Breitung, Jorg (2000): The Local Power of Some Unit Root Tests for Panel Data, in: Baltagi, Badi H. (ed.): *Advances in Econometrics*, Vol. 15, Elsevier Science, Amsterdam; New York and Tokyo.

Briseman, S. (1933): Some refections on the theory of foreign exchange, in: *Economic Essays in Honour of Gustav Cassel*, Allen and Unwin, London, pp. 69-74.

Bruggeman, Annick; Donati, Paola and Anders Warne (2003): Is the demand for euro area M3 stable?, ECB Working Paper No. 255.

Burgess, Robert; Fabrizio, Stefania and Yuan Xiao (2003): Competitiveness in the Baltics in the run-up to EU accession, IMF Country Report No. 114.

Calza, Alessandro; Gerdesmeier, Dieter and Joaquim Levy (2001): Euro area money demand: Measuring the opportunity costs appropriately, IMF Working Paper No. 01/179.

Calza, Alessandro and João Sousa (2003): Why has broad money demand been more stable in the euro area than in other economies? A literature review, ECB Working Paper No. 261.

Carlson, John B.; Hoffman, Dennis L.; Keen, Benjamin D.; and Robert H. Rasche (2000): results of a study of the stability of cointegrating relations comprised of broad monetary aggregates, *Journal of Monetary Economics*, Vol. 46, No. 2, pp. 345-383.

Carlson, John B. and Sharon E. Parrott (1991): The demand for M2, opportunity cost, and financial change, *Federal Reserve Bank of Cleveland Economic Review*, Vol. 27, No. 2, pp. 2-11.

Carlson, John B. and Jeffrey C. Schwarz (1999): Effects of movements in equities prices on M2 demand, *Federal Reserve Bank of Cleveland Economic Review*, Vol. 35, No. 1, pp. 2-9.

Cassel, Gustav (1918): Abnormal deviations in international exchanges, *Economic Journal*, Vol. 28, pp. 62-65.

Cheung, Yin-Wong and Kon S. Lai (1993a): A fractional cointegration analysis of purchasing power parity, *Journal of Business and Economic Statistics*, Vol. 11, pp. 103-112.

Cheung, Yin-Wong and Kon S. Lai (1993b): Finite sample sizes of Johansen's likelihood ratio test for cointegration, *Oxford Bulletin of Economics and Statistics*, Vol. 55, pp. 313-328.

Chinn, Menzie D. (2000): The empirical determinants of the euro: Short and long run perspectives, mimeo, National Bureau of Economic Research.

Chinn, Menzie D. (2004), Measuring real effective exchange rates in: DeBrouwer, Gordon and Yunjong Wang (eds.): *Exchange Rate Regimes in East Asia*, Routledge Curzon, London.

Chinn, Menzie D. and Ron Alquist (2000): Tracking the euro's progress, *International Finance*, Vol. 3, No. 3, pp. 357-373.

Chowdhury, Abdur R. and Fabio Sdogati (1993): Purchasing power parity in the major EMS countries: The role of price and exchange rate adjustment, *Journal of Macroeconomics*, Vol. 15, pp. 25-45.

Clark, Peter B. and Ronald MacDonald (1998): Exchange rates and economic fundamentals: A methodological comparison of BEERs and FEERs, IMF Working Paper No. 98/67.

Clarida, Richard and Jordi Gali (1994): Sources of real exchange rate fluctuations: How important are nominal shocks, *Carnegie-Rochester Series on Public Policy*, Vol. 41, pp. 1-56.

Clark, Peter B. and Ronald MacDonald (2000): Filtering the BEER: A permanent and transitory decomposition, IMF Working Paper No. 00/144.

Clostermann, Jörg and Bernd Schnatz (2000): The determinants of the euro-dollar exchange rate: Synthetic fundamentals and a non-existing currency, *Applied Economics Quarterly*, Vol. 46, pp. 274-302.

Coakley, Jerry and Ana-Maria Fuertes (1997): New panel unit root tests of PPP, *Economics Letters*, Vol. 57, pp. 17-22.

Coakley, Jerry and Stuart Snaith (2004): Testing for long run relative purchasing power parity in Europe, mimeo, University of Essex, Department of Accounting, Finance and Management and Essex Finance Centre.

Coenenm, Günter and Juan-Luis Vega (1999): The demand for M3 in the euro area, ECB Working Paper No. 6.

Corbae, P. Dean and Sam Ouliaris (1988): Cointegration and tests of purchasing power parity, *Review of Economics and Statistics*, Vol. 70, pp. 508-511.

Coricelli, Fabrizio and Bostjan Jazbec (2001): Real exchange rate dynamics in transition economies, *Structural Change and Economic Dynamics*, Vol. 15, pp. 83-100.

Coudert, Virginie and Cécile Couharde (2003): Exchange rate regimes and sustainable parities for CEECs in the run-up to EMU membership, *Revue Économique*, Vol. 54, No. 5, pp. 983-1012.

Crespo-Cuaresma, Jesús; Fidrmuc, Jarko and Ronald MacDonald (2005): The monetary approach to exchange rates in the CEECs, *Economics of Transition*, Vol. 13, No. 2, pp. 395-416.

Crespo-Cuaresma, Jesús; Fortin, Ines; and Jaroslava Hlouskova (2004): Evaluating euro exchange rate predictions from a battery of multivariate models, in: *Macroeconomic models and forecasts for Austria*, Proceedings of OeNB Workshops No. 5.

Crowder, William J. and Mark E. Wohar (2004): A cointegrated structural VAR model of the Canadian economy, *Applied Economics*, Vol. 36, pp. 195-213.

Cumby, Robert E. and John Huizinga (1990): The predictability of real exchange rate changes in the short run and in the long run, NBER Working Paper No. 3468.

Currie, David and Simon Wren-Lewis (1989): Evaluating blueprints for the conduct of international macro policy, *American Economic Review*, Vol. 79, No. 2, 264-269.

Darby, Michael R. (1980): Does purchasing power parity work?, NBER Working Paper No. 607.

De Broeck, Mark and Torsten Sløk (2001): Interpreting real exchange rate movements in transition countries, IMF Working Paper No. 01/56.

Detken, Carsten and Carmen Marín Martínez (2001): The effective euro equilibrium exchange rate since the 70's: A structural NATREX estimation, mimeo, European Central Bank.

Detken, Carsten; Dieppe, Alistair; Henry, Jérôme; Marín, Carmen and Frank Smets (2002), Model uncertainty and the equilibrium value of the real effective euro exchange rate, European Central Bank Working Paper No. 160.

Dickey, David A. and Wayne A. Fuller (1979): Distribution of the estimators for autoregressive time series with a unit root, *Journal of the American Statistical Association*, Vol. 74, pp. 427-431.

Diebold, Francis X. and Roberto S. Mariano (1995): Comparing predictive accuracy, Journal of Business and Economic Statistics, Vol. 13, No. 3, pp. 134-144.

Diebold, Francis X.; Husted, Steven and Mark Rush (1991): Real exchange rates under the gold standard, *Journal of Political Economy*, Vol. 99, pp. 1252-1271.

Dobrinsky, Rumen (2003): Convergence in per capita income levels, productivity dynamics and real exchange rates in the EU acceding countries, *Empirica*, Vol. 30, No. 3, pp. 305-334.

Dornbusch, Rudiger (1976): Expectations and exchange rate dynamics, *Journal of Political Economy*, Vol. 84, pp. 1161-1176.

Dornbusch, Rudiger (1979): Monetary policy under exchange rate flexibility, in: *Managed exchange-rate flexibility: The recent experience*, Federal Reserve Bank of Boston Conference Series No. 20, Federal Reserve Bank of Boston, Boston.

Dotsey, Michael; Lantz, Carl D.; and Santucci, Lawrence (2000): Is money useful in the conduct of monetary policy, *Federal Reserve Bank of Richmond Economic Quarterly*, Vol. 86, No. 4, pp. 23-48.

Driver, Rebecca L. and Peter F. Westaway (2004): Concepts of equilibrium real exchange rates, Bank of England Working Paper No. 248.

Duca, John V. (1995): Should bond funds be added to M2?, *Journal of Banking and Finance*, Vol. 19, pp. 131-152.

Dumas, Bernard (1992): Dynamic equilibrium and the real exchange in spatially separated world, *Review of Financial Studies*, Vol. 5, pp. 153-180.

Duval, Romain (2002): What do we know about long run equilibrium real exchange rates? PPPs vs. macroeconomic approaches, *Australian Economic Papers*, Vol. 41, pp. 382-403.

Edison, Hali J. and B. Dianne Pauls (1993): A re-assessment of the relationship between real exchange rates and real interest rates: 1974-90, *Journal of Monetary Economics*, Vol. 31, pp. 165-187.

Égert, Balázs (2002a): Investigating the Balassa-Samuelson hypothesis in the transition: Do we understand what we see? A panel study, *Economics of Transition*, Vol. 10, No. 2, pp. 273-309.

Égert, Balázs (2002b): Estimating the impact of the Balassa-Samuelson effect on inflation and the real exchange rate during the transition, *Economic Systems* Vol. 26. No. 1, pp. 1-16.

Égert, Balázs (2004): Assessing equilibrium exchange rates in CEE acceding countries: Can we have DEER with BEER without FEER? A Critical survey of the literature, BOFIT Discussion Paper No. 1.

Égert, Balázs (2005): The Balassa-Samuelson hypothesis in Estonia: Oil shale, tradable goods, regulated prices and other culprits, *The World Economy*, Vol. 28, No. 2. pp. 259-286.

Égert, Balázs; Drine, Imed; Lommatzsch, Kirsten and Christophe Rault (2003): The Balassa-Samuelson effect in Central and Eastern Europe: Myth or reality?, *Journal of Comparative Economics*, Vol. 31, No. 3, pp. 552-572.

Égert, Balázs and László Halpern (2006): Equilibrium exchange rates in central and eastern Europe: A meta-regression analysis. *Journal of Banking and Finance*, Vol. 30, No. 5, pp. 1359-1374.

Égert, Balázs, Halpern, László and Ronald MacDonald (2006): Equilibrium exchange rates in transition economies: Taking stock of the issues, *Journal of Economic Surveys*, Vol. 20, No. 2, pp. 257-324.

Égert, Balázs and Amina Lahrèche-Révil (2003): Estimating the fundamental equilibrium exchange rate of Central and Eastern European Countries: The challenge of EMU enlargement, *Review of World Economics*, Vol. 139, No. 4, pp. 683-708.

Égert, Balázs; Lahrèche-Révil, Amina and Kirsten Lommatzsch (2004): The stock-flow approach to the real exchange rate of transition economies, CEPII Working Paper No. 14.

Égert, Balázs and Kirsten Lommatzsch (2003): Equilibrium real exchange rates in acceding countries: How large is our confidence (interval)?, Focus on Transition 2/2003.

Eitrheim, Øyvind (1995): The demand for broad money and tests for neglected monetary effects on inflation: Empirical evidence for Norway 1969-1993, Norges Bank Working Paper No. 1995/8.

Eitrheim, Øyvind (1998): The demand for broad money in Norway, 1969-1993, *Empirical Economics*, Vol. 23, No. 3, pp. 339-354.

Enders, Walter (1988): ARIMA and cointegration tests of PPP under fixed and flexible exchange rate regimes, *Review of Economics and Statistics*, Vol. 70, pp. 504-508.

Engle, Robert F. and Clive W. J. Granger (1987): Co-integration and error correction: representation, estimation and testing, *Econometrica*, Vol. 55, No. 2, pp. 251-276.

European Central Bank (2005): *Review of the international role of the euro*, European Central Bank, Frankfurt am Main.

Fagan, Gabriel and Jérôme Henry (1998): Long run money demand in the EU: Evidence for area-wide aggregates, *Empirical Economics*, Vol. 23, No. 3, pp. 483-506.

Falk, Barry and Chun-Hsuan Wang (2003): Testing long-run PPP with infinite-variance returns, *Journal of Applied Econometrics*, Vol. 18, pp. 471-484.

Faruqee, Hamid and Guy Debelle (1998): Saving-investment balances in industrial countries: An empirical investigation, in: Isard, Peter and Hamid Faruqee (eds.): Exchange rate assessment: Extensions of the macroeconomic balance approach, IMF Occasional Paper No. 167.

Felmingham, Bruce and Qing Zhang (2001): The long run demand for broad money in Australia subject to regime shifts, Australian Economic Papers, Vol. 40, No. 2, pp. 146-155.

Filipozzi, Fabio (2000): Equilibrium exchange rate of the Estonian kroon, its dynamics and its impacts of deviations, Bank of Estonia Working Paper No. 3.

Fischer, Christoph (2004): Real currency appreciation in accession countries: Balassa-Samuelson and investment demand, *Review of World Economics*, Vol. 140, No. 2, pp. 179-210.

Fischer, Christoph and Karlhans Sauernheimer (2002): A history of the DMark's real external value, *Australian Economic Papers*, Vol. 41, pp. 480-498.

Fisher, Irving (1930): The Theory of Interest, The Macmillan Company, New York.

Fisher, Paul F. and Juna L. Vega (1993): An empirical analysis of M4 in the United Kingdom, Bank of England Working Paper No. 21.

Flood, Robert P. and Mark P. Taylor (1996): Exchange rate economics: What's wrong with the conventional macro approach?, in: Frankel, Jeffrey A.; Giampaolo, Galli and Alberto Giovannini (eds.): *The microstructure of foreign exchange markets*, University of Chicago Press, Chicago.

Frankel, Jeffrey A. and Andrew K. Rose (1996): A panel project on purchasing power parity: Mean reversion within and between countries, *Journal of International Economics*, Vol. 40, pp. 209-224.

Frankel, Jeffrey A. (1979): On the mark: A theory of floating exchange rates based on real interest differentials, *American Economic Review*, Vol. 69, pp. 610-622.

Frankel, Jeffrey A. (1984): Tests of monetary and portfolio balance models of exchange rate determination, in: Bilson, John F. O. and Richard C. Marston (eds.): *Exchange rate theory and practice*, University of Chicago Press, Chicago.

Frankel, Jeffrey A. (1996): How well do foreign exchange markets work: might a Tobin tax help?, in: Haq, Mahbub ul; Kaul, Inge; and Isabelle Grunberg (eds.): *The Tobin tax: Coping with financial volatility*, Oxford University Press, New York and Oxford.

Franses, Philip H. and Dick van Dijk (2006): A simple test for PPP among traded goods, *Applied Financial Economics*, Vol. 16, pp. 19-27.

Frenkel, Jacob A. (1976): A monetary approach to the exchange rate. Doctrinal aspects and empirical evidence, *Scandinavian Journal of Economics*, Vol. 78, No. 2, pp. 200-224.

Frenkel, Jacob A. (1981): The collapse of purchasing power parity during the 1970s, *European Economic Review*, Vol. 16, pp. 145-165

Frenkel, Jacob A. and Harry G. Johnson (1978): *The economics of exchange rates*, Addison-Wesley, Reading, Massachusetts.

Frenkel, Michael and Isabell Koske (2004): How well can monetary factors explain the exchange rate of the Euro, *Atlantic Economic Journal*, Vol. 32, No. 3, pp. 232-243.

Gandolfo, Giancarlo (1981): *Qualitative Analysis and Econometric Estimation of Continuous Time Dynamic Models*, North-Holland Publishing Company, Amsterdam.

Gandolfo, Giancarlo and Alberto Felettigh (1998): The NATREX: An alternative approach, Theory and empirical verifications, CIDEI Working Paper No. 52, La Sapienza, Rome.

Gerlach-Kristen, Petra (2001): The demand for money in Switzerland 1936-1995, *Swiss Journal of Economics and Statistics*, Vol. 137, No. 4, pp. 535-554.

Glen, Jack D. (1992): Real exchange rates in the short, medium, and ling run, *Journal of International Economics*, Vol. 33, pp. 147-166.

Golinelli, Roberto and Sergio Pastorello (2002): Modelling the demand for M3 in the euro area, *European Journal of Finance*, Vol. 8, No. 4, pp. 371-401.

Granger, Clive W. J. and Jesus Gonzalo (1995): Estimation of long-memory components in cointegrated systems, *Journal of Business Economics and Statistics*, Vol. 13, pp. 27-35.

Groen, Jan J. J. (2005): Exchange rate predictability and monetary fundamentals in a small multi-country panel, *Journal of Money, Credit, and Banking*, Vol. 37, No. 3, pp. 495-516.

Hadri, Kaddour (1999): Testing for stationarity in heterogeneous panel data, *Econometric Journal*, Vol. 3, pp. 148-161.

Halpern, László and Charles Wyplosz (1997): Equilibrium exchange rates in transition countries, *IMF Staff Papers*, Vol. 44, No. 4, pp. 430-461.

Halpern, László and Charles Wyplosz (2001): Economic transformation and real exchange rates in the 2000s: The Balassa-Samuelson connection, UNO Economic Survey of Europe, pp. 227-239.

Harris, David; Leybourne, Stephen; and Brendan McCabe (2005): Panel stationarity tests for purchasing power parity with cross-sectional dependence, *Journal of Business and Economic Statistics*, Vol. 23, No. 4, pp. 395-409.

Harvey, David; Leybourne, Stephen; and Paul Newbold (1997): Testing the Equality of Prediction Mean Squared Errors, International Journal of Forecasting, Vol. 13, No. 2, pp. 281-91.

Hasan, Mohammad S. (2006): A century of purchasing power parity: Evidence from Canada and Australia, *Applied Financial Economics*, Vol. 16, pp. 145-156.

Haug, Alfred A. and Robert F. Lucas (1996): Long-run money demand in Canada. In search of stability, *Review of Economics and Statistics*, Vol. 78, No. 2, pp. 345-348.

Haynes, Stephen E. and Joe A. Stone (1981): On the mark: Comment, *American Economic Review*, Vol. 71, pp. 1060-1067.

Hendry, David F. and Grayham E. Mizon (1998): Exogeneity causality, and co-breaking in economic policy analysis of a small econometric model of money in the UK, *Empirical Economics*, Vol. 23, No. 3, pp. 267-294.

Hodrick, Robert J. (1978): An empirical analysis of the monetary approach to the determination of the exchange rates, in: Frenkel, Jacob A. and Harry G. Johnson (eds.): *The economics of exchange rates*, Addison-Wesley, Reading, Massachusetts.

Hooper, Peter and John Morton (1982): Fluctuations in the dollar: A model of nominal and real exchange rate determination, *Journal of International Money and Finance*, Vol. 1, No. 1, pp. 39-56.

Hoque, Asraul and Naief Al-Mutairi (1996): Financial deregulation, demand for narrow money and monetary policy in Australia, *Applied Financial Economics*, Vol. 6, pp. 301-305.

Hubrich, Kirstin (1999): *Cointegration analysis in a German monetary System*, Physica-Verlag, Heidelberg and New York.

Huizinga, John (1987): An empirical investigation of the long-run behavior of real exchange rates, *Carnegie-Rochester Conference Series on Public Policy*, Vol. 27, pp. 149-214.

Husted, Steven and Ronald MacDonald (2000): The Asian currency crash: Where badly driven fundamentals to blame?, *Journal of Asian Economics*, Vol. 10, No. 4, pp. 537-550.

Isard, Peter and Hamid Faruqee (1998): Exchange rate assessment: Extensions of the macroeconomic balance approach, IMF Occasional Paper No. 167.

Jazbec, Bostjan (2002): Balassa-Samuelson effect in transition economies: The case of Slovenia, William Davidson Working Paper No. 507.

Johansen, Søren (1988): Statistical analysis of cointegration vectors, *Journal of Economic Dynamics and Control*, Vol. 12, pp. 231-254.

Johansen, Søren (1995): *Likelihood-based inference in cointegrated vector autoregressive models*, Oxford University Press, Oxford.

Johansen, Søren (2001): The interpretation of common trends, impulse responses and cointegrating coefficients in the cointegrated VAR model, mimeo.

Johansen, Søren and Katarina Juselius (1990): Maximum likelihood estimation and inference on cointegration - With applications to the demand for money, *Oxford Bulletin of Economics and Statistics*, Vol. 52, pp. 169-210.

Johansen, Søren and Katarina Juselius (1992): Testing structural hypothesis in a multivariate cointegration analysis of the PPP and the UIP for the UK, *Journal of Econometrics*, Vol. 53, pp. 211-244.

Jorion, Philippe and Richard J. Sweeney (1996): Mean reversion in real exchange rates: evidence and implications for forecasting, *Journal of International Money and Finance*, Vol. 15, No. 4, pp. 535-550.

Juselius, Katarina (1991): Long-run relations in a well defined statistical model for the data generating process. cointregration analysis of the PPP and UIP relations between Denmark and Germany, in: Gruber, Josef (ed.): *Econometric decision models: New methods of modelling and applications*, Springer Verlag, New York.

Juselius, Katarina (1995): Do purchasing power parity and uncovered interest parity hold in the long run? An example of likelihood inference in a multivariate time-series model, Journal of Econometrics, Vol. 69, pp. 211-240.

Juselius, Katarina and Ronald MacDonald (2000): The international parities between the USA, Germany, and Japan: A tripolar analysis, unpublished report, European University Institute.

Kao, Chihwa (1999): Spurious regression and residual-based tests for cointegration in panel data, *Journal of Econometrics*, Vol., 90, No. 1, pp. 1-44.

Karádi, Péter (2003): Structural and single equation estimation of the NATREX equilibrium real exchange rate of the Hungarian forint, National Bank of Hungary, mimeo.

Karfakis, Costas I. and Ashok Parikh (1993): A cointegration approach to monetary targeting in Australia, *Australian Economic Papers*, Vol. 32, pp. 53-72.

Kemme, David M. and Wenyuan Teng (2000): Determinants of the real exchange rate, misalignment and implications for growth in Poland, *Economic Systems*, Vol. 24, No. 2, pp. 171-205.

Kilian, Lutz and Mark P. Taylor (2001): Why is it so difficult to beat the random walk forecast of exchange rates?, ECB Working Paper No. 88.

Kilian, Lutz and Mark P. Taylor (2003): Why is it so difficult to beat the random walk forecast of exchange rates?, *Journal of International Economics*, Vol. 60, pp. 85-107.

Kim, Byung-Yeon and Iikka Korhonen (2005): Equilibrium exchange rates in transition countries: Evidence from dynamic heterogeneous panel models, *Economic Systems*, Vol. 29, No. 2, pp. 144-162.

Kim, Yoonbai (1990): Purchasing power parity in the long run: a cointegration approach, *Journal of Money, Credit, and Banking*, Vol. 22, 491-503.

Kimura, Takeshi (2001): The impact of financial anxieties on money demand in Japan, in: Hans-Joachim Klöckers and Caroline Willeke (eds.): *European Central Bank, Seminar on Monetary Analysis: Tools and Applications*, ECB, Frankfurt am Main.

Koedijk, Kees G.; Tims, Ben; and Mathijs A. van Dijk (2004): Purchasing power parity and the euro area, *Journal of International Money and Finance*, Vol. 23, pp. 1061-1107.

Kovács, Mihaly A. (2002): On the estimated size of the Balassa-Samuelson effect in five central and eastern European countries, National Bank of Hungary Working Paper No. 5.

Krajnyák, Kornelia and Jeromin Zettelmeyer (1998): Competitiveness in transition economies: What scope for real appreciation?, *IMF Staff Papers*, Vol. 45, pp. 309-362.

Kwiatkowski, Denis; Phillips, Peter C. B.; Schmidt, Peter and Yongcheol Shin (1992): Testing the null hypothesis of stationarity against the alternative of a unit root, *Journal of Econometrics*, Vol. 54, pp. 159-178.

Lamdany, Ruben; Mates, N.; Wagner, Nancy L.; Braumann, Benedikt and Thomas Dorsey (1998): Slovak Republic: Recent economic developments, IMF Staff Country Report No. 98/60.

Levin, Andrew and Chien-Fu Lin (1992): Unit root tests in panel data: asymptotic and finite-sample properties, Discussion Paper 92-23, Department of Economics, University of California, San Diego.

Levin, Andrew and Chien-Fu Lin (1993): Unit root tests in panel data: new results, Discussion Paper 93-56, Department of Economics, University of California, San Diego.

Lim, Guay C. and Jerome L. Stein (1997): The dynamics of the real exchange rate and current account in a small open economy: Australia, in: Stein, Jerome L., Allen, Polly R. (eds.): *Fundamental determinants of exchange rates*, Oxford University Press, Oxford.

Lommatzsch, Kirsten and Silke Tober (2004): What is behind the real appreciation of the accession countries' currencies? An investigation of the PPI-based real exchange rate, *Economic Systems*, Vol. 28, No. 4, pp. 383-403.

Lopez, Claude and David H. Papell (2003): Convergence to purchasing power parity at the commencement of the euro, University of Cincinnati, Department of Economics, University of Cincinnati, Economics Working Papers Series.

Lorenzen, Hans P. and Niels Thygesen (2000): The relation between the euro and the dollar, paper presented at the EPRU Conference, Copenhagen.

Lothian, James R. (1997): Multi-country evidence on the behavior of purchasing power parity under the current float, *Journal of International Money and Finance*, Vol. 16, pp. 19-35.

Lothian, James R. and Mark P. Taylor (1996): Real exchange rate behavior: The recent float from the perspective of the past two centuries, *Journal of Political Economy*, Vol. 104, pp. 488-510.

Lown, Cara S.; Peristiani, Stavros; and Kenneth J. Robinson (1999): What was behind the M2 breakdown?, Federal Reserve Bank of Dallas Financial Industry Studies Working Paper No. 02/99.

MacDonald, Ronald (1985): Do deviations from the real effective exchange rate follow a random walk?, *Economic Notes*, Vol. 14, No. 1, pp. 63-69.

MacDonald, Ronald (2000): Concepts to calculate equilibrium exchange rates: An overview, Deutsche Bundesbank Discussion Paper No 3.

MacDonald, Ronald and Ian W. Marsh (1997): On Casselian PPP, cointegration and exchange rate forecasting, *Review of Economics and Statistics*, Vol. 79, pp. 655-664.

MacDonald, Ronald and Ian W. Marsh (1999): *Exchange rate modelling*, Kluwer, Amsterdam.

MacDonald, Ronald and Phillip Swagel (2000): Real exchange rates and the business cycle, mimeo, IMF, Washington, D.C.

MacDonald, Ronald and Mark P. Taylor (1992): Exchange rate economics: A survey, *IMF Staff Papers*, Vol. 39, No. 1, pp. 1-57.

MacDonald, Ronald and Cezary Wójcik (2004): Catching up: The role of demand, supply and regulated price effects on the real exchange rates of four accession countries, *Economics of Transition*, Vol. 12, No. 1, pp. 153-179.

MacKinnon, James G. (1991): Critical values for cointegration tests, in: Engle, Robert F. and Clive W. J. Granger (eds.): *Long run economic relationships: Readings in cointegration*, Oxford University Press, Oxford.

MacKinnon, James G., Haug, Alfred A. and Leo Michelis (1999): Numerical distribution functions of likelihood ratio tests for cointegration, *Journal of Applied Econometrics*, Vol. 14, pp. 563-577.

Maddala, Gangadharrao S. (2001): *Introduction to Econometrics*, 3rd edition, Chichester, John Wiley & Sons, England.

Maddala, GGangadharrao S. and Shaowen Wu (1999): A comparative study of unit root tests with panel data and a new simple test, *Oxford Bulletin off Economics and Statistics*, Vol. 61, pp. 631-652.

Mark, Nelson C. (1990): Real and nominal exchange rates in the long-run: An empirical investigation, *Journal of International Economics*, Vol. 28, pp. 115-136.

Jiménez Martín, Juan A. and M. Dolores Robles Fernández (2005): Nonlinear adjustment to purchasing power parity: An analysis using Fourier approximations, mimeo, Instituto Complutense de Análisis Económico, Universidad Complutense de Madrid.

Maseo-Fernandez, Franciso; Chiara Osbat and Bernd Schnatz (2001): Determinants of the euro real effective exchange rate: A BEER/PEER approach, ECB Working Paper No. 85.

Maseo-Fernandez, Franciso; Chiara Osbat and Bernd Schnatz (2004): Towards the estimation of equilibrium exchange rates for CEE acceding countries: Methodological issues and a panel cointegration perspective, ECB Working Paper No. 353.

Masih, A. Mansur M. and Rumi Masih (2004): Fractional cointegration, low frequency dynamics and long-run purchasing power parity: An analysis of the Australian dollar over its recent float, *Applied Economics*, Vol. 36, pp. 593-605.

Masson, Paul (1998): A globally consistent conceptual framework, in: Isard, Peter and Hamid Faruqee (eds.): Exchange rate assessment: Extensions of the macroeconomic balance approach, IMF Occasional Paper No. 167.

Meese, Richard A. and Kenneth Rogoff (1983): Empirical exchange rate models of the seventies: Do they fit out of sample?, *Journal of International Economics*, Vol. 14, pp. 3-24.

Mehra, Yash P. (1997): A review of the recent behavior of M2 demand, *Federal Reserve Bank of Richmond Economic Quarterly*, Vol. 83, pp. 27-43.

Metzler, Lloyed A. (1951): Wealth, savings and the rate of interest, *Journal of Political Economy,* Vol. 59, pp. 930-946.

Michael, Panos; Nobay, A. Robert; and David A. Peel (1997): Transactions costs and nonlinear adjustment in real exchange rates: An empirical investigation, *Journal of Political Economy*, Vol. 105, pp. 862-879.

Mihaljek, Dubravko and Marc Klau (2004): The Balassa-Samuelson effect in central Europe: A disaggregated analysis, *Comparative Economic Studies*, Vol. 46, No. 1, pp. 63-94.

Miyao, Ryuzo (1996): Does a cointegrating M2 demand relation really exist in Japan?, *Journal of the Japanese and International Economies*, Vol. 10, pp. 1-10.

Narayan, Paresh K. (2005): New evidence on purchasing power parity from 17 OECD countries, *Applied Economics*, Vol. 37, pp. 1063-1071.

Neely Christopher J. and Lucio Sarno (2002): How Well Do Monetary Fundamentals Forecast Exchange Rates?, Review (Federal Reserve Bank of Saint Louis), Vol. 84, No. 5, pp. 51-74.

Newey, Whitney and Kenneth West (1987): A simple positive semi-definite, heteroskedasticity and autocorrelation consistent covariance matrix, *Econometrica*, Vol. 55, pp. 703-708.

Nurkse, Ragnar (1945): Conditions of international monetary equilibrium, Essays in International Finance, No. 4., Princeton University Press, Princeton, New Jersey.

Obstfeld, Maurice and Alan M. Taylor (1997): Nonlinear aspects of goods-market arbitrage and adjustment: Heckscher's commodity points revisited, *Journal of the Japanese and International Economies*, Vol. 11, pp. 441-479.

O'Connell, Paul G. J. (1998): The overvaluation of purchasing power parity, *Journal of International Economics*, Vol. 44, pp. 1-19.

Officer, Lawrence H. (1976): The purchasing-power-parity theory of the exchange rate: A review article, *IMF Staff Papers*, Vol. 23, pp. 1-60.

Oomes, Nienke (2005): Maintaining competitiveness under equilibrium real appreciation: The case of Slovakia, *Economic Systems*, Vol. 29, No. 2, pp. 187-204.

Orden, David and Lance A. Fisher (1993): Financial deregulation and the dynamics of money, price, and output in New Zealand and Australia, *Journal of Money, Credit, and Banking*, Vol. 25, pp. 273-292.

Orphanides, Athanasios and Richard D. Porter (2001): Money and inflation: the role of information regarding the determinants of M2 behavior, in: Hans-Joachim Klöckers and Caroline Willeke (eds.): *European Central Bank, Seminar on Monetary Analysis: Tools and Applications*, ECB, Frankfurt am Main.

Osbat, Chiara; Rüffer, Rasmus and Bernd Schnatz (2003): The rise of the yen vis-à-vis the ('synthetic') euro: Is it supported by economic fundamentals?, ECB Working Paper No. 224.

Papell, David H. (1988): Expectations and exchange rate dynamics after a decade of floating, *Journal of International Economics*, Vol. 25, pp. 303-317.

Pedroni, Peter (1999): Critical values for cointegration tests in heterogeneous panels with multiple regressors, *Oxford Bulletin of Economics and Statistics*, Vol. 61, p. 653-670.

Pesaran, M. Hashem; Shin, Yongcheol and Ron P. Smith (1999): Pooled mean group estimation of dynamic heterogeneous panels, *Journal of the American Statistical Society*, Vol. 94, pp. 621-634.

Pesaran, M. Hashem; Smith, Ron P. and Kyung S. Im (1996): Dynamic linear models for heterogeneous panels, in: Mátyás, Laslo and Patrick Sevestre (eds.): *The econometrics of panel data: A handbook of theory with applications*, 2nd edition, Kluwer Academic Publishers, Dordrecht.

Peytrignet, Michel and Christof Stahel (1998): Stability of money demand in Switzerland: A comparison of the M2 and M3 cases, *Empirical Economics*, Vol. 23, pp. 437-454.

Phillips, Peter C. B. and Mico Loretan (1991): Estimating long-run economic equilibria, *Review of Economic Studies*, Vol. 58, pp. 407-436.

Putnam, Bluford H. and John R. Woodbury (1979): Exchange rate stability and monetary policy, *Review of Business and Economics Research*, Vol. 15, No. 2, pp. 1-10.

Rahn, Jörg (2003): Bilateral equilibrium exchange rates of EU accession countries against the euro, Bank of Finland Discussion Paper No. 11.

Rich, Georg (2003): Swiss monetary targeting 1974-1996: The role of internal policy analysis, ECB Working Paper No. 236.

Rogoff, Kenneth (1996): The purchasing power parity puzzle, *Journal of Economic Literature*, Vol. 34, pp. 647-668.

Rubaszek, Michal (2004): A model of balance of payments equilibrium exchange rate: Application to the Zloty, *Eastern European Economics*, Vol. 42, No. 3, pp. 5-22.

Samuelson, Paul A. (1964): Theoretical problems on trade problems, *Review of Economics and Statistics*, Vol. 46, pp. 145-154.

Sarno, Lucio and Mark P. Taylor (2002): Purchasing power parity and the real exchange rate, *IMF Staff Papers*, Vol. 49, No.1.

Scharnagl, Michael (1998): the stability of German money demand: Not just a myth, *Empirical Economics*, Vol. 23, pp. 355-370.

Schnatz, Bernd; Vijselaar, Focco and Chiara Osbat (2004): Productivity and the euro-dollar exchange rate, Review of World Economics, Vol. 140, No. 1, pp. 1-30.

Sekine, Toshitaka (1998): Financial liberalization, the wealth effect, and the demand for broad money in Japan, Bank of Japan, *Monetary and Economic Studies*, Vol. 16, No. 1, pp. 35-55.

Šmídková, Katarina; R. Barrell; and D. Holland (2002): Estimates of fundamental real exchange rates for the five EU pre-accession countries, Czech National Bank Working Paper No. 3/2002.

Stein, Jerome L. (1994): The natural real exchange rate of the US dollar and determinants of capital flows, in: Williamson, John (ed.): *Estimating equilibrium exchange rates*, Institute for International Economics, pp. 133-175, Washington, D.C.

Stein, Jerome L. (1997): The equilibrium real exchange rate of Germany, in: Stein, Jerome L., Allen, Polly R. (eds.): *Fundamental determinants of exchange rates*, Oxford University Press, Oxford.

Stein, Jerome L. and Polly R. Allen (1997): *Fundamental determinants of exchange rates*, Oxford University Press, Oxford.

Stein, Jcrome L. and Karlhans Sauernheimer (1996): The equilibrium real exchange rate of Germany, *Economic Systems*, Vol. 20, pp. 97-132.

Stock, James H. and Mark W. Watson (1988): Testing for common trends, *Journal of the American Statistical Association*, Vol. 83, pp. 1097-1107.

Stracca, Livio (2001): The functional form of the demand for euro area M1, ECB Working Paper No. 51.

Swan, Trevor W. (1963): Longer-run problems of the balance of payments, in: Arndt, Heinz W. and W. Max Corden (eds.): *The Australian economy: A volume of readings*, F. W. Cheshire, Melbourne.

Taylor, Alan M. and Mark P. Taylor (2004): The purchasing power parity debate, *Journal of Economic Perspectives*, Vol. 18, No. 4, pp. 135-158.

Taylor, Mark P. (1988): An empirical examination of long-run purchasing power parity using cointegration techniques, *Applied Economics*, Vol. 20, pp. 1369-1381.

Taylor, Mark P. (2004): Is official exchange rate intervention effective?, *Economica*, Vol. 71, pp 1-11.

Taylor, Mark P. (2006): Real exchange rates and purchasing power parity: mean-reversion in economic thought, *Applied Financial Economics*, Vol. 16, pp. 1-17.

Taylor, Mark P.; Peel, David A.; and Lucio Sarno (2001): Nonlinear mean-reversion in real exchange rates: Towards a solution to the purchasing power parity puzzles, CEPR Discussion Paper No. 2658.

Taylor, Mark P. and Lucio Sarno (1998): The behavior of real exchange rates during the post-Bretton Woods Period, *Journal of International Economics*, Vol. 46, pp. 281-312.

Thomas, Ryland (1997a): The demand for M4: A sectoral analysis, Part 1 - The personal sector, Bank of England Working Paper No. 61.

Thomas, Ryland (1997b), The demand for M4: A sectoral analysis, Part 2 - The corporate sector, Bank of England Working Paper No. 62.

van Aarle, Bas; Boss, Michael; and Jaroslava Hlouskova (2000): Forecasting the euro exchange rate using vector error correction models, *Review of World Economics*, Vol. 136, No. 2, pp. 232-258.

Verrue, Johan L. and Jan Colpaert (1998): A dynamic model of the real Belgian franc, CIDEI Working Paper No. 47, La Sapienza, Rome.

Whitesell, William (1997): Interest rates and M2 in an error-correction macro model, Board of Governors of the Federal Reserve System, Financial and Economics Discussion Paper No. 97-59.

Williams, Jeffrey C. and Brian D. Wright (1991): *Storage and commodity markets*, Cambridge University Press, Cambridge, England.

Williamson, John (1985): *The exchange rate system*, 2nd ed., Institute for International Economics, Washington, D.C.

Williamson, John (1994): *Estimating equilibrium exchange rates*, Institute for International Economics, Washington, D.C.

Williamson, John and Molly Mahar (1998): Current account targets, in: Wren-Lewis, Simon and Rebecca L. Driver (eds.): *Real exchange rates for the year 2000*, Appendix A, Institute for International Economics, Washington, D.C.

Williamson, John and Marcus H. Miller (1987): Targets and indicators: A blueprint for the international coordination of economic policy, Policy Analysis in International Economics, No. 22, Institute for International Economics, Washington, D.C.

Wren-Lewis, Simon and Rebecca L. Driver (1998): *Real exchange rates for the years 2000*, Institute for International Economics, Washington, D.C.

Wu, Yangru (1996): Are real exchange rates non-stationary?: Evidence from a panel-data test, *Journal of Money, Credit, and Banking*, Vol. 28, No. 1, pp. 54-63.

Yamada, H. (2000): M2 demand relation and effective exchange rate in Japan: A cointegration analysis, *Applied Economic Letters*, Vol. 7, pp. 229-232.

Studien zu Internationalen Wirtschaftsbeziehungen

Herausgegeben von Prof. Dr. Michael Frenkel

Band 1 Christiane Nickel: Insider und Outsider bei der Osterweiterung der Europäischen Währungsunion. 2002.

Band 2 Georg Stadtmann: Noise-Trader auf Devisenmärkten. Viel Lärm um Nichts? 2002.

Band 3 Wolf-Heimo Grieben: Trade and Technology as Competing Explanations for Rising Inequality. An Endogenous Growth Perspective. 2003.

Band 4 Alexander Mende: Order Flow Analyses and Foreign Exchange Dealing. 2005.

Band 5 Torsten Wezel: Determinants of Foreign Direct Investment in Emerging Markets. An Empirical Study of FDI Flows from Germany and its Banking Sector. 2005.

Band 6 Steffen Kern: The Behaviour of Interest Groups in Trade and Industry Towards Monetary Policy and Central Banks. Theory and Evidence on Germany and the Euro Area. 2006.

Band 7 Holger Michaelis: Kapitalbilanzliberalisierung in der Volksrepublik China und ihre Einbettung in den volkswirtschaftlichen Reformprozess. 2006.

Band 8 Ralf Fendel: Monetary Policy, Interest Rate Rules, and the Term Structure of Interest Rates. Theoretical Considerations and Empirical Implications. 2007.

Band 9 Katja Funke: Balance of Payments Issues in Central and Eastern European Countries' Run-Up to Euro Area Accession. 2007.

Band 10 Isabell Koske: Equilibrium Exchange Rate Models, the Euro and the 2004 Expansion of the EU. 2007.

www.peterlang.de

Peter Lang · Internationaler Verlag der Wissenschaften

Jörg Rahn

Equilibrium Exchange Rates of Central and Eastern European Countries on the Road to the European Monetary Union

Frankfurt am Main, Berlin, Bern, Bruxelles, New York, Oxford, Wien, 2005.
199 pp., num. tab. and graf.
European University Studies: Series 5, Economics and Management. Vol. 3161
ISBN 978-3-631-54243-9 · pb.€ 39.–*

The upcoming enlargement of the European Monetary Union involves the selection of appropriate reference rates at which the exchange rates of the accession countries will be fixed against the euro in order to avoid economic distortions as consequences of serious exchange rate misalignments. Determination of an exchange rate that is neither undervalued nor overvalued raises the issue of equilibrium exchange rates. Based on time series as well as panel estimation techniques three different concepts – BEER, PEER and PPP – are applied in this study to calculate equilibrium exchange rate levels for ten Central and Eastern European countries. The results indicate significant real misalignments in a number of accession countries.

Contents: Developments of exchange rates and exchange rate regimes in ten Central and Eastern European Countries · Concepts to calculate equilibrium exchange rates · Appliance of three methods based on time series as well as panel estimation techniques: BEER, PEER and PPP · Determination of misalignments in real effective terms as well as in nominal terms against the euro